Naturalism and Religion

This book guides readers through an investigation of religion from a naturalistic perspective and explores the very meaning of the term 'religious naturalism'. Oppy considers several widely disputed claims: that there cannot be naturalistic religion; that there is nothing in science that poses any problems for naturalism; that there is nothing in religion that poses any serious challenges to naturalism; and that there is a very strong case for thinking that naturalism defeats religion.

Naturalism and Religion: A Contemporary Philosophical Investigation is an ideal introduction for undergraduate and postgraduate students of religious studies and philosophy who want to gain an understanding of the key themes and claims of naturalism from a religious and philosophical perspective.

Graham Oppy is Professor of Philosophy in the School of Philosophical, Historical and International Studies at Monash University, Australia.

Investigating Philosophy of Religion

Series editors: Chad Meister, Bethel College, and Charles Taliaferro, St. Olaf College

This is a series of interfaith texts that philosophically engage with the major world religions in light of central issues they are currently facing. Each work is an original contribution by a leading scholar from that religious tradition and incorporates the latest developments in scholarship in the field. The texts are written for students, scholars, and all those who want a fairly detailed but concise overview of the central issues in contemporary philosophy of religion from the perspective of the major world religions.

Judaism: A Contemporary Philosophical Investigation
Lenn E. Goodman

Buddhism: A Contemporary Philosophical Investigation
David Burton

Islam: A Contemporary Philosophical Investigation
Imran Aijaz

Naturalism and Religion: A Contemporary Philosophical Investigation
Graham Oppy

For more information about this series, please visit: https://www.routledge.com/Investigating-Philosophy-of-Religion/book-series/IPR

Naturalism and Religion
A Contemporary Philosophical Investigation

Graham Oppy

LONDON AND NEW YORK

First published 2018
by Routledge
2 Park Square, Milton Park, Abingdon, Oxon OX14 4RN

and by Routledge
711 Third Avenue, New York, NY 10017

Routledge is an imprint of the Taylor & Francis Group, an informa business

© 2018 Graham Oppy

The right of Graham Oppy to be identified as author of this work has been asserted by him in accordance with sections 77 and 78 of the Copyright, Designs and Patents Act 1988.

All rights reserved. No part of this book may be reprinted or reproduced or utilised in any form or by any electronic, mechanical, or other means, now known or hereafter invented, including photocopying and recording, or in any information storage or retrieval system, without permission in writing from the publishers.

Trademark notice: Product or corporate names may be trademarks or registered trademarks, and are used only for identification and explanation without intent to infringe.

British Library Cataloguing in Publication Data
A catalogue record for this book is available from the British Library

Library of Congress Cataloging in Publication Data
A catalog record has been requested for this book

ISBN: 978-0-8153-5464-2 (hbk)
ISBN: 978-0-8153-5466-6 (pbk)
ISBN: 978-0-429-48786-6 (ebk)

Typeset in Times New Roman
by Taylor & Francis Books

Contents

	Preface	vi
1	Introduction	1
2	What is naturalism?	11
3	What is religion?	26
4	Can there be naturalistic religion?	43
5	Does science defeat naturalism?	56
6	Does religion defeat naturalism?	86
7	Does science defeat religion?	126
8	Does naturalism defeat religion?	151
9	Conclusion	185
	Bibliography	186
	Index	195

Preface

Chad Meister and Charles Taliaferro wrote to me in early August, 2011, to invite me to contribute a book on naturalism and religion to their book series *Investigating Philosophy of Religion*. Initially, I agreed to deliver a finalised version of the book to them by the end of July, 2015. However, at that point, I only had drafts for Chapter 4 and the first half of Chapter 5, and no prospects of making any immediate further progress. Fortunately, I had sabbatical scheduled for the second half of 2017, and I was able to complete the book during that time. I am very grateful to Chad and Charles for inviting me to write this book, and for their forbearance during the excessively long time that it took me to actually get it done; I hope that they are pleased enough with the outcome.

I am grateful to Monash University for the sabbatical in the second half of 2013, during which I wrote Chapter 4 and the first half of Chapter 5, and for the sabbatical in the second half of 2017, during which I completed the remaining chapters. This gratitude extends to all of the staff and students at Monash who have supported me throughout the years during which I was working on this book. I must mention, in particular, the honours and graduate students I have supervised during this time with whom I have discussed themes in this book, including: Lok Chi Chan, Ben Kemmann, Paul Litchfield, Shang Lu, Jane McDonnell, James Molesworth, Jenny Munt, Paul Podosky, Shaff Rahman, Maxwell Reiss, Mark Saward, Dwayne Schulz, and Brendan Vize.

As always, I owe a special debt to family, friends, and the organisations to which I belong that take me away from academic pursuits. Big thanks to everyone at the Glen Waverley Cougars Cricket Club and the Monash Blues Football Club; to Neville Bryan, Owen Davies, and Ian Rennie; and, especially, to Camille, Gilbert, Calvin, and Alfie.

1 Introduction

> Philosophical naturalism has consistently shown itself to be a non-scientific religious perspective that is adverse to impartial inquiry into the nature of reality according to the scientific principles of methodological naturalism. Its adherents and defenders have consistently shown by their writings and opinions a prejudicial intolerance of fundamentally human intuitive understandings of reality and an anti-intellectual rejection of compelling evidence, evidence that has proven acceptable to profound thinkers and researchers. It is not science, nor is it a scientific approach. Ipso facto, by its a priori rejection of the possibility of the supernatural ... philosophical naturalism represents an approach that is militantly ... and overtly hostile to religion and human culture.
> ('Philosophical Naturalism' *Conservapedia* 21/08/17, 3:09 p.m., http://www.conservapedia.com/Philosophical_naturalism)

It takes no effort or searching skill to find criticisms of (philosophical) naturalism. The above quotation from the *Conservapedia* entry on philosophical naturalism serves as well as any. Among the commonly encountered criticisms of philosophical naturalism that are displayed in this quotation, there are at least the following:

1. Philosophical naturalism is a religion, or, at any rate, a religious perspective.
2. Philosophical naturalism is adverse to impartial inquiry.
3. Philosophical naturalism is anti-scientific, or, at any rate, non-scientific.
4. Philosophical naturalism is inherently prejudicial and intolerant of natural basic human beliefs.
5. Philosophical naturalism is an anti-intellectual rejection of compelling evidence.
6. Philosophical naturalism makes an *a priori* rejection of the supernatural.
7. Philosophical naturalism is militantly and overtly hostile to religion.
8. Philosophical naturalism is militantly and overtly hostile to human culture.

That's quite a rap sheet. But can any of the charges be made to stick? I don't think so, and I hope to get you to agree with me (if you do not already do so).

2   *Introduction*

The rap sheet makes use of a number of difficult terms (or forms thereof): *philosophy, religion, science, culture, evidence,* and *impartial inquiry.* In all cases, the application of these terms is contested. In each case, there are many people who claim to be in favour of what the term denotes – philosophy, religion, science, culture, evidence, impartial inquiry – but there is heated disagreement about exactly what these things are. In this work, I'm particularly interested in getting clear about (philosophical) naturalism, philosophy, science, religion and the ways in which they are related to one another.

Naturalism is a claim: roughly, the conjunctive claim that (a) there are none but natural causal entities with none but natural causal powers and (b) well-established science is our touchstone for identifying natural causal entities and natural causal powers. There are many claims that are appropriately compared with naturalism. Consider, for example, theism: the claim that there is at least one god. It makes just as much sense to claim that naturalism is a religion as it does to claim that theism is a religion: none. There are many theistic religions: what makes a religion theistic is that the family of big pictures associated with that religion all entail that there is at least one god. Theism, *per se*, is not a religion: to think that is to conflate religions with big pictures. Nor is theism intrinsically linked to religion. There are religions whose associated big pictures do not entail that there is at least one god. Moreover, there are non-religious big pictures that entail that there is at least one god. But it is even more obvious that naturalism is not a religion than it is that theism is not a religion. After all, there is no religion whose associated big pictures entail (a) that there are none but natural causal entities with none but natural causal powers and (b) that well-established science is our touchstone for identifying natural causal entities and natural causal powers.

Given that naturalism entails that well-established science is our touchstone for identifying natural causal entities and natural causal powers, it is hard to see how naturalism *per se* could be either anti-scientific or non-scientific. Certainly, naturalism has another commitment: there are none but natural causal entities with none but natural causal powers. But (a) well-established science has not identified any non-natural causal entities or non-natural causal powers; and (b) well-established science has not embraced any methods that will identify non-natural causal entities or non-natural causal powers at some point in the future. Science is, roughly speaking, a collective enterprise of data-driven description, prediction and understanding in which universal expert agreement functions as regulative ideal. The only methods that science embraces are methods that are consonant with the regulative ideal of producing universal expert agreement. We are not currently in possession of even one method consonant with the production of universal expert consensus about the existence of non-natural entities or the exercise of non-natural causal powers.

The project of philosophical naturalism is the defence and elaboration of naturalistic big pictures. The ideal method that I propose for choosing between big pictures is utterly impartial. Roughly, if we follow this method, we develop all the big pictures in which we are interested with the same level of care to the same level of detail, and then we make an objective comparative assessment of their theoretical virtues relative to all of the available evidence. Among the big pictures that we are assessing, the best are those that do best in balancing the full range of theoretical virtues given all of the available evidence.

Given the ideal method that I propose, accusations of prejudice, intolerance, and anti-intellectual rejection of evidence are completely out of bounds. Everything on which all parties to big picture disputes agree counts as evidence; nothing on which all parties agree can be properly set aside. Anything on which the parties in dispute disagree is a theoretical difference; it gets weighed when we assess the theoretical virtues of the big pictures in question. Central theoretical virtues include: consistency, breadth and depth of explanation of evidence, fit with established science, and so on. (In the discussion in this work, I shall assume – with accompanying justification – that the evaluative and the normative are theoretically independent from the causal. So the theoretical virtues to which we appeal will be just those virtues that are appropriate to assessing theorising about the causal domain.)

Given my account of the philosophical assessment of big pictures, it is clear that (philosophical) naturalism does not involve an *a priori* rejection of the supernatural. What justifies (philosophical) naturalism – if, indeed, it is justified – is that the best big pictures are best naturalistic big pictures. And whether best naturalistic big pictures are the best big pictures depends upon which best big pictures win out at balancing theoretical virtues in the light of total evidence. It is true that naturalism is characterised – 'defined' – by its exclusive commitment to the natural. But that doesn't mean that naturalists – those who endorse naturalistic big pictures – have an *a priori* commitment to naturalistic big pictures.

It is a controversial question how naturalism is related to religion. In part, this is because it is controversial exactly what counts as religion. On my account – taken from the work of Scott Atran – *very* roughly, religions are passionate communal displays of costly commitments resulting from evolutionary canalisation and convergence of (a) widespread beliefs in non-natural entities with non-natural causal powers, (b) mastery of people's existential anxieties, and (c) ritualised coordination in communion and intimate fellowship. Given this account, it follows that naturalism and religion exclude one another: no one can be both a naturalist and a genuine follower of a religion. However, it does not follow from this that naturalists are militantly and overtly hostile towards religions and religious believers. Certainly, naturalists maintain that the supernatural beliefs of religious believers are *false*; but, equally, religious believers hold that the defining naturalistic beliefs of naturalists are false. Nothing further follows in either case about attitudes that members of the one group have towards members of the other group, either individually or collectively.

The claim that naturalism is militantly and overtly hostile to human culture is absurd on its face. So, too, is the claim that naturalistic worldviews are militantly and overly hostile to human culture. It is, I think, plausible to claim that naturalism runs counter to many 'natural' human beliefs. When we examine the full range of human cultures, we find non-naturalistic beliefs wherever we look. But those 'natural' non-naturalistic beliefs are never beliefs on which there is universal expert consensus; those 'natural' non-naturalistic beliefs typically divide people rather than bring them together. Everyone – no matter what else they believe – agrees that the vast majority of 'natural' non-naturalistic beliefs are false. That naturalists go a little further, and claim that all of these 'natural' non-naturalistic beliefs are false, does not make the beliefs of naturalists any more militantly and overtly hostile to human culture than are the beliefs of everyone else. If more argument is needed, it is worth noting that there is no reason to suppose that naturalists contribute less per capita than non-naturalists to the arts, humanities, and sciences, or to the political, business, and social spheres. On any measure, that's not hostility to human culture.

While there may be legitimate criticisms of philosophical naturalism, I doubt that there is any major criticism of philosophical naturalism that is as easy as the *Conservapedia* entry suggests. For at least the past seventy years, naturalism has been enormously popular among professional philosophers. Of course, the naturalistic big pictures adopted by naturalistic philosophers have varied considerably, and some of those big pictures have been subject to relatively easy refutation. But naturalism itself is a much smaller target than many of its opponents imagine, and it is not threatened when even quite widely shared naturalistic big pictures fall. Part of the driving force behind the writing of this book is the ambition to set out and defend a small target naturalism that can nonetheless be put to useful work in serious philosophical arguments.

1. The plan

Here's the plan for the book.

The second chapter – 'What is naturalism?' – is a discussion of some controversial questions about naturalism. The first section – 'First pass' – introduces my characterisation of naturalism and then briefly discusses a large range of issues on which naturalists disagree, including whether there are non-causal entities, whether all properties are causal powers, whether there are mental causal powers, whether to endorse physicalism, whether to endorse materialism, whether to endorse scientism, whether to endorse humanism, whether to eschew first philosophy, whether to endorse empiricism, and whether to hold that all causal entities have spatiotemporal location. The second section – 'Natural and non-natural' considers some issues raised by the characterisation of naturalism, including, in particular, the question of exactly what is involved in the distinction between the natural and the non-natural;

here, I defend the view that, while completed science is the ultimate arbiter of what counts as natural and non-natural, current *established* science is an excellent guide to the verdicts of completed science on this question. The third section – 'What might have been' – takes up the question of whether naturalists should suppose that naturalism is necessarily true; while I argue that it is fine for naturalists to disagree in their responses to this question, I also provide a sketch of my preferred metaphysical view, on which naturalism turns out to be necessarily true. The fourth section – 'Big pictures' – gives a preliminary account of big pictures as, roughly, the best approximations that we have to philosophical theories of everything, and then introduces a couple of naturalistic supervenience claims that are controversial among naturalists. The fifth section – 'Attitudes' – takes up some questions about the kinds of doxastic attitudes that naturalists can have towards naturalism, considering this matter both from the standpoint that takes belief to be an all-or-nothing matter, and the standpoint that takes belief to involves assignments of probabilities. The sixth, and final, section – 'Critics' – notes that many critics of naturalism make extraordinarily uncharitable assumptions about what else, besides naturalism, might – or must – be part of naturalistic big pictures; in particular, it notes that the various papers in Craig and Moreland (2000a) are universally attacks on strawmen.

The third chapter – 'What is religion?' – is a discussion of some controversial questions about religion. The first section – 'Data' – is a summary of data about religions and religious affiliation that pays some attention to the methodological difficulties that arise for those engaged in demographic studies of religions. The second section – 'Definition' – briefly discusses the history of attempts to define 'religion', and settles on a working definition that is adapted from the stipulative definition adopted by Atran (2002). The third section – 'Inside/Outside' – responds to the objection, that the working definition fails to pay proper respect to 'insider' religious perspectives, (primarily) by explaining why there simply cannot be an 'insider' definition of religion. The fourth section – 'Spirituality' – responds to the suggestion, that it would be better to define religion in terms of religious spirituality, (primarily) by noting that the definition of 'spirituality' is in far worse shape than the definition of 'religion'. The fifth section – 'Is naturalism a religion?' – explains why neither naturalism nor naturalistic big pictures are religions: while being a religious adherent requires not merely having a religious big picture but also engaging in the practices of a religion, being a naturalist requires no more than having a naturalistic big picture. The sixth section – 'Is philosophy a religion?' – explains why philosophy is not a religion: being a philosopher requires no more than being a participant in a particular theoretical discipline; being a philosopher does not require any kind of engagement in the types of practices that are characteristic of religions. The seventh section – 'Theories of religion' – provides a brief overview of various kinds of theories of religion, and notes that the adopted working definition fits well with contemporary cognitive evolutionary theories of religion while also preserving the grains of truth in earlier social and psychological theories of religion.

The fourth chapter – 'Can there be naturalistic religion?' – gives more detailed attention to the question of whether it is an unacceptable consequence of the working definition of 'religion' that it rules it impossible that there are naturalistic religions. The first section – 'Pantheism' – takes up the question whether there is reason to say that natural reality is divine, and argues that the claim that natural reality is divine contradicts the naturalistic claim that causal reality is just natural causal reality. The second section – 'Panentheism' – argues that panentheism is even more clearly ruled out by naturalism than is pantheism; this section includes a fairly careful discussion of the allegedly 'naturalistic' panentheism defended by Johnston (2009). The third section – 'Religious naturalism' – criticises the work of a bunch of theorists whose guiding ambition is to develop naturalistic big pictures that include beliefs and values often associated with religion, noting, in particular, that the characterisation of naturalism places very minimal constraints upon the evaluative, normative, and emotional commitments of naturalistic big pictures. The fourth section – 'Naturalistic religion' – criticises the claim that there are coherent big pictures that are both naturalistic and religious, with a particular focus on Bishop (2018), who claims to be both a naturalist and a believer in 'the received Christian faith'. The fifth section – 'Religion of humanity' – considers and criticises the claims of those – such as Comte and Mill – who have called for the establishment of a morally credible naturalistic religion, noting, in particular, that no proposed 'religion of humanity' has included plausible mechanisms for mastering existential anxieties. The sixth section – 'Religious humanism' – considers and criticises proposals by humanist organisations to take on some of the trappings of religion in order to provide for mastery of some existential anxieties, including, perhaps, loneliness and alienation, noting that, while this would not make religious humanism a religion, it also would not allow religious humanism to play the role that religions currently play.

The fifth chapter – 'Does science defeat naturalism?' – provides a detailed discussion and analysis of the argument of Plantinga (2011), with the aim of showing that Plantinga fails to provide any support for the implausible claim that science defeats naturalism. The discussion begins by establishing some background (Section 1: 'Background' and Section 2: 'Epistemology'), and then critically assesses Plantinga's attempts to show that: (a) there is merely superficial conflict between, on the one hand, Christian theism, and, on the other hand, evolutionary psychology and higher Biblical criticism (Section 3: 'Superficial conflict'); (b) there is merely apparent conflict between theism and evolutionary theory, and between natural science and theistic claims of special divine action in the world (Section 4: 'Merely apparent conflict'); (c) 'fine-tuning' and 'protein machine' arguments offer slight support for theism over naturalism (Section 5: 'Arguments for theism'); (d) 'design discourse' offers some – hard to quantify – support for theism over naturalism (Section 6: 'Support for theism'); and (e) there is deep concord between theism and science (Section 7: 'Deep concord'). My conclusion is that none of the arguments that Plantinga offers for these claims succeed (Section 8: 'Interim conclusion'). Attention then turns to a careful discussion of Plantinga's Evolutionary Arguments against Naturalism, EAAN and EAAN* (Section 9: EAAN*). After giving reasons for thinking that Plantinga's argument cannot succeed, and noting that Plantinga's assumptions about the reliability of our cognitive mechanisms are false (Section 10: 'Reliability'), I set out the cases to which Plantinga appeals in attempting to justify his first premise, i.e. the claim that: the conditional probability that our cognitive mechanisms are reliable, given naturalism and evolutionary theory, is low (Section 11: 'Cases'). I argue that Plantinga's account of the cases stands to the truth pretty much as behaviourist accounts of human beings stand to the truth (Section 12: 'Analysis'). I then argue that, while naturalists have good reason to suppose that our evolutionary and social history explains why established science is almost all true (Section 13: 'Contra'), naturalists also have good reason to suppose that our positive philosophical and religious beliefs are mostly false (Section 14: 'Truth'). After brief consideration of the second premise (Section 15: 'Premise 2'), the third premise (Section 16: 'Premise 3'), and the fourth premise (Section 17: 'Premise 4'), of Plantinga's argument, I conclude that Plantinga's EAAN fails (Section 18: 'Upshot'). I wind up the chapter by noting that, *en passant*, we have also shown that EAAN* fails (Section 19: 'EAAN*').

The sixth chapter – 'Does religion defeat naturalism?' – has two parts. The first section of the chapter provides a detailed discussion of the argument of Rea (2002) (Section 1: 'Rea's argument against naturalism'); the second section of the chapter provides discussion of a generic challenge posed by contemporary Thomism (Section 2: 'The Thomist challenge to naturalism').

After listing some controversial claims to which Rea commits himself, I begin with some discussion of relatively minor points of detail (Section 1.1 'Initial quibbles'), and then move on to critical discussion of more significant points of dispute (Section 1.2 'Dispositions, experience, and evidence'; Section 1.3 'Methodological dispositions'; Section 1.4 'Sources of basic belief', and Section 1.5 'Big picture conflict'), setting the background for my criticism of Rea's claim that there can be no substantive characterisation of naturalistic commitments. I argue against his claim that there can be no substantive characterisation of metaphysical naturalistic commitments – which he defends on the grounds that there is nothing informative that naturalists can say about the distinction between the natural and the non-natural – by arguing for the substantive role that current science plays in limiting the commitments of completed or ideal science (Section 1.6 'Metaphysical commitments of naturalism'; Section 1.7 'Armstrong'; Section 1.8 'Pettit'). I argue against Rea's claim that there can be no substantive characterisation of epistemological naturalistic commitments – which he defends with an alleged demonstration that any epistemological characterisation of naturalism is self-defeating – by insisting on an unambiguous understanding of the relationship between scientific methods and 'pre-scientific methods' (Section 1.9 'Epistemological commitments of naturalism'). Since Rea's defence of the claim that there can be no substantive characterisation of methodological naturalistic commitments assumes the success of his prior arguments in connection with metaphysical naturalistic commitments and epistemological naturalistic commitments, my counterargument is mercifully brief (Section 1.10 'Methodological commitments of naturalism'), as is my discussion of characterisations of naturalism that draw upon more than one of these kinds of commitments (Section 1.11 'Combined characterisations of naturalism'). The substantive conclusion of this part of the discussion is that Rea fails to show that the basic commitments of naturalism cannot be metaphysical, or epistemological, or methodological, or some combination of all three, and so Rea fails to show that naturalism can only be a 'research program' (Section 1.12 'Substantive conclusions'). This section concludes with critical discussion of some other less important matters: Rea's claim that his account of naturalism is charitable (Section 1.13 'Charity'), Rea's claim that there is no sense in which naturalists can appeal to rational intuitions (Section 1.14 'Rational intuition'), and Rea's claim that naturalism is both a movement and a tradition (Section 1.15 'Tradition'). The overall conclusion of this discussion is that Rea provides no good reason to think that naturalists cannot be realists about material objects and the mindedness of others, and no good reason to deny that there are naturalistic big pictures with substantive metaphysical, epistemological, and methodological commitments.

The discussion of Thomistic arguments for the existence of non-natural entities with non-natural causal powers begins with a discussion of interpretations of, and expositions of, Aquinas' Five Ways (Section 2.1 '*Summa Theologiae*'). Some Thomists maintain that, while the Five Ways, as presented, are invalid, the presentation is deliberately incomplete, with missing premises supplied elsewhere in Aquinas' work. Against this interpretation, I argue that nothing in the *Summa Contra Gentiles* (Section 2.2 '*Summa Contra Gentiles*') or in *De Ente Et Essentia* (Section 2.3 '*De Ente Et Essentia*') provides premises that could turn the Five Ways into valid arguments; and I add that it is highly implausible to suppose that the 'missing premises' are given in other works by Aquinas. Some Thomists maintain that the Five Ways are valid, but not proofs of the existence of God; the most that these arguments establish is that there is at least one unmoved mover, at least one uncaused cause, at least one necessary being that does not owe its necessity to anything else, at least one cause of being for all other beings, and at least one intelligent being by which all natural things are ordered to their ends, with the further premises needed to complete the proof(s) of the existence of God supplied elsewhere in Aquinas' work. I argue that there is nothing elsewhere in the *Summa Theologiae* (Section 2.4 '*Summa Theologiae* revisited') or in *De Ente et Essentia* (Section 2.5 '*De Ente et Essentia* revisited') that supplies the missing premises, and I also argue that the independent argument(s) for the existence of God that can be extracted from the text of *De Ente et Essentia* are not arguments that should cause naturalists any loss of sleep.

I conclude that there is nothing in Aquinas' arguments for the existence of God that poses a serious challenge to naturalists.

The seventh chapter – 'Does science defeat religion?' – mounts a case for the controversial conclusion that science does not defeat religion. The first section (What is science?) gives a characterisation of science, a brief taxonomy of the different kinds of sciences, and a more extensive discussion of the institutions of science that protect its integrity and help non-scientists to identify the results of genuinely established science. The second section ('Is science a religion?') sets out some of the major differences between science and religion that suffice to establish that science is not a religion, and that religion is not a science, but goes on to note that one important similarity between science and religion is that both require particular commitments: science requires commitment to the values and imperatives generated by the regulative ideal of universal expert agreement, and religion requires taking on, and giving public expression to, certain kinds of costly commitments. The third section ('Are scientists religious?') reviews studies of the religious beliefs of scientists and academics that suggest that, while those who lack religion are over-represented in the sciences and in the academy relative to the population at large, there are questions about how this under-representation of the religious in the sciences and the academy should be understood; in particular, I critically examine the suggestion that there is bias against the religious in the sciences and in the academy, and the suggestion that the under-representation is explained by the fact that religious people internalise negative societal stereotypes. The fourth section ('How is science related to religion?') considers the widely accepted claim that there are four views that one might take about 'the relation' between science and religion – 'conflict', 'independence', 'dialogue', and 'integration' – and argues for the conclusions that (a) whether there is conflict or independence between religion and science depends entirely upon the claims made by given religions; and (b) that any 'dialogue' or 'integration' can only be a matter of acceptance of the deliverances of science by given religions. The fifth section ('What do religions say about science?') examines the wide range of teachings about science – rejection, partial acceptance, (mistakenly) claimed full acceptance, genuine full acceptance – that are to be found among the religions of the world, paying special attention to the kinds of religious worldviews that are compatible with full acceptance of the teachings of science, and arguing against those – such as Tyson, Dawkins, Hitchens, Harris, Stenger, and Krauss – who suggest that it is impossible for there to be any such religious worldviews. The sixth section ('What does science say about religion?') gives a very brief overview of branches of sciences – such as anthropology, sociology, economics, political science, psychology, and cognitive science – that study religion, including a few remarks about meta-analyses in psychology of religion.

The eighth chapter ('Does naturalism defeat religion?') sketches the best case that I have been able to make for the conclusion that best naturalistic big pictures are better than best religious big pictures. The first section ('Outline') sets out the main contours of the case, which relies upon the following three claims: (Premise 1) all the other best big pictures have weightier theoretical commitments than best naturalistic big pictures; (Premise 2) no other best big pictures have greater explanatory breadth, depth, and adequacy than best naturalistic big pictures; and (Premise 3) if, among best big pictures, there is a type of big picture that is minimal with respect to theoretical commitment and maximal with respect to breadth, depth, and adequacy of explanation, then those big pictures are the very best big pictures. The next five sections ('Background: big pictures', 'Background: idealisation', 'Background: method', 'Background: theoretical virtues', and 'Background: shortcut') set out the theoretical framework within which the case is developed, and provide a defence of Premise 3. The seventh section ('Premise 1') defends the claim that best naturalistic big pictures are only committed to that to which all other best big pictures are committed. The next eight sections ('Premise 2: overview', 'Premise 2: general causal features', 'Premise 2: general design features', 'Premise 2: mind', 'Premise 2: anomalies', 'Premise 2: experience', 'Premise 2: artifacts', and 'Premise 2: communication') provide a case-based defence of Premise 2, taking into account the various cases where some have thought that religious big pictures have explanatory advantage over naturalistic big pictures. After drawing the conclusions that my overall case supports – i.e. that best naturalistic big pictures are the best big pictures, hence that best naturalistic big pictures are better than religious big pictures, hence that naturalism defeats religion – I note some of the ways in which this case falls short of being fully persuasive: each of the three premises is controversial and each is rejected by some philosophical experts.

2. Tips to readers

This book is written to be read from beginning to end. There are various ways in which later material depends upon earlier material; but there are also ways in which earlier material depends upon later material. (For example, I start talking about big pictures in the Introduction, but do not begin to explain what they are until Chapter 2, Section 4, and go on to give a fuller account in Chapter 8, Section 2. In this case, it may be close enough to read 'big picture' as 'worldview' until you get to the fuller explanation.) Despite the occasional cases of content dependence, the issues that are taken up in the various chapters are largely independent of one another. So – perhaps with judicious use of the index – it should be possible to read any of the chapters independently.

There are many excellent works on naturalism (and religion) that have preceded this book. Readers of this book who are interested in reading back into the literature might consider: Dawes (2011), Dennett (2006), Draper (2005), Horgan (2006), Maddy (2011), Nielsen (2001), Papineau (1993) (2015), Pettit (1992), Price (2011), and Stroud (1996).

2 What is naturalism?

For some, the term 'naturalism' is a badge of honour; for others, it is a term of abuse. On these grounds alone, it is predictable that the term admits a wide range of conflicting interpretations. Moreover, it is plausibly predicted that those for whom it is a term of abuse often load far more into it than do those for whom it is a badge of honour.

This chapter begins with rough characterisations of ontological (metaphysical) naturalism and methodological naturalism, and the suggestion that, at least roughly, naturalism should be taken to be the conjunction of these two claims. It is noted immediately how little this characterisation settles, i.e., how much remains upon which naturalists do not agree.

My characterisation of naturalism relies on controversial notions – causal powers, causal reality – and a controversial distinction – natural versus non-natural. In the second part of this chapter I argue that, while the distinction is not problematic, we should allow freedom in the metaphysical primitives that we use to characterise naturalism.

My characterisation of naturalism is a thesis about what is actually the case. In the third part of this chapter, I consider what naturalists may say about what might be the case. While I allow that permissible naturalist opinion on this matter varies considerably, I express my preference for a view on which the ontological claim that characterises naturalism holds of necessity.

My characterisation of naturalism is not framed in terms of what is fundamental, or grounding, or subvenient. In the fourth part of this chapter, I suggest that, since naturalistic big pictures can permissibly disagree about what they take to be primitive, it is no black mark against my characterisation of naturalism that it is not framed in terms of what is fundamental, or grounding, or subvenient.

My characterisation of naturalism does not address the doxastic attitudes that naturalists might take towards the propositions that characterise naturalism. In the fifth part of this chapter, I note that there is wide permissible variation in the magnitude and resilience of naturalistic all-or-nothing beliefs and naturalistic credences.

Finally, in the sixth part of this chapter, I canvass some of the work of critics of naturalism. In particular, I observe that many critics of naturalism characterise it in terms that many naturalists do not themselves accept. I note, for example, that most of the essays in Craig and Moreland (2000a) are attacks on strawmen.

1. First pass

There is a widely accepted distinction between *ontological naturalism* and *methodological naturalism*. Ontological naturalists maintain, roughly, that natural reality exhausts causal reality: there are none but natural causal entities with none but natural causal powers. Methodological naturalists maintain, roughly, that well-established science is our touchstone for identifying the denizens of causal reality: we have no reason to believe in causal entities and causal powers beyond those recognised by science. Naturalists typically accept both ontological naturalism and methodological naturalism; at least for now, we shall suppose that it is best for naturalists to do this.

Naturalists disagree about whether there are non-causal entities: for example, some, but not all, naturalists allow that there are non-causal abstract objects. Consider numbers. Some naturalists suppose that numbers are non-causal abstract objects: our use of mathematical vocabulary is best explained by appeal to a domain of non-causal abstract objects. Other naturalists suppose that talk about numbers does not incur commitment to a domain of non-causal abstract objects; rather, at least in principle, our use of mathematical vocabulary has a complete nominalist or fictionalist explanation.

Naturalists disagree about what kinds of causal powers there are: for example, some, but not all, naturalists allow that there are mental causal powers. Naturalists who allow that there are mental causal powers identify mental causal powers with neural causal powers: mental states and processes are just neural states and processes. Naturalists who deny that there are mental causal powers reject the identification of mental causal powers with neural causal powers: on their view, properly scientific psychological explanation is all formulated exclusively in the vocabulary of neural events and processes.

Naturalists disagree about whether all properties are causal powers. In part, this may be a purely verbal dispute about the term 'property'. Some, but not all, naturalists accept that there are normative properties: moral properties, aesthetic properties, and the like. Typically, these naturalists deny that there are normative causal powers: moral properties and aesthetic properties are not causal powers of the objects that possess them. Other naturalists deny that there are moral properties and aesthetic properties: on their view, moral and aesthetic talk is properly given an error-theoretic, or fictionalist, or otherwise anti-realist explanation.

Naturalists do not uniformly allow that they are (ontological) physicalists. Roughly, (ontological) physicalists maintain that there are none but physical causal entities with none but physical causal powers. Some naturalists suppose that there are non-physical natural causal powers. Consider chemical powers. Some naturalists suppose that chemical powers are just (suitably configured) physical powers. But other naturalists say that chemical powers are 'emergent' with respect to physical powers; and these naturalists make similar claims for biological powers, psychological powers, and so forth.

Naturalists may allow that they are (ontological) materialists. Roughly, (ontological) materialists maintain that there are none but material causal entities with none but material causal powers. If we understand 'material causal entities' in the way that pre-Newtonians did, then contemporary naturalists deny that they are (ontological) materialists: few, if any, contemporary naturalists are committed to the claim that, fundamentally, the universe is composed of indivisible atoms that interact solely via contact. However, if we understand 'material causal entities' to be 'natural causal entities', then, of course, naturalists are 'materialists' in this stipulated sense.

Naturalists do not uniformly endorse scientism. Roughly, scientism maintains that scientific inquiry is the only proper form of inquiry. Some naturalists accept that science is the only reliable source of knowledge about any topic, including those topics traditionally studied in the humanities: philosophy, human history, literature, music, and the arts. Other naturalists insist on the autonomous authority of the humanities: while it is true that the causal entities studied in the humanities are all recognised by science, there are properties – but not causal powers – of those causal entities that are only properly understood from the standpoint of the humanities; and, if there are non-causal entities – e.g. abstract objects – that are studied in the humanities, then those entities may lie entirely beyond the purview of the sciences.

Naturalists do not uniformly endorse 'humanism', in at least one sense of that contested term. Roughly, in the sense I have in mind, humanists are naturalists who take human agency, human freedom, and human progress to be of fundamental value. Some naturalists suppose that humanism is unacceptably parochial: if agency, freedom, and progress are fundamental values, then they are so quite apart from any considerations about *humanity*. Other naturalists question the values that humanists take to be fundamental, either because they suppose that these values are not fundamental, or because they suppose that what humanists claim to be values are not really values at all. (Disputes about whether what the humanists claim to be values really are values may rest on merely verbal disagreements about 'agency', 'freedom', and 'progress'. For example, those who deny that we have libertarian freedom will not accept that *libertarian* freedom is a fundamental value, though they may accept that *compatibilist* freedom is a fundamental value.)

Naturalists disagree about whether there is 'first philosophy'. Some naturalists are entirely dismissive of any alleged investigation of the first causes of things, that which does not change, and 'being as such'. However, particularly if we allow some latitude in the interpretation of these topics – so that we do not insist that they be understood exactly as they are in Aristotle's *Metaphysics* – then there is no reason why naturalists cannot embrace them. For example, naturalists who suppose that there is an initial state of the causal order are bound to accept that there is at least one kind of 'first cause';

and naturalists who accept that there are certain kinds of conserved quantities that characterise our universe are bound to accept that there are features of our universe that do not change.

Naturalists disagree about the stance to take on disputes between rationalists and empiricists. Some naturalists suppose that we have innate concepts and innate knowledge; other naturalists suppose that experience is the ultimate source of all of our concepts and knowledge. More generally, naturalists differ markedly from one another in their epistemological views, including their views about proper responses to philosophical scepticism.

Perhaps surprisingly, naturalists even disagree about whether all causal entities are spatiotemporally located entities. Some naturalists suppose that, fundamentally, the universe is a distribution of fields over a single spatiotemporal manifold; for these naturalists, all causal entities are spatiotemporally located entities. But other naturalists suppose that, fundamentally, the universe is something other than a distribution of fields over a single spatiotemporal manifold; for these naturalists, it is at least an open question whether there are parts of our universe that are causal but not spatiotemporal.

2. Natural and non-natural

Given that naturalists disagree about so much, is there anything that they agree upon, beyond the claim that there are none but natural causal entities, with none but natural causal powers? Clearly enough, they agree on anything that is *entailed by* the claim that there are none but natural causal entities, with none but natural causal powers. In particular, they agree that there are no non-natural causal entities with non-natural causal powers. But what would count as non-natural causal entities? And what would count as non-natural causal powers?

It is not controversial that science does not recognise ancestor spirits, astral intelligences, demons, devas, fairies, ghosts, gods, gremlins, mermaids, trolls, vampires, werewolves, witches, wizards, yeti, zombies, and the like. Moreover, it is not controversial that science does not allow that ch'i, kami, karma, samsara, Sat, the Tao, and so forth, play causal roles in our universe. So, given that naturalists do not believe in causal entities and causal powers beyond those recognised by science, it is no surprise that naturalists do not believe that these entities exist or that these powers are exercised. But it doesn't follow – at least not immediately – that all of the listed entities are non-natural causal entities and that all of the listed powers are non-natural causal powers.

Our characterisation of naturalism relies upon distinctions between (a) natural and non-natural causal entities and (b) natural and non-natural causal powers. But can these distinctions be informatively explained? And, if these distinctions cannot be informatively explained, does that somehow cast doubt on the characterisation of naturalism? Would anything be lost if naturalists gave up on ontological naturalism, and nailed their colours exclusively to the mast of methodological naturalism? Why not say that naturalists believe in just those causal entities and causal powers that are recognised by science?

One response to these questions is to take the distinctions to be primitive. It is not implausible to suppose that some distinctions are primitive; that is, it is not implausible to suppose that some distinctions do not admit of illuminating explication in other terms. Moreover, it is not implausible to suppose that ordinary distinctions between the natural and the non-natural are in reasonably good working order: it is not as if we simply draw blanks – or reach for our revolvers – when other people make use of the words 'natural' and 'non-natural' in the kinds of contexts in which we are now operating. And it seems to be consonant with the ways in which we ordinarily use these terms that the entities and powers listed above are non-natural. Perhaps it is unsatisfying to go without an illuminating explication of these distinctions; but, as even rock stars have noted, at least *inter alia*, desires must sometimes remain unsatisfied.

Another response to these questions is to suggest that natural causal entities and natural causal powers are just those causal entities and causal powers that are recognised by science. If we take up this response, then, in effect, we are nailing our colours to the mast of methodological naturalism: naturalists do believe in just those causal entities and causal powers that are recognised by science, and it is in virtue of being recognised by science that causal entities and causal powers are natural causal entities and natural causal powers.

However, if we take up this response, we open ourselves up to certain pointed questions. Are the natural causal entities and natural causal powers those that are recognised by *current* science? Are the natural causal entities and natural causal powers those that are recognised by *best future* science? Are the natural causal entities and natural causal powers those that are recognised by *ideal* science? And, if what matters is recognition by best future science or ideal science, why should we suppose that science really does fail to recognise the entities and powers listed above?

In response to the last of the pointed questions, it seems reasonable to suggest that it is not just that the listed entities and powers are not recognised by current science: there is no reason to doubt that the listed entities and powers will not be recognised by any future science, and nor would they be recognised by ideal science, if there were such a thing. While it is true that current science is incomplete in all kinds of ways – and while it is true that some parts of current science are mistaken – we have enough securely established science to rule it out that future science will, or that ideal science would, recognise the listed entities and powers.

Given this response to the last of the pointed questions, our response to the first three pointed questions is clear: natural causal entities and natural causal powers are those that would be recognised in *ideal* science; and non-natural causal entities and non-natural causal powers are those that would not be recognised in *ideal* science. While we do not know *all* of the natural causal entities and natural causal powers that would be recognised in ideal science, we do know *many* of the natural causal entities and natural causal powers that would be recognised in ideal science. And while we cannot identify *all* of the non-natural causal entities and non-natural causal powers that would not be recognised in ideal science, we can identify *many* of the non-natural causal entities and non-natural causal powers that would not be recognised in ideal science. No future science is going to tell us – and ideal science would not tell us – that there are ancestor spirits, astral intelligences, demons, devas, fairies, ghosts, gods, gremlins, mermaids, trolls, vampires, werewolves, witches, wizards, yeti, zombies, and the like. No future science is going to tell us – and ideal science would not tell us – that ch'i, kami, karma, samsara, Sat, the Tao, and so forth, play causal roles in our universe.

I have some sympathy for *both* responses to the request for explanation of the distinctions between the natural and the non-natural. On the one hand, it seems to me that we have a pretty good pre-theoretical grasp of these distinctions: we can accurately predict which entities and powers naturalists will classify as 'natural' and which entities and powers naturalists will classify as 'non-natural'. On the other hand, it seems to me to be reasonable to think that pre-theoretical application of these distinctions yields the same verdicts that we get if we ask whether ideal science would count given causal entities or causal powers as natural or non-natural. Current science – the current application of scientific method – is our touchstone for identifying the denizens of causal reality. But current science is also our guide to ideal science. And our judgments about what is natural or non-natural are not merely judgments about the deliverances of current science; they are also judgments about what would be the deliverances of ideal science.

Use of the distinction between the natural and the non-natural is not the only respect in which my characterisation of naturalism is controversial. Recall that, on my characterisation, naturalists are committed to the following two claims: (a) current science is our touchstone for identifying the denizens of causal reality; and (b) natural reality exhausts causal reality: there are none but natural causal entities with none but natural causal powers. This characterisation adverts to causal entities, causal powers, and causal reality. Some philosophers will be unhappy that the characterisation is framed in terms of *causation*; other philosophers will be unhappy that it is framed in terms of *powers*. In particular, given the various areas of disagreement between naturalists that I discussed earlier, it might be suspected that some naturalists would prefer something like the following formulation: (a) current science is our touchstone for identifying what there is; and (b) natural reality exhausts reality: there are none but natural entities with none but natural properties.

I'm inclined to think that the characterisation of naturalism should not depend upon the stance taken on the various questions on which I say that naturalists disagree. For example, I don't think that we should characterise naturalism in ways that rule out the existence of abstract objects, even though some naturalists do maintain that there are no abstract objects, and even though I am, myself, sympathetic to the view that there are no abstract objects. Since it seems to me right to say that, if there are abstract objects, then there are non-natural objects, I think that the alternative formulation proposed at the end of the previous paragraph is too restrictive: it fails to count as naturalistic views that are naturalistic.

But then what about those naturalists who wish to eschew powers (and perhaps even causation)? I'm inclined to think that the characterisation of naturalisation can be allowed to vary with some of the hitherto unmentioned philosophical commitments on which naturalists disagree. Where I have adverted to powers and causation, another naturalist might appeal to laws, or to counterfactual dependencies, or some other combination of denizens of the Goodmanian nomological circle. Those philosophers who do not like powers and causes are free to reformulate the characterisation of naturalism that I have given in their own favoured vocabulary. Such reformulation will not affect the identification of ancestor spirits, astral intelligences, demons, devas, fairies, ghosts, gods, gremlins, mermaids, trolls, vampires, werewolves, witches, wizards, yeti, zombies, and the like, as non-natural entities; and nor will it affect the identification of ch'i, kami, karma, samsara, Sat, the Tao, and so forth, as non-natural properties.

3. What might have been

So far, I have considered what naturalists have to say about *actual* causal reality. On the account given, actual causal reality consists of none but natural causal entities with none but natural causal powers. But this account leaves it open what naturalists say about *possible* causal reality. Could it have been the case that, among the denizens of causal reality, there are non-natural causal entities and non-natural causal powers? Naturalists differ in their answers to this question.

Some naturalists think that, while there actually are none but natural causal entities with none but natural causal powers, there could have been non-natural causal entities with non-natural causal powers. Typically, naturalists who think this way have fairly loosely constrained views of what is possible. Such naturalists may suppose that conceivability is a good guide to possibility – roughly, if we can coherently conceive that p, then it is possible that p – whence, since we can coherently conceive of the entities and powers listed earlier figuring in causal reality, it is possible that those entities and powers figure in causal reality. Such naturalists may suppose that any recombinations of parts of actual entities and powers are possible entities and powers, whence, since we can plausibly suppose that the entities and powers listed earlier are recombinations of parts of actual entities and powers, it is possible that those entities and powers figure in causal reality. No doubt there are other routes that such naturalists might take to reach or justify the claim that there could have been non-natural causal entities with non-natural causal powers.

Other naturalists think that it is not merely that there actually are none but natural causal entities with none but natural causal powers, but also that there

18 *What is naturalism?*

could not possibly have been non-natural causal entities with non-natural causal powers. Since this view will be less familiar to many readers, and since it is a view that I find attractive, I shall spend more time developing one version of it here. On the view that I favour, the following three claims are true:

Shared History: Necessarily, any possible way for causal reality to be shares an initial history with the way that causal reality actually is.
Actual Naturalness: Actual causal reality is entirely natural.
Conservation of Naturalness: Necessarily, if, at some point, causal reality is entirely natural, then it remains entirely natural at all subsequent points.

These three claims entail that there could not possibly have been non-natural causal entities with non-natural causal powers.

All naturalists are committed to *Actual Naturalness*; and, plausibly, all naturalists are committed to *Conservation of Naturalness* as well. After all, if you think that it is possible for non-natural causal entities with non-natural causal powers to arise in a possible causal reality in which, hitherto, there have been none but natural causal entities with none but natural causal powers, then what grounds do you have for being confident that no non-natural causal entities with non-natural causal powers will arise in actual causal reality?

So the controversial claim here is *Shared History*. If you suppose that conceivability is a good guide to possibility, or that any recombinations of parts of actual entities and powers are possible entities and powers, then you will deny *Shared History*. However, if you suppose that possibility – real, ontic, metaphysical possibility – is closely tied to chance – real, ontic, metaphysical chance – then you may also accept:

Chance Divergence: Necessarily, the only way that causal histories diverge is by having chances play out differently.

If we accept *Shared History* and *Chance Divergence*, and if we suppose that there are ways that causal reality might have been other than the way that it actually is, then we must suppose that chance is operative in causal reality. While it may be that some of the causal relations in causal reality are deterministic – there is only one possible effect given the cause – there are some causal relations in causal reality that are indeterministic or probabilistic: given the cause, there is a probability distribution over a range of possible effects, and there is nothing that determines which of those effects is the one that eventuates. On some interpretations of quantum mechanics, there are chance quantum events; on some ways of understanding libertarian freedom, there are chance free actions of human beings. Even if we suppose that quantum mechanics is deterministic and that nothing has libertarian freedom, it may still be that there is a fundamental level at which chance enters into causal reality: there is much that we do not yet know about causal reality.

Accepting *Shared History* and *Chance Divergence* does not entail rejection of ordinary probabilistic talk. Suppose I roll a die, and that the roll of the die is not subject to real, ontic, metaphysical chance. In order to calculate fair odds for those who wish to bet on the roll of the die, we need to assign probabilities to the epistemically or doxastically possible outcomes of the roll. While, given our assumption that real, ontic, metaphysical chance is not in play, there is only one really, ontically, metaphysically possible way for the roll to end, none of those privy to the roll of the die possess any information that favours one of the epistemically or doxastically possible outcomes of the roll over other epistemically or doxastically possible outcomes of the roll. Given our ignorance, we can do no better than to suppose that all of the epistemically or doxastically possible outcomes of the roll are equally likely. (Of course, we could have evidence – from previous rolls of the die – that it is loaded towards particular outcomes. But let's suppose that we have no evidence that contradicts the claim that the die is fair.) Moreover, even if we suppose that real, ontic, metaphysical chance is in play – or, at any rate, might be in play – when we roll a die, so long as we are ignorant of the chances, we still can do no better than to suppose that all of the epistemically or doxastically possible outcomes of the roll are equally likely.

Obviously enough, there is nothing special about the rolling of dice; across a vast range of cases, we need to use epistemic or doxastic probabilities in order to accommodate our ignorance, whether or not there are real, ontic, metaphysical chances in play. True enough, if we know that real, ontic, metaphysical chances are in play, and we know what the real, ontic, metaphysical chances are, then our epistemic or doxastic probabilities should be keyed to those chances. But, when we do not know the real, ontic, metaphysical chances and nonetheless have need of epistemic or doxastic probabilities, we may be permitted to appeal to (appropriately restricted) versions of conceivability and recombination – and to other related principles – in order to generate the epistemic or doxastic possibilities that populate the relevant probability space.

As we have already noted, acceptance of *Shared History, Actual Naturalness, Conservation of Naturalness*, and *Chance Divergence* does not entail that there are chances and alternative ways that causal reality can be. If we suppose that there are chances and alternative ways that causal reality can be, then we should also add the following principle:

Actual Chance: Actual causal reality is chancy.

Given these five principles, while there are ways that causal reality could have been other than the way that it actually is, there are no ways that causal reality could have been in which there are non-natural causal entities with non-natural causal powers. Moreover, given *Shared History*, if actual causal reality has a finite history, then there is an initial part of causal reality that is necessary: natural causal reality exists of necessity, as do any natural causal entities that belong to that initial part of causal reality.

No doubt there are other ways of developing naturalistic views according to which there could not possibly have been non-natural causal entities with non-natural causal powers. However, we shall not attempt to canvass alternatives here.

4. Big pictures

The claim that naturalism says that there are none but natural causal entities with none but natural causal powers does not fix what naturalists says about what is *fundamental*, or what *grounds* all else, or what belongs to the base upon which all else *supervenes*. Moreover, our earlier treatment of the distinction between natural causal entities and powers and non-natural causal entities and powers does not speak at all to the distinction between natural properties and non-natural properties. Should we suppose that these are reasons for thinking that our characterisation of naturalism is inadequate?

Suppose that a *worldview* is a theory of everything: a comprehensive descriptive, evaluative, and normative account of reality. Even in principle, it is impossible for any of us to have a worldview: there are propositions that we lack the conceptual resources to formulate; and there are so many propositions that we do have the conceptual resources to formulate that, even collectively, we cannot entertain them all. However, while we cannot have worldviews, we can have *big pictures*: theories that are the best approximations that we can make to worldviews. While we cannot expect big pictures to answer all questions, we can expect that they will provide answers to the perennial big philosophical questions. Moreover, while we cannot expect big pictures to be held in optimally axiomatised form, we can expect that big pictures will exhibit aspirations to systematicity: big pictures will include powerful general principles as well as detailed lower-level claims.

Naturalistic big pictures may include carefully formulated claims about grounding and/or fundamentality, and/or supervenience. For example, a naturalistic big picture might include the following, relatively precise, way of spelling out the claim that everything supervenes on the natural:

(a) There are no parts of minimal natural variants of actual causal reality that have no qualitative intrinsic natural properties; and (b) there are no parts of minimal natural variants of actual causal reality that are exactly alike in all qualitative intrinsic natural properties and yet that differ in some qualitative intrinsic properties.

But, among the naturalistic big pictures that include this claim, some – and only some – will also include the following claim:

(a) There are no parts of minimal physical variants of actual causal reality that have no qualitative intrinsic physical properties; and (b) there are no parts of minimal physical variants of actual causal reality that are exactly alike in all qualitative intrinsic physical properties and yet that differ in some qualitative intrinsic properties.

No matter what account we adopt of natural properties and physical properties, it is clear that this latter claim entails the former. Consequently, it is clear that, even if we thought that the former claim is a requirement for naturalistic big pictures, we would not think that it is a requirement for naturalistic big pictures that the former claim is taken to be primitive or fundamental.

Each of the above principles is controversial among naturalists. While it might seem reasonable to suppose that naturalists will agree that there is some *loose* sense in which reality is fundamentally natural, or in which everything is grounded in the natural, or in which everything supervenes upon the natural, there is no reason to expect that naturalists will agree on any very precise formulation of these claims. It is a familiar feature of philosophical investigation that increasing precision in formulation does not necessarily lead to increasing convergence of opinion. Our big pictures are always works in progress; in particular, the precise formulations of the commitments of our big pictures are always works in progress.

The first of the two principles given above makes use of a distinction between natural and non-natural properties, and the second makes use of a distinction between physical and non-physical properties. While it is certainly possible to make heavy weather of both of these distinctions, I'm inclined to repeat here what I said earlier about the distinctions between (a) natural and non-natural causal entities and (b) natural and non-natural causal powers. These distinctions are in no worse shape than most of the distinctions upon which we rely; and, as happens everywhere else, attempts to precisify these distinctions secure *less* agreement than is typically found in their pre-theoretical application.

5. Attitudes

So far, we have considered some basic definitional questions. We have said that *naturalists* are those who have *naturalistic* big pictures, and that naturalistic big pictures are those that include or entail *naturalism*. Further, we have said that naturalism is the view that: (a) science is our touchstone for identifying the denizens of causal reality; and (b) there *are* none but natural causal entities with none but natural causal powers. Moreover, we have noted that it is controversial among naturalists whether – though I myself accept that – there *must be* none but natural causal entities with none but natural causal powers. Finally, we have noted that, while naturalists are typically committed to some version of the claim that reality is *fundamentally* natural, it is controversial among naturalists how this claim might properly be made more precise.

This discussion of basic definitional questions leaves open exactly what attitudes naturalists have to the propositions that we take to define naturalism.

If we suppose that belief is an all or nothing matter, then we must suppose that naturalists are committed to – and, in the typical case, *believe* – the propositions that define naturalism. But to say this much is to say nothing about what kind of believing attitude naturalists might have towards the propositions that define naturalism. As with many kinds of beliefs, these defining naturalistic beliefs may be held unreservedly, or tentatively, or with some intermediate degree of conviction. Perhaps relatedly, these defining naturalistic beliefs may be relatively immune to revision – located centrally in the web of belief – or they may be relatively exposed to revision – located somewhere near the periphery of the web of belief. Perhaps also relatedly, these defining naturalistic beliefs may be strongly supported by other beliefs – associated with a panoply of strong supporting reasons – or they may be only weakly supported by other beliefs – associated with few, weak supporting reasons.

If we suppose that beliefs are really point credences, then we must suppose that naturalists are committed to – and, in the typical case, assign – a credence greater than 0.5 to the conjunction of the two propositions that define naturalism. If we suppose that beliefs are really interval credences, then we must suppose that naturalists are committed to – and, in the typical case, assign – a credence with lower bound greater than 0.5 to the conjunction of the two propositions that define naturalism. And, for more complicated views about the credences that constitute beliefs, we need to make similar suppositions. But to say these things about credences leaves open other questions about the believing attitudes that naturalists might take towards the propositions that define naturalism. In particular, information about credences tells us nothing about the resilience or robustness of those credences. No matter what credences are held concerning the propositions that define naturalism, those credences may be only very weakly robust or resilient, or they may be very strongly robust or resilient.

No matter how we think about beliefs, we need to acknowledge the obvious point that it is *possible* for the beliefs that are characteristic of naturalism to be held dogmatically, or irrationally, or unreasonably, or on the basis of middling to weak reasons, and so forth. Moreover, we *should* acknowledge the equally obvious point that there *are* naturalists whose naturalism is dogmatic, or irrational, or unreasonable, or held on the basis of middling to weak reasons, and so on.

If we wish to draw general conclusions about naturalistic big pictures, then we need to focus our attention on *best* naturalistic big pictures. Showing that less than best naturalistic big pictures suffer from various deficits tells us nothing about the virtues of naturalism. Moreover, showing that best *extant* naturalistic big pictures suffer from various deficits teaches no definitive lesson about the virtues of naturalism: we can be sure, before we look, that any extant naturalistic big pictures are susceptible of improvement. Of course, similar points hold for non-naturalistic big pictures that are in competition with naturalistic big pictures: proper doxastic humility entails that claims about the comparative virtues of big pictures are given no more than tentative advance.

6. Critics

'Naturalism' has many critics. There are many volumes devoted to arguments against 'naturalism'. Consider, for example, Craig and Moreland (2000a). This volume collects together essays that are intended to show that 'naturalism' cannot give an adequate account of knowledge, intentionality, properties, ordinary objects, minds, free agency, morality, the origins of the universe, and the origins of life, among other things. The contributions to that volume work with diverse characterisations of 'naturalism' and its commitments. It is worth listing some of the parts of these characterisations.

> Every legitimate method of acquiring knowledge consists of, or is grounded in, the hypothetically completed methods of the empirical sciences (that is, in natural methods).
>
> (Moser and Yandell 2000: 10)

> All knowledge is ... reducible to (or in some manner continuous with) sense perception.
>
> (Willard 2000: 25)

> Human knowledge and intentionality are to be explained entirely in terms of scientifically understandable causal connections between brain states and the world.
>
> (Koons 2000: 50)

> The only explanations that count are scientific explanations.
>
> (Moreland 2000: 74)

> The naturalistic program consists primarily of a plan to use the methods of the natural sciences, and those methods alone, in the development of philosophical theories.
>
> (Rea 2000: 110–111)

> The fundamental explanation of any event is non-psychological in nature.
>
> (Goetz 2000: 157)

> Scientific naturalism would have us understand the universe entirely in terms of the undirected causes studied by science. In particular, since human beings are a part of the universe, who we are and what we do must ultimately be understood in [these] terms.
>
> (Dembski 2000: 253)

While it is true that, for each of these claims, there are some naturalists who accept them – and while it is also true that there are some very wellknown naturalists who accept all of them – it is important to recognise that there are many naturalists who accept none of these claims. There are naturalists – that is, people who suppose that there are none but natural causal entities with none but natural causal powers – who accept that, for example, the humanities afford methods of acquiring knowledge, e.g. the reading of fiction, that are not grounded in the hypothetically completed methods of the empirical sciences; that, for example, philosophy yields knowledge, e.g. about logic and reasoning, that is not reducible to sense perception; that, for example, our thought about and our knowledge of our own conscious states is not explained in terms of scientifically understandable causal connections between brain states and the world; that, for example, there are important normative and evaluative explanations that are not scientific explanations; that, for example, philosophers may legitimately develop philosophical theories about normative and evaluative domains without making use of any natural scientific methods; that fundamental psychological explanation is psychological in nature; and that, for example, our ultimate understanding of human virtue is not cast solely in terms of the causes studied by science.

All big pictures – including naturalistic big pictures – are works in progress; all big pictures – and not merely naturalistic big pictures – are subject to strawman attacks. But, of course, that a vast amount of criticism of 'naturalism' is largely attacks on strawmen does not entail that there are no legitimate objections to naturalism, and, in particular, to current formulations of naturalism. Moreover, as I have already noted, it is not the case that the works to which I have just been adverting are *entirely* attacks on strawmen: there certainly have been naturalists – sometimes very prominent naturalists – who have advanced some of the claims that these critics take to be canonical for naturalists. But no family of big pictures is to be rejected merely on the grounds that some of its members are badly behaved. After all, apart from anything else, it is no less true of any other family of big pictures that some of its members are badly behaved.

Perhaps it is also worth adding a methodological observation at this point. Given that there is a large family of naturalistic big pictures, and given that these naturalistic big pictures differ considerably from one another, it is implausible to suppose that it can be shown, in one fell swoop, that naturalistic big pictures are self-defeating: internally inconsistent, inconsistent with uncontroversial data, etc. If we are interested in the merits of naturalistic big pictures, then we should be thinking about the *comparative* merits of naturalistic big pictures. When, for example, we compare naturalistic big pictures with theistic big pictures, does it turn out that we can be fairly confident that the best big pictures belong to just one of these two families? When we compare naturalistic big pictures with all of the other families of big pictures, does it turn out that we can be fairly confident that the best big pictures belong to just one of those families?

Given that it is implausible to suppose that it can be shown that all naturalistic big pictures are self-defeating, and given that we wish to assess the comparative merits of naturalistic big pictures, what we should be doing is setting particular naturalistic big pictures against competing big pictures, and assessing the comparative merits of these big pictures. Part of the reason why Craig and Moreland (2000a) – and the many books similar to it – are so unsatisfactory is that they don't (a) give detailed articulations of the competing big pictures that make clear the commitments of those competing big pictures; and (b) engage in detailed comparison, on particular points of data, of the explanations that the competing big pictures offer of that data. The approach taken in Craig and Moreland (2000a) leaves it entirely open for readers to conclude that naturalistic big pictures are the very worst big pictures, except for all of the other big pictures.

7. Concluding remarks

Naturalism is roughly best characterised by the following two claims: (1) natural reality exhausts causal reality; and (2) scientific method is the touchstone for identifying the denizens of causal reality. More carefully: (1) there are none but natural causal entities with none but natural causal powers; and (2) scientific method is the touchstone for identifying natural causal entities and natural causal powers.

Naturalism is distinct from – and naturalists differ in their attitudes towards – nominalism, empiricism, physicalism, materialism, scientism, mental eliminativism, modal eliminativism, rejection of first philosophy, and the fundamentality of spacetime.

Naturalists do not agree on whether it is necessarily true that there are none but natural causal entities with none but natural causal powers; and naturalists do not agree on whether it is necessarily true that scientific method is the touchstone for identifying natural causal entities and natural causal powers.

Naturalists do not agree about what is fundamental, or about what grounds all else, or about what belongs to the base on which all else supervenes.

Naturalists differ in the nature, strength, and resilience of their commitments to naturalism. Most naturalists are fallibilists; few naturalists are dogmatists.

Much contemporary criticism of naturalism misses the mark. In particular, much contemporary criticism of naturalism works with characterisations of naturalism that fail to capture what many – often enough, most – contemporary naturalists believe. It is very important to distinguish between the contents of particular naturalistic big pictures, and the claims that are common to all naturalistic big pictures.

3 What is religion?

For some, religion is the core of their existence; for others, religion is a blight on humanity. Much as we suspected about naturalism prior to our discussion of it, we might guess that religion is subject to a wide range of conflicting interpretations. However, unlike in the case of naturalism, the matter is greatly complicated by the fact that proponents of particular religions often enough suppose that other religions are blights on humanity. In consequence, it is not plausible to suppose that the initially reported conflict turns on differences in the use of the term 'religion'.

This chapter starts out with a review of familiar data about religion. We begin with a reminder about standard taxonomies of religions. Then, after noting the difficulties involved in collecting accurate data concerning membership in religions, we provide some rough contemporary demographic data, including data about naturalists, atheists, agnostics, and those who have no religious affiliation.

The second part of this chapter takes up questions about the definition of 'religion'. After noting the inadequacies of familiar definitions of 'religion', I adopt a definition adapted from one constructed in Atran (2002). This rather lengthy and complicated definition makes commitment to the non-natural a necessary condition for religion, while eschewing both the suggestion that religion relates humanity to the supernatural and the suggestion that religion relates humanity to the spiritual.

In the third part of this chapter, I respond to the objection that the adopted definition of 'religion' fails to accord with 'insider' religious perspectives. Among the responses that I provide, perhaps the most important is that there just is no serious prospect of giving an adequate 'insider' definition of 'religion'.

The fourth part of this chapter provides my response to the objection that the adopted definition of 'religion' fails to make the religious a special case of the spiritual. I argue that, apart from seeking to explain the well-defined in terms of the ill-defined, this objection overlooks the many dimensions of religion that simply cannot be explained in terms of spirituality.

In the fifth part of this chapter, I take up the question whether – as critics often enough allege – naturalism is a religion. Given my accounts of naturalism and religion, it is obvious that naturalism is not a religion. And the same is true for atheism, materialism, physicalism, and so forth: these, too, are obviously not religions.

In the sixth part of this chapter, I take up the question whether – as some have suggested – philosophy is a religion. I give an account of philosophy – as theoretical discipline – on which it is obvious that philosophy is not a religion. Moreover, I argue that we should not agree with those who say that philosophy is, or, at any rate, should be, a way of life.

Finally, in the seventh part of this chapter, I discuss theories of religion, and the correlations between my adopted definition of 'religion' and those theories of religion. I claim that, while there is some grain of truth in most theories of religion that have been proposed over the past few centuries, we are a long way from having a fully satisfactory theory of religion.

1. Data

Standard reference works typically divide the religions of the world, by origin, into something like the following major categories: Semitic religions, Indian religions, East Asian religions, Indigenous religions, and New religions.

Semitic religions include Judaism, Christianity, and Islam; these three religions are sometimes known as the great post-Axial Abrahamic religions. All Abrahamic religions are taken to profess adherence to the God of Abraham. Smaller, more recent, Semitic religions – which may also be classified as New Religions – include Bahá'í and Rastafarianism.

Indian religions include Hinduism, Buddhism, Jainism, and Sikhism; these four religions are sometimes known as the great post-Axial Dharmic religions and are taken to share some teachings about dharma, karma, and reincarnation. While Hindus, Jains, and Sikhs remain primarily concentrated in India, there are now more Buddhists in China, Thailand, Japan, Burma, and South Korea than there are in India.

East Asian religions include Taoism and Confucianism; these two religions are sometimes known as the great post-Axial Taoic religions. All East Asian religions are taken to share some teaching about the Tao or Dō. Smaller East Asian religions, which may also be classified as Indigenous religions or New Religions, include Shinto, Tenriism, Korean Shamanism, Cheondoism, Caodaism, Hoahaoism, Falun Gong, and Han Folk Religion.

Indigenous – local, folk – religions with pre-Axial foundations are found in all parts of the world, sometimes – but not always – in syncretism with post-Axial religions that threaten them with extinction. For example, there are various minority Iranian religions – Zoroastrianism, Mandaeism, and Yazdânism – that are a thousand years older than Islam. There are so many indigenous African, indigenous American, indigenous Asian, indigenous Australian, indigenous Austronesian, and indigenous European religions that it is not possible to identify them all here.

New religions come in various forms. Some new religions are off-shoots from the great post-Axial religions, e.g. Hindu reform movements such as

Ananda Marga, and Jewish innovations such as Noahidism. Some new religions are revivals, or contemporary patterning, of ancient religious practices: Druidry, Heathenry, Hellenism, Kemeticism, Wicca, and the like. Some new religions are apparently made up from whole cloth: Eckankar, Raëlism, Scientology, Unitarian Universalism, and so forth.

Of course, the great post-Axial religions themselves divide into sub-classes in various different ways. Jews may be, for example, Conservative, Orthodox, or Reform. Christians may be, for example, Eastern Orthodox, Catholic, Protestant, Restorationist, Mormon, or Jehovah's Witness; and if, for example, Protestant, then they may be, for example, Adventist, Anabaptist, Anglican, Baptist, Calvinist, Lutheran, Methodist, or Pentecostal; and if, for example, Methodist, then they may be – though they need not be – one of the eighty denominations that belongs to the World Methodist Council. Muslims may be, for example, Ahmadiyya, Ibadi, Mahdavi, Salafi, Shiite, Sufi, Sunni, or Wahhabi; and if, for example, Sunni, then they may be, for example, Hanafi, Hanbali, Maliki, Shafi'i, or Zāhirī. Buddhists may be, for example, Theravada, Mahayana, or Vajrayana (though some think that Vajrayana is merely a branch of Mahayana); and, if, for example, Mahayana, then they may be, for example, Chan, Nichiren, Pure Land, Seon, or Zen (and, if Vajrayana is merely a branch of Mahayana, then they may also be, for example, Shingon, Tendai, Tiantai, or Tibetan). Hindus may be classified – with varying precision – in several different ways, for example, according to primary deities, for example Vaishnavi, Shaivi, Shakti, or Smarti; or according to the weight of historical sources, for example Folk, Vedic, Vedantic, Yogic, Dharmic, or Bhakti; or according to type of religiosity, for example karma-marga, jnana-marga, bhakti-marga, or virya-marga; or even, perhaps, according to darśanas – Samkhya, Yoga, Nyaya, Vaisheshika, Mimamsa, or Vedanta.

Estimating the number of adherents of the religions of the world is fraught with difficulty. Not all countries collect data about religious adherence in national censuses. Even when countries do collect national census data about religious adherence, they do so under different categories, and with differing degrees of reliability. Other agencies or organisations that attempt to collect data about religious adherence have found that estimates vary considerably depending exactly how requests for information are framed. Moreover, other agencies and organisations that attempt to collect data about religious adherence often have motivating agendas that may introduce deliberate or unintended bias into their results.

When setting out to collect data about religious adherence, agencies and organisations need to consider: what typology to use for the categories of religious adherence; whether to make some level of active practice a necessary condition for religious adherence; whether to make self-identification a necessary condition for religious adherence; whether to include children among those who count as religious adherents; whether to recognise that there are people who belong to more than one religion; and whether to allow that individuals can 'belong' to religions even if they are not adherents of those religions (e.g. atheistic Jews or merely 'cultural' Christians). Moreover, those who wish to use already collected data to construct demographic profiles for the religions of the world must decide which data to use and how to use it, bearing in mind the various ways in which the data may be both inaccurate and difficult to aggregate.

The Pew Research Centre (2012) gives the following breakdown for global religious affiliation: Christian 31.5%; Muslim 23.2 %; Unaffiliated 16.3%; Hindu 15.0%; Buddhist 7.1%; Folk Religionist 5.9%; and Other 1.0%.

Adherents.com (2017) gives the following breakdown for global religious affiliation: Christian 33%; Muslim 21%; Unaffiliated 16%; Hindu 14%; Buddhist 6%; Folk Religionist 6%; Chinese Traditional 6%; and Other 5%. Adherents.com notes that the aim of this list is only to generate an order; the percentages are 'not normalised', and 'tend towards the high end of reasonable estimates'.

The Pew Research Centre and Adherents.com both note that the Unaffiliated category includes many who hold some religious or spiritual belief even though they do not identify with a particular faith. The Pew Research Centre – Masci and Smith (2016) – gives the following breakdown for the 22.8% Unaffiliated in the United States: 7.1% Atheists and Agnostics (3.1% Atheists); 8.8% Don't Care about Religion; and 6.9% Care about Religion. Perhaps it is a reasonable conjecture that 3.0% of US adults are naturalists. Boldly projecting this onto global levels of the Unaffiliated, we might guess that somewhere between 1% and 2% of the world's adult population are naturalists. This estimate is obviously highly imprecise. No agencies or organisations collect data about *naturalists*. Moreover, collection of data about *atheists* is notoriously unreliable. In many parts of the world, atheists have strong incentives not to disclose their religious views. In addition, many atheists are happy to make merely cultural identifications, as Jews, or Hindus, or even as Christians.

Across the globe, there are many more religious adherents than there are naturalists, perhaps by as much as 80:1. And, across the globe, there are some religions with more religious adherents than there are naturalists: Christianity (perhaps by as much as 33:1), Islam (21:1), Hinduism (14:1), Buddhism (6:1), Confucianism (3:1), and Taoism (3:1). But, for almost all of the world's religions, there are more naturalists than there are adherents of those religions; and moreover, perhaps unsurprisingly, for almost all of the denominations of the world's religions, there are more naturalists than there are adherents of those denominations. When we consider the fine structure of big picture disagreement, the various kinds of naturalistic big pictures are no less well-subscribed than the multifarious kinds of religious big pictures.

2. Definition

Despite the familiarity of the considerations that I have just rehearsed, talk that uses the term 'religion' is taken to be problematic in some parts of the modern academy. This suspicion about the term 'religion' begins with the observation that our use of this term has its origins in seventeenth-century Western Europe, and that, while there are earlier terms in other languages – e.g. 'din', 'dharma', 'halakha', 'threskeia' – that we sometimes translate with the term 'religion', those earlier terms really didn't mean anything like what the term 'religion' means. To this observation about the origins of the term 'religion', it is added that, while the term 'religion' is a good fit for Christianity – and perhaps also for Judaism and Islam – it misleads us into thinking that what we call 'eastern religions', 'indigenous religions', 'new religions', and so on, are best thought of as 'variations' on the 'Abrahamic religions'.

These suspicions about the term 'religion' may seem to be strengthened by examination of the kinds of definitions of 'religion' that have been given by scholars since the second half of the nineteenth century. Consider:

> Religion is belief in spiritual beings.
> (Tylor 1871: 8)

> Religion is a unified system of beliefs and practices related to sacred things.
> (Durkheim 1915: 62)

> Religion is a system of beliefs and practices – by means of which a group of people struggles with the ultimate problems of human life – that expresses its refusal to capitulate to death, to give up in the face of frustrations, to allow hostility to tear apart their human aspirations.
> (Yinger 1948: 7)

> Religion is a system which acts to establish powerful, pervasive, and long-lasting moods and motivations in men by formulating conceptions of a general order of existence and clothing these conceptions with such an aura of factuality that the moods and motivations seem uniquely realistic.
> (Geertz 1971: 4)

> Religion is an institution consisting of culturally patterned interactions with culturally postulated superhuman beings.
> (Spiro 1971: 96)

> Religion, in a given society, is that instituted process of interaction among the members of that society – and between them and the universe as they conceive it to be constituted – that provides them with meaning, coherence, direction, unity, easement, and whatever degree of control over events they perceive is possible.
> (Klass 1995: 38)

Among these definitions – and the wider class to which they belong – there is a common, but not universal, tendency to select defining features that hold for the 'Abrahamic religions', and, perhaps, for some of the other classes of 'religions', but that clearly do not hold for other classes of 'religions'. Not all 'eastern religions' and 'new religions' suppose that there are spiritual beings. Not all 'eastern religions', 'new religions', and 'indigenous religions' express a refusal to capitulate to death. Not all 'eastern religions' postulate superhuman beings. Moreover, where these definitions do not select defining features that fail to hold for some classes of 'religions', they exhibit the common, but not universal tendency to allow things that manifestly do not belong to any of the classes of 'religions' to count as religion. In particular, secular political ideologies and practices can be what the definitions of Durkheim, Geertz, and Klass say that religions are.

While it might seem that the failure of these definitions supports the claim that talk that uses the word 'religion' is problematic, it would be hasty to leap to that conclusion. To this point, we have nothing that rules out the claim that, while talk that uses the word 'religion' is perfectly in order, attempts to define the word 'religion' have often turned out to be problematic for the very reason that has led some to be suspicious about the word 'religion' itself. Moreover, while some contemporary theorists – e.g. McKinnon (2002) – maintain that 'religion' is a family resemblance term for which we can do no more than provide a list of examples, it would also be hasty to leap to the conclusion that there is nothing better that we can do if asked to explain the proper use of the term.

Consider the following definition of 'religion' that is adapted from Atran and Norenzayan (2004):

> Religions are passionate, communal displays, of costly commitments to the satisfaction of non-natural causal beings – e.g. gods and/or ancestor spirits – and/or the overcoming of non-natural causal regulative structures – e.g. cycles of reincarnation, reward and punishment – resulting from evolutionary canalisation and convergence of:
>
> 1   widespread belief in non-natural causal agents and/or non-natural causal regulative structures;
> 2   hard to fake public expressions of costly material commitments – offerings and/or sacrifices of goods, property, time, and/or life – to the satisfaction of those non-natural causal agents and/or the overcoming of, or escape from, those non-natural causal regulative structures;
> 3   mastering of people's existential anxieties – death, deception, disease, catastrophe, pain, loneliness, injustice, want and loss – by those costly commitments to the satisfaction of those non-natural causal agents and/or the overcoming of, or escape from, non-natural causal regulative structures; and
> 4   ritualised, rhythmic, sensory co-ordination of (1), (2), and (3) in communion, congregation, intimate fellowship, or the like.

While Atran and Norenzayan offer the definition from which this one is adapted as a merely stipulative definition – i.e., as a definition of what they mean by 'religion' for the purposes of their work – it seems to me that this definition gives a decent account of what ordinary speakers are talking about when they are talking about religion. Of course, that's not to say that ordinary speakers think about religion in these terms; nor is it to say that ordinary speakers would immediately agree that this is an adequate definition of the term 'religion'. But this definition – unlike the definitions that we considered earlier – clearly has the resources to classify what we call 'Abrahamic religions', 'Iranian religions', 'Indian religions', 'East Asian religions', 'African religions', 'Indigenous religions', and 'New religions' as religions, while also correctly identifying that merely secular political ideologies and practices – e.g., Communism, Nazism, and Fabianism – are not religions.

The definition that we have adapted from Atran and Norenzayan is much longer, and much more complicated, then the earlier definitions that we considered. This seems right and proper; the definitions that we have considered and rejected typically fail because they overlook significant features of religions. Elements that we expect to see in religions (even if we do not find all of them in every religion) include: big pictures; designated behaviours and practices (art, dance, feasts, festivals, funerary rites, initiations, marriage ceremonies, meditation, music, prayer, rituals, sacrifices, sermons, trances, and veneration); faith or belief in entities postulated in the relevant big pictures; hierarchies; institutions and organisations; moral codes; public service; religious leaders and/or holy people; sacred objects; sacred sites; and religious texts (histories, narratives, and symbolic stories).

The definition that we have adapted from Atran and Norenzayan has the interesting feature that it builds commitment to the non-natural into the definition of religion: religions are, by definition, in the business of satisfying non-natural agents and/or escaping from non-natural regulative structures. In the next chapter, we shall return to the question of whether this is acceptable.

The definition that we have adopted from Atran and Norenzayan, unlike many competing definitions, does not have it that religion relates humanity to the 'supernatural'. The 'non-natural' is a very broad category that includes, at least, the 'supernatural', the 'preternatural', and the 'paranormal'. Roughly speaking, the paranormal is concerned with non-religious subject matters that allegedly lie beyond the range of scientific explanation: cryptids, ESP, psychic abilities, UFOs, and so forth; the preternatural is concerned with religious marvels and deceptive trickery that are not due to divine powers, but are rather the workings of demons, witches, wizards, and the like; and the supernatural is concerned with ghosts, spirits, and other entities not essentially tied to religion that neither produce marvels and engage in deceptive trickery nor possess and exercise divine powers. While naturalists certainly deny that there is anything that is supernatural, or preternatural, or paranormal, religious believers are not required to believe that there are things that are paranormal, or preternatural, or supernatural, though they may believe that there are things that fall under all three of these categories.

The definition that we have adopted from Atran and Norenzayan, unlike many competing definitions, does not have it that religion relates humanity to the 'spiritual'. While it is quite common for participants in the Abrahamic religions – and in a range of 'new religions' – to claim that their religion is, somehow, 'spiritual', the definition leaves it open that there are participants in religions who would deny that their religion is, in any sense, 'spiritual'. Perhaps – though this is less clear – the definition that we have adapted from Atran and Norenzayan also does not have it that religion relates humanity to the 'transcendent'. Here, it depends exactly how 'transcendence' is understood. If the 'transcendent' is just the non-natural, then, of course, the definition does have it that religion relates humanity to the transcendent. But if the 'transcendent' is a sub-category of the non-natural, then the definition leaves it open whether it must be that religion relates humanity to the transcendent.

3. Inside/Outside

One objection, hinted at above, that some religious adherents may wish to lodge against the definition of 'religion' that I have adopted, is that it does not mention those features of their own religions that they take to be of the greatest significance and value. Perhaps, when you look at religions from the *outside*, what you see is what the definition presents: belief in 'the transcendent'; costly commitment to its satisfaction or overcoming; passionate public affirmation of that commitment; soothing of existential anxieties by the commitment and its public affirmation; and ritualised, rhythmic, sensory coordination in communion, congregation and intimate fellowship that figures centrally in both the passionate expression and the soothing. However, when you look at a religion from the *inside*, what you take to be of the greatest significance and value are encounters with, and/or experiences of, 'the transcendent', and the emotions, feelings, and attitudes generated and sustained by those encounters and/or experiences, whether these encounters and/or experiences, and the related emotions, feelings, and attitudes, are given to you first-hand, or second-hand, or third-hand.

There are several things to say in response to this objection.

First, it seems that there is no prospect of giving an *insider* account of religion: no one belongs to more than a tiny fraction of the religions of the world, so who could possibly be well-placed to give, or to assess, putative insider definitions? Unless we wish to say that there is really only one religion, it seems that the requirements of definition will force us to give an outside account.

Second, it is important that what we have given is only a *definition* of 'religion'; in particular, it should not be supposed that what is offered is intended to be a *theory* of religion. What is required of a definition is just that it tells you enough about its target to distinguish the target from everything else. It is not a requirement of a definition that it tells you

34   *What is religion?*

everything – or even everything important – about its target. So far as this point goes, it could be true that what is of the greatest significance and value in religions is encounters with and/or experiences of 'the transcendent' that generate and sustain certain kinds of emotions and feelings and attitudes, even though none of this rates a mention in perfectly acceptable definitions of 'religion'.

Third, it is wrong to suppose that what has the greatest significance and value in *all* religions is encounters with and/or experiences of 'the transcendent' that generate and sustain certain kinds of emotions and feelings and attitudes. Perhaps it is true that encounters with and/or experiences of 'the transcendent' that generate and sustain certain kinds of emotions and feelings and attitudes have the greatest significance and value in *some* religions; or, more weakly and so more likely, perhaps it is true that encounters with and/or experiences of 'the transcendent' that generate and sustain certain kinds of emotions and feelings and attitudes have the greatest significance and value for *some* members of some religions. But in at least some religions, what is taken to have the greatest significance and value is right practice: doing those things that the religion requires one to do. As it is sometimes said, some religions – including some folk religions – value orthopraxy above orthodoxy (of attitudes, feelings, and emotions); indeed, some religions – including some folk religions – recognise little value in orthodoxy (of attitudes, feelings, and emotions).

Fourth, it won't do to respond here with the claim that the definition of 'religion' should be the definition of 'true religion'. We can take it for granted that, if there is a true religion, then it is the one among the religions that is true. But, in order to take this for granted, we need an understanding of 'religion' that is prior to our understanding of 'true religion'. This chapter began with an uncontroversial discussion of the many different world religions; there is no mileage to be gained from the insistence that only one of them really is a religion.

Fifth, we should not suppose that the proposed definition is merely 'nominal', and that, in consequence, we should continue to seek a 'real' definition of religion. The definition that we have proposed does an equally good job of sorting actual and merely possible cases; there is no further definitional work that remains to be done. Of course, as noted above, there is plenty of theoretical work still to be done; but there is no reason to suppose that further attempts to refine our definition will help with that task.

4. Spirituality

Another objection, also hinted at in the preceding discussion, is that we should think of the *religious* as a special case of the *spiritual*: rather than defining 'religion', we should be defining 'spirituality', and then explaining what distinguishes religious spirituality from non-religious spirituality. There are various things to say in response to this objection.

First, there is much less agreement about the use of the term 'spirituality' than there is about the use of the term 'religion', both in everyday contexts and in academic contexts. Among the things that are sometimes said to be constitutive of spirituality there are at least the following: (a) questing for 'ultimate meaning'; (b) experiencing awe, wonder, or reverence, particularly in connection with natural reality; (c) encountering one's own 'inner dimension'; (d) reaching a state of 'inner peace'; (e) enjoying 'mystical' or 'quietist' experiences; (f) engaging in meditative or 'self-expressive' practices; and (f) achieving 'personal growth' (against a background of 'issues' or 'difficulties'). Many of the items in this list also use terms whose use is contested, both in everyday contexts and in academic contexts.

There are naturalistically acceptable interpretations of much of (a)–(f). Naturalists sometimes investigate, and endorse, fundamental norms and values. Naturalists sometimes experience awe and wonder in contemplation of natural reality. Naturalists sometimes meditate. Naturalists sometimes engage in self-reflection. Naturalists sometimes have experiences that non-naturalists report as 'religious', or 'mystical', or 'quietist'. Naturalists sometimes overcome substance abuse, or marital difficulties, or parenting difficulties, or some kinds of mental health problems, at least in part through their own efforts. If we suppose that 'spirituality' is no more than what is available to naturalists, then 'spirituality' turns out to have nothing in particular to do with religion.

There are also naturalistically unacceptable interpretations of (a)–(f). Naturalists do not engage in quests for non-natural ultimate meaning. Naturalists do not claim to have encounters with their own non-natural inner reality. Naturalists do not claim to have mystical or quietist experiences of the non-natural. Naturalists do not claim to have found non-natural resources for personal growth. Naturalists do not claim that meditation and self-expression put them in touch with a non-natural dimension. If we suppose that 'spirituality' is essentially concerned with the non-natural, then it is not automatically foreclosed that 'spirituality' is also essentially connected to religion.

Second, even if it is accepted that religious people are all spiritual, in the naturalistically unacceptable sense of 'spiritual', it is implausible that religion can be explained in terms of spirituality. There is nothing in 'spirituality', as such, that mandates, or legitimises, or even explains passionate communal displays of costly commitments to the satisfaction of non-natural causal beings and/or the overcoming of non-natural causal regulative structures. 'Spirituality', as such, can be – and often seems to be – no more than a bare commitment to the existence of a non-natural dimension or aspect of causal reality. That commitment is insufficient to motivate any kind of passionate communal display; in particular, it is insufficient to motivate displays of costly commitments: offerings and/or sacrifices of goods, property, time, life, and so forth.

Third, as we noted, at least *inter alia*, in discussion of the previous objection, it seems doubtful that we should accept that all religious people are spiritual, in the naturalistically unacceptable sense of 'spiritual'. Of course, it is clearly true that many religions, including many mainstream parts of all of

36 *What is religion?*

the great post-Axial religions, are centrally concerned with spiritual development, in the naturalistically unacceptable sense of 'spiritual'. But some religions – including, in particular, indigenous religions – attach negligible significance to individual development, spiritual or otherwise. For religions focussed on social orthopraxy, considerations about non-natural 'spirituality' may have no particular importance or significance.

5. Is naturalism a religion?

The definition of 'religion' that we have given can do useful work. For example, we can appeal to it to make short work of the claim that naturalism is a religion. Recall that our definition says:

> Religions are passionate communal displays of costly commitments to the satisfaction of non-natural beings and/or the overcoming of non-natural regulative structures resulting from evolutionary canalisation and convergence of:
>
> 1   widespread belief in non-natural causal agents and/or non-natural regulative causal structures; and
> 2   hard to fake public expressions of costly material commitments to the satisfaction of those non-natural causal agents and/or the overcoming of those non-natural causal regulative structures; and
> 3   mastery of people's existential anxieties by those costly commitments; and
> 4   ritualised, rhythmic, sensory coordination of (1), (2), and (3) in communion, congregation and intimate fellowship.

Naturalism is the claim that there are none but natural causal entities with none but natural causal powers. Naturalistic big pictures include naturalism. Naturalists are those who have naturalistic big pictures. There is nothing more to being a naturalist than having a naturalistic big picture. (Caveat. If we want to allow that big pictures can include claims merely by entailing them, then we might want some fancy footwork to accommodate worries about inconsistency. Where big pictures are logically consistent, we can happily say that big pictures that entail naturalism are naturalistic big pictures. But, at least if we are working with classical logic, inconsistent big pictures trivially entail – and so include – all claims. Perhaps the simplest solution is to allow that inconsistent big pictures are *trivially* naturalistic: the only *interesting* naturalists are those who have logically consistent naturalistic big pictures.)

Religious people are adherents of religions. Religious big pictures are big pictures had by religious people. Directly from our definition, religious big pictures include non-natural causal beings and/or non-natural causal regulative structures. Directly from our definition, there are no logically consistent naturalistic religious big pictures. It cannot be that religious people have logically consistent naturalistic big pictures. It cannot be that naturalists are religious. It cannot be that naturalism is a religion.

As we noted two paragraphs back, there is nothing more to being a naturalist than having a naturalistic big picture. Being a naturalist does not require hard to fake public expressions of costly material commitments to anything; in particular, being a naturalist does not require hard to fake public expressions of costly material commitments to the satisfaction of non-natural causal agents and/or the overcoming of non-natural causal regulative structures. Furthermore, being a naturalist does not require mastery of one's existential anxieties by anything; in particular, being a naturalist does not require mastery of one's existential anxieties by costly commitments to the satisfaction of non-natural causal agents and/or the overcoming of non-natural causal regulative structures. Again, being a naturalist does not require any ritualised, rhythmic, sensory coordination in communion, congregation and intimate fellowship; in particular, being a naturalist does not require the kind of ritualised, rhythmic, sensory coordination in communion, congregation and intimate fellowship that is characteristic of religion. The claim that naturalism is a religion imputes to naturalists commitments that they are not required to have, and that, as a matter of fact, many of them do not have.

What goes for naturalism goes for atheism as well. Atheism is the claim that there are no gods. (To accommodate those who deny that God is a god, we might say: atheism is the claim that there is no God *and* there are no gods. Henceforth, those who require this adjustment should take it as read.) Atheistic big pictures include or entail atheism. Atheists are those who have atheistic big pictures. By exactly the same kind of reasoning that we went through in connection with naturalism, we can conclude that it cannot be that atheism is a religion; and we can also conclude that the claim that atheism is a religion imputes to atheists commitments that they are not required to have, and that, as a matter of fact, many of them do not have.

Our definition of 'religion' also tells us something interesting about the relationship between theism and religion. Theism is the claim that there is at least one god. Theistic big pictures include or entail theism. Theists are those who have theistic big pictures. While it is plausible to suppose that there is a strong correlation between having a theistic big picture and being an adherent of a religion, there are people who have theistic big pictures and yet are not adherents of any religion. Such people believe that there is at least one god, but do not participate in, and do not otherwise support, passionate communal displays of costly commitments to the satisfaction of whatever gods they take there to be, while also not participating in, or otherwise supporting, passionate communal displays of costly commitments to the overcoming of non-natural causal regulative structures. Theism is neither necessary nor sufficient for religion.

38   *What is religion?*

6. Is philosophy a religion?

The definition of 'religion' that we have given can also do useful work in helping us to understand the ways in which religion differs from philosophy.

Philosophy is a theoretical discipline. The subject matter of philosophy is those claims for which we do not have, and cannot see how we might come to have, expert agreement on the methods to be used in settling them. In other disciplines – such as mathematics, computer science, physics, biology, psychology, economics, sociology, media studies, and history – there are core claims on which there is expert agreement: these core claims are taught as settled fact to students and used without question by researchers in other disciplines. Beyond these core claims, there is the domain of regular research: while there is not yet expert agreement on the claims in this domain, there is expert agreement on the methods, or kinds of methods, that will eventually settle these claims, if, indeed, they are eventually to be settled. At the boundary of the discipline, where it slides into the philosophy of that discipline, there are claims for which there is not even expert agreement on whether those claims properly belong to the discipline and so might yield to current or future methods that are proper to the discipline. (Think, for example, about current disputes about string theory. Some expert physicists maintain that string theory is the future of fundamental physics; other expert physicists maintain that, at least as things now stand, string theory is not any kind of physics.)

On this way of thinking about philosophy, other disciplines start out as philosophy, and claims cease to be philosophical only when other disciplines contain a sufficient number of independent experts who agree (a) on the methods by which those claims are to be assessed; and (b) on the assessment of a sufficient number of those claims. Furthermore, every discipline borders on philosophy: for every discipline, there are borderline claims on which there is no expert agreement, even concerning whether those claims will eventually yield to claims proper to the discipline in question. Moreover, beyond all of the other disciplines, there are domains – for example, ethics, aesthetics, and political philosophy – that remain resolutely philosophical despite millennia of attention: in these domains, there is no more expert agreement on answers to significant questions than there was in Plato's time.

The overall assessment of religious big pictures is something that falls at least partly in the domain of philosophy: there is no expert agreement on the overall assessment of religious big pictures, and nor is there expert agreement on the methods to be used in the overall assessment of religious big pictures. More generally, the overall assessment of big pictures is something that falls at least partly in the domain of philosophy: there is no expert agreement on the overall assessment of big pictures, and nor is there expert agreement on the methods to be used in the overall assessment of big pictures.

The assessment of religion is also something that falls partly in the domain of philosophy: there is, of course, no expert agreement on the methods to use in assessing *some* claims about religion. However, there is a panoply of disciplines – including, for example, anthropology, archaeology, cultural studies, demography, economics, history, human geography, law, linguistics, literary studies, musicology, neuroscience, political science, psychology, religious studies, and sociology – that provide expert agreement on some claims, and some methods for investigating further claims, about religion. Depending upon exactly what falls into religious big pictures, it may also be that these disciplines provide expert agreement on some claims and some methods for investigating further claims that belong to religious big pictures.

To be a philosopher is to be an exponent of a theoretical discipline, just as it is for mathematicians, computer scientists, physicists, biologists, psychologists, economists, sociologists, and historians. To be a philosopher does not require participation in, or support of, passionate communal displays of costly commitments to anything. Hence, in particular, to be a philosopher does not require participation in, or support of, passionate communal displays of costly commitments to the satisfaction of non-natural causal agents and/or to the overcoming of non-natural causal regulative structures. Of course, this is not to say that no philosophers incur costly commitments as a result of their participation in philosophy; the point is just that philosophy is not religion, and philosophers, merely as such, are not required to have religion.

Some philosophers maintain that philosophy is, or should be, more than a theoretical discipline; philosophy is, or should be, a *way of life*. In my view, the most that can sensibly be required is that, for those philosophers who work on developing particular big pictures, there is an appropriate fit between the normative and evaluative aspects of their big pictures and the lives that they lead. Say that someone leads a *philosophical life* just in case they devote a significant part of their life to the pursuit of the theoretical discipline that is philosophy. If, while leading a philosophical life, someone develops a big picture that says that a philosophical life is a life wasted, then that one is not a good candidate to be leading a fully flourishing life. However, someone who, while leading a philosophical life, develops a big picture that says that a philosophical life can be a fully flourishing life – and, in particular, that their *own* philosophical life can be a fully flourishing life – is, at the very least, a much better candidate to be leading a fully flourishing life.

There is nothing in my definitions of 'religion' and 'philosophy' that rules it out that there are religious philosophers, i.e., that there are philosophers who belong to particular religions. To be a philosopher requires commitment to the practice of a theoretical discipline. To be religious requires participation in, or support of, passionate communal displays of costly commitments to the satisfaction of non-natural causal agents and/or to the overcoming of non-natural causal regulative structures. In the general case, there is no reason why people cannot manage both commitment to a theoretical discipline and participation in, or support of, religious passionate communal display. Of course, it is possible that some might feel that they must give up commitment to the practice of a theoretical discipline in order to have sufficient resources for participation in or support of the religious passionate communal display. (Perhaps Pascal's renunciation of mathematics might be taken to be an example.) But, equally, some might feel that their commitment to participation in, or support of, the religious passionate communal display provides them with reason to commit to the practice of the theoretical discipline: perhaps the assessment and development of big pictures is, itself, to be counted as significant support for the religious passionate communal display.

7. Theories of religion

The definition of religion that we have adopted is not committed to any particular theory of religion. Nonetheless, it is framed with an eye to possible accommodation of whatever is true in extant theories of religion. Here, we shall give no more than the roughest thumbnail sketches of theories of religion.

Some theories of religion make fundamental appeal to explanation of data. Tylor (1871) and Frazer (1890) both suppose that religious beliefs are overarching explanations of natural phenomena: birth, death, and everything in between. Otto (1917) explains religious beliefs as responses to numinous experience: religion is the product of our causal connection to transcendental reality.

Some theories of religion make fundamental appeal to psychological function. Hume (1770) suggests that religious beliefs express and satisfy needs that arise from the uncertainties of human life, including the need to manage hopes and fears about events that are neither controllable nor comprehensible. Feuerbach (1841) claims that religious beliefs project fundamental forms of human thought and feeling embodying moral aspirations arising from social interactions between human beings. Freud (1927) holds that religion offers fulfilment for some of our deepest, most repressed, unconscious desires and wishes, including, in particular, the Oedipus complex. Malinowski (1944) argues that religion is born out of the conflict between plans and realities, particularly in connection with death. Eliade (1971) asserts that religion arises from a nostalgia for origins or a yearning to return to a mythical age.

Some theories of religion make a fundamental appeal to social function. Marx (1844) says that religious thought is part of an ideology that leads everyone to accept that their position in social hierarchy is justified. Durkheim (1915) maintains that the primary social role of religion is to establish and support group cohesion through collective participation in religious rituals. Stark and Bainbridge (1987) take religions to be 'systems of compensation' that vie for followers in a religious economy, selling 'non-natural' compensation for goal frustration and personal deficit.

Some theories of religion make appeal to evolutionary theory, treating religion as adaptation or exaptation. Simple exaptationist accounts of religious beliefs view them as non-functional products of human cognitive mechanisms that are functional in other domains. Some exaptationists follow Guthrie (1993) in positing a hyperactive agency detection device whose false positive errors give rise to postulation of non-natural agents. Some exaptationists follow Boyer (1994) in adding that the mistaken postulation makes use of minimally counterintuitive concepts: invisible hands, incorporeal actors, and the like. Simple adaptationist accounts of religious beliefs typically view them as mechanisms for producing adaptive prosocial behaviour. Some adaptationists follow Irons (1996) and Wilson (2002) in suggesting that religious practices are costly signals of willingness to cooperate with others; others follow Steadman and Palmer (2008) in suggesting that what is signalled is preferability as potential mate. More complex accounts seek to meld the simple exaptationist and adaptationist approaches: e.g., Atran (2002) says that the non-functional products of human cognitive mechanisms become the locus of emotionally motivated self-sacrifice that stabilises in-group order and assuages existential anxiety.

Given that our definition of religion traces back to Atran (2002), it is hardly surprising that it fits well with evolutionary accounts; and nor is it surprising that it has some degree of fit with both social accounts and psychological accounts. In almost all of the psychological accounts and social accounts that we have mentioned, there is some grain of truth. But none of these psychological accounts and social accounts considered individually, nor the sum of these psychological accounts and social accounts considered collectively, provides a plausible, comprehensive, explanatory theory of religion. Moreover, while it is clear that evolutionary theories promise to provide good explanatory accounts of religion, there is much work to be done to capitalise on the initial promise that they exhibit.

I anticipate that some readers may worry that the fit between evolutionary accounts of religion and my favoured definition indicates that the definition is loaded against the claim that at least some religious big pictures get things right, or, at any rate, get things more nearly right than do any competing big pictures. There are at least two salient points to make in response to this worry. First, on any remotely plausible view, almost all religious big pictures do not get things right. No plausible theory of religion has the consequence that a sizeable proportion of religious big pictures get things right. Second, while naturalists may well suppose that evolutionary accounts debunk the claims of religion, there are proponents of religion – see, for example Barrett (2004), and De Cruz and De Smedt (2015) – who see no inconsistency between evolutionary accounts and the truth of their favoured religious big picture, and, indeed, who suppose that evolutionary accounts of religion actually provide support for their favoured religious big picture.

8. Concluding remarks

Religions are passionate communal displays of costly commitments to the satisfaction of non-natural beings and/or the overcoming of non-natural regulative structures resulting from evolutionary canalisation and convergence of:

1 widespread belief in non-natural causal agents and/or non-natural regulative causal structures; and
2 hard to fake public expressions of costly material commitments to the satisfaction of those non-natural causal agents and/or the overcoming of those non-natural causal regulative structures; and
3 mastery of people's existential anxieties by those costly commitments; and
4 ritualised, rhythmic, sensory coordination of (1), (2), and (3) in communion, congregation and intimate fellowship.

Because religions involve big pictures, designated attitudes (e.g. faith), designated behaviours (e.g. fasting), designated practices (e.g. prayer), hierarchies, institutions, leaders, moral codes, public service, sacred objects, sacred sites, sacred texts, and saints, and much more besides, naturalism is not a religion.

Philosophy is a theoretical discipline. The subject matter of philosophy is those claims for which we do not have, and cannot see how we might come to have, expert agreement on the methods to be used in settling them. Philosophy is not a religion.

Theories of religion that appeal to data, or to psychological function, or to social function often contain a grain of truth, but are inadequate as theories of religion. The adopted definition makes it clear that any adequate theory of religion must appeal to data, *and* to psychological function, *and* to social function, *and* to more besides. Moreover, while evolutionary theories potentially make a good fit with the adopted definition, we do not yet have anything that approaches an adequate theory of religion.

4 Can there be naturalistic religion?

Given my account of naturalism and religion, it seems that 'naturalistic religion' is a contradiction in terms. On the one hand, given my account, naturalism entails that there are no non-natural causal entities with non-natural causal powers. On the other hand, given my account, religion requires belief in non-natural causal agents and/or non-natural causal regulative structures. A believer who belonged to a 'naturalistic religion' would be required to believe both that there are non-natural causal agents and/or non-natural causal regulative structures and that there are no non-natural causal entities with non-natural causal powers. That is to say, a believer who belonged to a 'naturalistic religion' would be required to have contradictory beliefs simply by virtue of belonging to that 'naturalistic religion'. While it is not impossible for people to hold contradictory beliefs – and while it is not even impossible for people to hold contradictory beliefs while recognising that they hold contradictory beliefs – most of us suppose that no one can rationally embrace the contradiction that seems to be embedded in the very idea of a naturalistic religion, given my account of naturalism and religion.

However, there are many philosophers who claim to embrace 'naturalistic religion'; and there are many other philosophers who claim to aspire to establish 'naturalistic religion'. Some philosophers say that pantheistic religions are naturalistic religions. Some philosophers say that panentheistic religions are naturalistic religions. Some philosophers say that they are religious naturalists. Some philosophers say that there are versions of the great post-Axial religions that are naturalistic religions. Some philosophers claim that naturalists need to build naturalistic religions. Some philosophers claim that they are religious humanists. My aim in this chapter is to work through the various cases, to see how they are classified by my definitions, and to determine whether any of these cases provides good reason to reconsider those definitions.

1. Pantheism

Pantheists typically claim two things: (a) natural reality exhausts causal reality; and (b) natural reality is divine. Since naturalists accept (a), the only question is whether naturalists can also accept (b). On the account that I have given, the central question is whether being divine either is a non-natural causal power, or else entails possession of non-natural causal powers.

Mander (2016) canvasses – without himself endorsing – a list of putative reasons for supposing that natural reality is divine. These reasons include: that natural reality is a unity; that natural reality is an appropriate object of pro-attitudes; that natural reality supports a grand narrative; that natural reality is – or might be – infinite, eternal, and necessary; that natural reality is ineffable; that natural reality is personal; and that natural reality is axiologically perfect.

Among the putative reasons that Mander canvasses, there are several that can happily be embraced by naturalists who deny that natural reality is divine: that natural reality is a unity; that natural reality is an appropriate object of pro-attitudes; that natural reality supports a grand narrative; that natural reality is – or might be – infinite, eternal, and necessary. Of course, it is controversial whether natural reality is infinite; and it is controversial whether natural reality is eternal; and it is controversial whether natural reality is necessary. But, even if natural reality possesses all three of these attributes, this provides no independent reason at all to suppose that natural reality is divine. Much the same goes for the other properties mentioned here: that natural reality is one, that it supports a grand narrative, and that it is the appropriate object of awe and wonder provides no independent reason at all to suppose that natural reality is divine.

Among the putative reasons that Mander canvasses, there are a couple that are really just non-starters. No naturalist can accept that natural reality is ineffable: that's ruled out by the claim that scientific method is our touchstone for identifying the denizens of natural reality. Since science does inform us about natural reality it is not true that natural reality is ineffable. Moreover, no naturalist can accept that natural reality is axiologically perfect: it is the most straightforward common sense that there are many ways in which natural reality could be better than it is.

Once we eliminate the reasons that clearly are not up to the task, the only reason that we are given for thinking that natural reality is divine is that natural reality is personal, at least in some kind of analogical sense. But, even if it is consistent with naturalism to suppose that natural reality is personal, at least in some kind of analogical sense, we then need to ask whether the attribution of personality entails the attribution of non-natural causal powers. It seems to me that it does. Even if we suppose that personality is to be understood in an analogical sense, it seems to me that being a person entails having certain kinds of causal powers, such as those involved in thinking, feeling, sensing, and so on, where these, too, are understood in the same kind of analogical sense. Clearly, there is nothing in science that tells us that natural reality has these powers; so the proper conclusion to draw is that they are non-natural causal powers.

Not all pantheists suppose that the divine is personal. But those pantheists who suppose that the divine is not personal face the task of explaining how to understand their claim that natural reality is divine. If we follow the lead provided by Mander, it is hard not to reach the conclusion that pantheists who suppose that the divine is not personal are unable to discharge this debt. And, for reasons just given, those pantheists who do suppose that the divine is personal are not naturalists, on the account of naturalism that I have adopted.

Elsewhere – e.g., in Oppy (2014a) – I have suggested that a minimal characterisation of 'metaphysical naturalism' should include (a) the claim that the distribution of mindedness in the universe is late and local – that is, the only minded entities are evolved creatures with relatively complex biological structures and, perhaps, minded entities that are the end results of the creative activities of those evolved creatures – and (b) the claim that nothing is divine, or sacred, or worthy of worship. In the present work, I'm suggesting that we should define 'naturalism' as a product of 'scientific naturalism' and 'metaphysical naturalism' and that, if we do so, we get (a) and (b) as plausible consequences of that definition. If I'm right, then, even though pantheists *say* that natural reality exhausts causal reality, it is still the case that pantheists are not naturalists: their further claim that natural reality is divine *contradicts* the claim that natural reality exhausts causal reality.

2. Panentheism

Panentheists are distinguished from pantheists by their views about exactly what it is that is divine. Panentheists, just like pantheists, *say* that natural reality exhausts causal reality. But rather than say that natural reality *is* divine, panentheists say that there is something further that is divine. Given the long history of those who have been labelled 'panentheists', or, at any rate, who have been claimed to exhibit panentheistic tendencies – late antique Neo-Platonists (e.g., Plotinus, Proclus, Pseudo-Dionysius); medieval Neo-Platonists (e.g. Erigena, Eckhart, Cusano, Böhme); modern Neo-Platonists (e.g., Cudworth, More, Astell, Edwards, Schleiermacher); German Idealists (e.g., Hegel, Schelling); American Transcendentalists (e.g. Emerson, Thoreau, Fuller, Alcott); British Idealists (e.g., Green, Ward, Pringle-Pattison, Alexander); Process Philosophers (e.g., Whitehead, Bergson, Hartshorne, Morgan); and contemporary enthusiasts (e.g., Clayton, Griffin, Wegter-McNelly, Johnston) – it is unsurprising that there are many different distinctive theses that are accepted by at least some who have been called, or who self-identify as, panentheists.

Some panentheists suppose that that which is divine is greater than natural causal reality, both including and interpenetrating it. Some panentheists suppose that that which is divine is a transcendent soul or spirit. Some panentheists suppose that that which is divine is constituted from, but, in some sense, goes beyond, natural causal reality. Some panentheists suppose that there is an internal relationship between natural causal reality and that which is divine: that which is divine influences what natural causal reality is like, and natural causal reality affects what that which is divine is like. Some panentheists are panpsychists, committed to 'neutral monism', or 'strong emergence', or the like. Some panentheists claim that quantum entanglement provides a model for understanding the relationship between that which is divine and natural causal reality.

The claims that are characteristic of panentheism are pretty clearly inconsistent with the account of naturalism that I have adopted. If that which is divine *includes* and *interpenetrates* natural causal reality, then that which is divine is a non-natural causal entity with non-natural causal powers. (This follows because 'inclusion' and 'interpenetration' must here be understood in causal terms: the causal powers of that which 'includes' [and 'interpenetrates'] natural causal reality cannot be natural causal powers.) If that which is divine is a *transcendent* soul or spirit, then that which is divine is a non-natural causal entity with non-natural causal powers. (This follows because souls and spirits have causal powers, and the causal powers of *transcendent* souls and spirits must be non-natural.) If that which is divine is *internally related* to natural causal reality in the way suggested above, then that which is divine is a non-natural causal entity with non-natural causal powers. (This follows because the causal powers of that which interacts causally with natural causal reality cannot be natural causal powers.) If that which is divine is *strongly emergent* from natural causal reality, then that which is divine has non-natural causal powers. (This follows because the causal powers of that which is strongly emergent from natural causal reality must be non-natural causal powers.)

One of the most interesting recent defences of panentheism is provided in Johnston (2009). Johnston defends a 'process panentheism' that he claims has no truck with the 'supernatural', i.e., with 'invisible spiritual agencies whose putative interventions would violate the laws of nature' (2009: 40). According to Johnston, his process panentheism encompasses 'legitimate naturalism': the view that the domain of the natural sciences is 'complete on its own terms: every causal interaction ultimately consists in some utterly natural process, for example, mass-energy transfer' (2009: 127). However, according to Johnston, his process panentheism involves a rejection of 'scientism', i.e., a rejection of the view that 'only the natural realm exists' (2009: 127). For, in addition to the natural realm, there is also an autonomous 'realm of sense, the realm in virtue of which things are intelligible' (2009: 128). While repudiating 'pantheism' – the view that the Highest One *is* the natural realm – Johnston defends 'panentheism' – the view that the Highest One is wholly constituted by the natural realm (2009: 127). Moreover, he tells us that, as a matter of definition, the Highest One is 'the outpouring of Existence Itself by way of its exemplification in ordinary existence for the sake of self-disclosure of Existence Itself' (2009: 116, 120, 123, 158). He also says: 'The [Highest One] is the true object of our innermost wills, the very thing we obscurely desire in everything we desire' (2009: 25). '... We know of the Highest One that there could not be one higher. ... We also know that the Highest One could not have evil intent, nor a contempt for the truth' (2009: 36).

Can there be naturalistic religion? 47

An immediate tempting response to all of this is to observe that, if the Highest One can have intent – as implicated in the claim that we know that the Highest One cannot have *evil* intent – then the Highest One has causal powers that are clearly not natural causal powers. So, on the account of naturalism that I have adopted, Johnston's process panentheism is not naturalistic. However, Johnston does warn that:

> We are forced to draw on analogy in thinking and speaking of the Highest One. Accordingly, the Love of the Highest One is analogised as its outpouring in ordinary existents; its Will as self-disclosure, its Mind as the most revealing presentations found in the realm of sense, and its Power as the totality of the laws of nature.
>
> (2009: 158)

Perhaps we should not be too quick to conclude that Johnston supposes that it is literally true that the Highest One loves, and wills, and intends, and establishes natural law. Nonetheless, even if we suppose only that the Highest One 'outpours', and 'self-discloses', and 'presents', it is still surely the case that the Highest One is taken to have, and to exercise, non-natural causal powers. And that is enough to establish that, on the account of naturalism that I have adopted, Johnston's process panentheism is not naturalistic.

Johnston also has interesting views about religion that conflict with the account that I have given. These views are developed against the background of the observation that:

> There are certain large-scale structural defects in human life that no amount of psychological adjustment or practical success can free us from. These include arbitrary suffering, aging (once it has reached the corrosive stage), our profound ignorance of our condition, the isolation of ordinary self-involvement, the vulnerability of everything we cherish to time and chance, and, finally, to untimely death.
>
> (2009: 15, 124)

Johnston claims that: 'Religion is a complex and open-ended collection of cultic practices from which the practitioners derive a deepened capacity to deal with the manifest large-scale structural defects in human life' (2009: 44). 'The religious life is a form of life in which we are reconciled to these large-scale defects of ordinary life. ... [I]t provides a reservoir of energy otherwise dissipated in denial of, and resistance to, necessary suffering.' (2009: 15, 125). He also adds that: 'Salvation is a new orientation that authentically addresses the large-scale defects of human life' (2009: 16, 125). '[It is] an orientation out of which one can live without denying or resisting the necessary suffering that is inherent in the large-scale defects of human life' (2009: 17). '[It is a] transformed outlook in which those defects are somehow overcome (healed, or addressed, or rendered irrelevant, redeemed [but not removed])' (2009: 124). 'True salvation consists in the right relation to the Highest One' (21).

While Johnston is happy to allow that almost everything that is commonly called 'religion' is not really religion properly so-called, it seems to me that he mistakes something that is not even essentially religious for the whole of religion. On the account of religion that I have adopted, it is one important aspect of religion that it provides mastery of people's existential anxieties – in Johnston's terms, it provides adherents with a deepened capacity to deal with the manifest large-scale structural defects in human life. But it is not merely religion that provides resources for dealing with people's existential anxieties; despite what Johnston suggests, there are naturalistically acceptable alternatives whose efficacy is visible in the flourishing lives led by some naturalists. While Johnston's favoured religious resources involve 'life-orientation towards the Highest One' (2009: 37n.1), there is no good reason to suppose that this is the only way to achieve genuine mastery of existential anxieties.

3. Religious naturalism

In some quarters, there is developing interest in what gets called 'religious naturalism'. (See, for example, Goodenough [2000], Crosby [2002], Hague [2010], Rue [2011], and Wildman [2014].) Roughly speaking, the guiding idea seems to be to develop naturalistic big pictures that include beliefs and values often associated with religion. Whether this is a reasonable ambition depends, in part, upon exactly which beliefs and values are up for inclusion.

Some 'religious naturalists' claim to be pantheists or panentheists. We have already seen that pantheistic and panentheistic big pictures cannot be naturalistic: if you are committed to the claims that there are none but natural causal entities with none but natural causal powers and that scientific method is our touchstone for identifying the denizens of causal reality, then you cannot consistently go on to say either that natural causal reality is divine or that natural causal reality participates in the divine. But, of course, rejection of the claim that natural causal reality is divine or that natural causal reality participates in the divine is perfectly consistent with, for example, awed responses to natural causal reality. More generally, there is a vast range of intellectual and emotional responses to natural causal reality that are no less appropriate for naturalists than they are for religious adherents; there is no special work that naturalists need to do in order to justify these responses.

The idea that we need to develop naturalistic big pictures that include values often associated with religion depends upon the assumption that naturalists do not already have big pictures that include those values. This assumption does not withstand even the lightest and most momentary inspection. There is nothing in the claims that there are none but natural causal entities with none but natural causal powers and that scientific method is our touchstone for identifying the denizens of causal reality that is inconsistent with valuing – and embodying and displaying – charity, compassion, courage, diligence, generosity, gratitude, honesty, humility, impartiality, integrity, kindness, love, loyalty, prudence, rectitude, spontaneity, temperance, tolerance, trust, and a host of other virtues. Moreover, there is no compelling evidence that, collectively, naturalists fare worse – or better – with respect to embodying and displaying virtue than do religious adherents. (See, for example, Paul [2005].) Of course, it is true that you cannot read off evaluative and normative commitments from the claims that there are none but natural causal entities with none but natural causal powers and that scientific method is our touchstone for identifying the denizens of causal reality: but it is no less true that, for example, you cannot read off evaluative and normative commitments from the claim that there is at least one god, or from the claim that someone's big picture is religious.

Some of those who claim to be 'religious naturalists' accept that any naturalists can be virtuous, and moral, and emotionally responsive to the wonders of natural causal reality. Rue (2011: 110–111) says that the relevant difference is that 'religious naturalists' take these things to heart and are more actively interested in them. But there are many naturalists who have no interest in taking on the 'religious naturalist' tag who are actively interested in – and who take to heart – concern with virtue, morality, and care for natural causal reality. There is no reason at all to relabel those naturalists who, in previous generations, have worked on developing naturalistic accounts of virtue, morality, and care for natural causal reality.

4. Naturalistic religion

Some claim to have big pictures that are both 'naturalistic' and 'religious', where the 'religious' content of these big pictures is in full conformity with the big pictures of one or another of the great world religions. I shall consider one example here.

Bishop (2018) claims to 'believe the received Christian faith' (2018: 6). True enough, he says that 'there is a good deal of open-ended contestability' (2018: 4) about exactly what Christians are required to believe about how our universe is. While he admits that some other Christians would not allow this, he interprets his own baptismal promise to believe all of the articles of the Christian faith as formulated in the historic creeds as a commitment to 'trust that the received tradition (in creed and scriptures) conveys divine revelation' (2018: 4).

Bishop claims to have a 'naturalistic' understanding of the divine 'just in the sense that it is *anti-supernaturalist*: it rejects the ontological realm separate from and prior to the natural universe that is required for personal omniGod theism' (2018: 14). He insists, however, that there is no implication 'that the divine is graspable through natural scientific inquiry: any viable theism will reject such "natural scientism"' (2018: 14).

At the heart of Bishop's big picture is the suggestion that 'theological explanation of the universe [can] be (uniquely) an irreducible teleological explanation' (2018: 14). In his view, there is no need to postulate a 'productive agent'. Rather, the universe is seen to have an efficient cause because it is 'explicable in terms of its actually realised ultimate and supremely good *telos*' (2018: 14). While he expects that some will be scandalised by the thought that 'in the order of productive causality, the Creator is dependent on his own creatures' (2018: 14), he thinks that this kind of scandal is actually entrenched in Christian tradition.

The core of Bishop's *euteleological* explanation of existence is that 'why everything exists that does exist and counts as created is that it belongs to a unified order whose telos is the supreme good that is actually fully realised' (2018: 15). Initially, it seems that what Bishop commits himself to is the claim that 'the divine is to be identified with [the sum total of] loving interpersonal relationships within the universe' (2018: 15). But he also says that even the most exemplary loving relations – those manifested by Jesus while he was being put to death by combined political and religious authority – do not exhaust the divine: 'What is divine is not just actual Christ-like relationships, but the *full cosmic meaning* of such loving relationship' (2018: 17). And he says that real, salvific, transformative, divine agency in the world is 'the "agency" of love itself, understood as a power that *emerges* from individual loving actions in relationship' (2018: 19). Rather than being the result of external supernatural agency, the Resurrection is the 'inherent effect of absolute steadfastness in living lovingly' (2018: 19).

Bishop's account of his view is not easy to understand. Some of what Bishop says suggests that he thinks that 'final causes' can also be efficient causes: the efficient cause of the existence of the universe is that, within it, there is realisation of the ultimate, supreme good of loving interpersonal relationships. But, whatever others may think about the prospects for an axiarchic explanation of the existence of the universe, it seems to me that naturalists are committed to rejecting this proposal. Science does not recognise efficient 'final causes'; the efficient causes that science does recognise are all such that it makes sense to suppose that they are necessarily associated with – perhaps even grounded in, or constituted from, or supervenient upon – transfers of conserved fundamental natural quantities. However, there is no way that the coming into existence of the universe could be associated with – or grounded in, or constituted from, or supervenient upon – transfer of conserved fundamental natural quantities *from* realisations of the ultimate, supreme good of loving interpersonal relationships. It is simply inconsistent with naturalism to suppose that the realisation of the ultimate, supreme good of loving interpersonal relationships is an efficient cause of the existence of the universe.

Some of what Bishop says suggests that he thinks that individual loving actions in relationship have emergent causal powers that somehow constitute further real, salvific, transformative agency in the world. But, whatever others may say, it seems to me to be very hard to make sense of the idea that 'love itself' has any agency that goes beyond the agency of individuals in loving relationship. People in loving relationships can act together to make real, transformative improvements to the world and to the lives of others; but there is no need to appeal to 'emergent' causal powers in order to explain their achievements. Moreover, it is not clear how an explanation that appealed to such 'emergent' causal powers would run: what is it that has these 'emergent' causal powers, and how does it get to exercise them? In my view, it is inconsistent with naturalism to suppose that individual loving actions in relationship have emergent causal powers that somehow constitute further real, salvific, transformative agency in the world.

Some of what Bishop says suggests uncertainty about exactly what should be claimed to be 'divine'. If Bishop identifies 'the divine' with the sum total of loving interpersonal relationships in the universe, then, while naturalists can accept that there is a sum total of loving interpersonal relationships in the universe, the question that naturalists will want to ask is: What makes it the case that the sum total of loving interpersonal relationships in the universe deserves the label 'divine'? Naturalists can agree – and many, if not all, do agree – that loving interpersonal relationships are a very good thing; but recognising that loving interpersonal relationships are a very good thing doesn't seem to take us any distance at all towards the view that loving interpersonal relationships deserve the label 'divine'. If, on the other hand, Bishop maintains that what is divine is the full cosmic meaning of interpersonal loving relationships, then the question that naturalists will want to ask him is: What do you take the full cosmic meaning of interpersonal loving relationships to be? If the answer to that question is that individual loving actions in relationship have emergent causal powers that somehow constitute further real, salvific, transformative agency in the world, then, as we have already seen, naturalists will deny that there are such emergent causal powers. But, of course, in making this denial, naturalists need not be denying that there is very little, if anything, in our universe that is better than loving interpersonal relationships.

In his discussion of the justifiability of his Christian commitment, Bishop notes that 'though the Christian commitment is to an ethical ideal, it is also a commitment to the world's being fit for hopefully and steadfastly seeking that ideal' (2018: 20). If we understand this commitment in the way that Bishop does – as a commitment to the claim that 'existence is ultimately for the sake of the good' (2018: 21) – then it seems to me that naturalists cannot accept it, for the reasons given above. However, if we take the ethical ideal to be that one should live virtuously – where that is understood to include living lovingly – then I can see no reason why naturalists cannot also be committed to that ideal. While the nature of our universe may make it difficult, for some, some of the time, in some places, to pursue this ideal, it seems to me that naturalists can perfectly well suppose that our universe is, on the whole, a place in which we can 'hopefully and steadfastly' pursue that ideal.

5. Religion of humanity

There is a very long history of calls for new religions that do not have the vices of existing religions. In particular, there is a long history of calls for new religions that lack most, if not all, of the non-natural commitments of existing religions. Here, I shall discuss part of the Western history of calls for new religions that lack most, if not all, of the non-natural commitments of Christianity.

The emergence of deism established various precedents for would-be reformers of religion. In its earliest formulation – in the work of Herbert of Cherbury – deism was presented as a simple, rational alternative to the dogmas of organised Christianity. Cherbury held that the whole content of acceptable religion could be summarised in a few brief claims: there is one Supreme God who deserves to be worshipped through virtuous and pious action, and who distributes rewards and punishments in this life and the next; we should both regret and repent our sins; and we can successfully petition the one Supreme God for assistance. While Cherbury gave short shrift to revelation, scripture, prophecies, miracles, mysteries, dogma, and demagogy, he made some concessions to special divine action. However, many later deists – e.g., the theophilanthropists – made no such concession: for them, the content of acceptable religion came down to, roughly, belief in God and a life to come.

While deism preserved central non-natural elements of organised religion – a Supreme God and the venue of the life to come – more radical alternatives to organised Christianity began to appear from the time of the French Revolution. In particular, the Cult of Reason – led by Jacques Hébert and Pierre Chaumette – aspired to become a civic religion, focussed on the perfection of humanity via the exercise of reason in pursuit of truth and liberty, which encouraged worship of, and devotion to, the ideal of reason. While the Cult of Reason was soon overthrown in favour of Robespierre's deistic Cult of the Supreme Being, enthusiasm for anthropocentric civic religion was not so readily defeated.

During the nineteenth century, there was widespread intellectual interest in the development of systems of belief and ritual in which humanity is the object of public veneration. Famously, Auguste Comte's 'Religion of Humanity' was intended to be a complete religion, with ecclesiastical hierarchy, congregation of saints, liturgy, and sacraments. While not enamoured of Comte's authoritarianism, John Stuart Mill – in company with many other progressive intellectuals of the age – agreed that altruistic virtue required nurturing in a religion of humanity that could foster a sense of unity, ideals of duty and service, and a feeling for the general good. Alongside those who called for the creation of a morally credible naturalistic religion, there were others – such as Henri Saint-Simon – who called for the creation of a new Christianity that had a primary focus on fraternal love.

In the twentieth century, Bertrand Russell, while not accepting the need for a religion of humanity, was very interested in the prospects for 'a free man's worship': a big picture that enables those who possess it to act with compassion in ways that transcend belittling self-concern. Despite the choice of words, it is probably more accurate to take Russell to be looking for an ethically compelling alternative to religion, and not for a naturalistic religion.

Given my account of religion, I think that there are good reasons for naturalists not to be seeking naturalistic religions. I take it that, if there were to be a naturalistic religion, then there would be some naturalistically acceptable entity X towards which that naturalistic religion would provide passionate communal displays of costly commitments dependent upon:

a   belief in X;
b   hard to fake expressions of costly commitments to X;
c   mastery of people's existential anxieties by these costly commitments to X; and
d   ritualised, rhythmic, sensory co-ordination of (a), (b), and (c) in communion, congregation, intimate fellowship, and the like.

The sticking point, I think, lies with (c): it is very hard to see how there could be a naturalistically acceptable entity that provides mastery of people's existential anxieties by supplying a focus for costly commitments.

For example, while the religion of humanity holds out some prospect of managing some existential anxieties – for example, concerning deception, immorality, injustice, and loneliness – it is very hard to see what it has to offer in the face of death, disease, catastrophe, loss, pain, and want. It's not too hard to see, in the designs of the proponents of the religion of humanity, anxieties about class conflict, immorality, social cohesion, trust, and the like. But it is not plausible to suppose that the drivers of religion are exhausted by ethical, moral, and social concerns.

Certainly, if we follow Atran (2002) in supposing that, in religions, non-functional products of human cognitive mechanisms become the locus of emotionally motivated self-sacrifice that stabilises in-group order and assuages existential anxiety, then there is no prospect of manufacturing religions around functional products of human cognitive mechanisms.

6. Religious humanism

The term 'humanism' is used in a variety of different ways that, in part, reflect its interesting history.

One use of the term connects it to the medieval revival of late antique philology and grammar that, in the nineteenth century, became known as 'Renaissance Humanism'. This use of the term became coupled with positive estimation of the wider study of the liberal arts ('humanities').

Another use of the term connects it to a feeling of benevolence towards human beings. Many of the philanthropic societies and institutes that sprang up during the nineteenth century took themselves to be pursuing 'humanistic' goals.

Yet another use of the term – close to the sense that is our primary interest – connects it to big pictures that are characterised by the importance and significance they attach to human understanding, human values, and human agency. Since these big pictures typically have strong commitments to altruism and distributive justice, and to a positive estimation of the liberal arts, these big pictures are often 'humanistic' in both of the previously discussed senses.

There is some global coordination of what I shall call 'humanism'. For example, the International Humanist and Ethical Union (IHEU) brings together rationalist, atheist, irreligious, freethought, humanist, secular, and ethical culture organisations. Typically, the member organisations of the IHEU are committed to critical evidence-based rationality, and to secular morality that promotes individual and collective virtue; typically, the member organisations of the IHEU are opposed to religious dogma, revelation, and any invocation of the non-natural. However, the member organisations of the IHEU divide when it comes to the question of the adoption of ritual and other elements that imitate religion. On the one hand, *secular* humanists reject any truck with religions and religiosity: they have no interest in imitating the rituals and practices of organised religion. On the other hand, *religious* humanists adopt rituals and practices that they take to promote human flourishing and to yield the social goods of religious rituals and practices, but that eschew religious dogma, revelation, and commitment to the non-natural. A current example of religious humanism is provided by Sunday Assembly, which was reported to be establishing local assemblies across the globe. The program for Sunday gatherings comprises a secular talk, some moments of contemplation, some singing, and some socialising. (See Addley [2013].)

The significant difference between the religion of humanity and religious humanism is that, in the case of religious humanism, there is no ambition to find a naturalistically acceptable X, towards which religious humanists would provide passionate communal displays of costly commitments dependent upon:

a   belief in X;
b   hard to fake expressions of costly commitments to X;
c   mastery of people's existential anxieties by these costly commitments to X; and
d   ritualised, rhythmic, sensory co-ordination of (a), (b), and (c) in communion, congregation, intimate fellowship, and the like.

Rather, in the case of religious humanism, the ambition is merely to take on some of the trappings of religion in order to alleviate some of the existential anxieties for which religion provides mastery: loneliness, alienation, and – perhaps – immorality and deception.

Given the ambitions of religious humanism, there is, of course, no conflict between religious humanism and naturalism. But, given the ambitions of religious humanism, it is hard to believe that anything like Sunday Assembly will have wide and prolonged uptake. While it is clear that, if proponents of the religion of humanity could find a suitable X, then they would have a naturalistically acceptable alternative to religion, it seems no less clear that religious humanism is simply not up to the task of providing a substitute for religion.

7. Concluding remarks

The answer to the question posed at the beginning of this chapter is negative. There cannot be a naturalistic religion: there is no naturalistically acceptable entity that can play the role that religion assigns to non-natural entities.

While pantheism and panentheism might be thought to be foundations for naturalistic religions, it turns out that pantheism and panentheism are both inconsistent with naturalism. Moreover – though I have not emphasised this point – it also turns out that pantheism and panentheism are inadequate foundations for religion.

While 'religious naturalism' sounds like a plausible candidate for naturalistic religion, it turns out that the ambitions that are held for 'religious naturalism' really have nothing to do with religion.

While some think that one can be both a naturalist and a proponent of one of the great post-Axial religions, it turns out that those who claim to be, for example, Christian naturalists, have naturalistically unacceptable commitments.

While the religion of humanity sounds like an excellent candidate for naturalistic religion, it turns out that there is no prospect that the design specifications for the religion of humanity will ever be met.

And, while religious humanism – and, for example, the Sunday Assembly – might have *prima facie* similarity with religion, it does not require much inspection to see these really are nothing at all like religions.

5 Does science defeat naturalism?

It might seem odd to suppose that science could defeat naturalism. After all, it is characteristic of naturalism that it supposes that scientific method is our touchstone for identifying the denizens of causal reality. Given that naturalists suppose that causal reality is just as science says that it is, how could it possibly be that science defeats naturalism?

Put aside thoughts that there might be more to natural reality than our universe; that is, put aside the thought that our universe might belong to a wider multiverse. Think of science as an investigation of our universe: physics investigates the physics of our universe; chemistry investigates the chemistry of our universe; biology investigates the biology of our universe; and so on. Given that naturalism says that our universe exhausts causal reality, how could it be that physics, and chemistry and biology, and so forth, say anything that is in conflict with naturalism?

Despite the *prima facie* implausibility of the claim that science defeats naturalism, there are many contemporary philosophers eager to take up the challenge of showing that science does defeat naturalism. Perhaps the best and most carefully elaborated defence of the claim that science defeats naturalism is provided by Plantinga (2011). The plan for this chapter is to have a careful look at the arguments that Plantinga provides.

1. Background

Plantinga argues: (1) that there is much merely alleged conflict between theism and science; (2) that there is superficial conflict but deep concord between theism and science; and (3) that there is superficial concord but deep conflict between naturalism and science.

According to Plantinga: (a) there is merely alleged conflict between theism and evolutionary theory, and between science and the claim that God acts in the world; (b) there is only superficial conflict between theism and evolutionary psychology, and between theism and historical Biblical criticism; (c) some parts of cosmology and molecular biology at least weakly support theism over naturalism; (d) a range of considerations concerning reliability, regularity, simplicity, necessity, natural law, and mathematics very strongly support theism over naturalism; and (e) there is deep conflict between naturalism and evolutionary theory.

Plantinga takes *theism* to be the claim that God exists and is the all-powerful, all-knowing, and perfectly good personal creator of the world (2011: ix); and he takes ('philosophical' or 'ontological') *naturalism* to be the claim that there is no such person as God or anything like God (2011: ix), where this latter claim 'includes materialism with respect to human beings' (2011: xiv) and excludes 'any other supernatural beings' (2011: 122). Plantinga also distinguishes two kinds of 'methodological' naturalism: *weak* methodological naturalism, which says that a scientific evidence base does not include the proposition that there is such a person as God or some other supernatural being, and *strong* methodological naturalism, which says that a scientific evidence base includes the proposition that there is no such person as God or any other supernatural being (2011: 174).

Plantinga defines a person's *evidence base* to be the set of beliefs that that person uses, or appeals to, in conducting an inquiry (2011: 167):

> One of the main functions of one's evidence base ... is that of evaluating possible hypotheses ... Some hypotheses ... will (given my background knowledge or evidence base) be very unlikely, perhaps so unlikely as not to be worth thinking about at all. ... It is important to see in this connection that the evidence base of a Christian theist will include theism, belief in God and also the main lines of the Christian faith; therefore it will assign a high probability to hypotheses probable with respect to the Christian faith.

At least roughly speaking, Bayesians identify 'evidence bases' with *probability distributions*: prior to the introduction of new evidence – data, arguments, etc. – Christian theists assign high probabilities to the claims that are characteristic of Christian theism.

2. Epistemology

Plantinga's epistemology gives a significant role to *defeaters of beliefs*.

Suppose that a person believes that p. If that person acquires a new belief that q, where q entails not p, and adopts the belief that not p in place of the belief that p for this reason, then that person's acquisition of the belief that q is a *rebutting* defeater for their previous belief that p. Weaker relationships than entailment may also suffice for rebutting defeat: for example, it might be enough that it is very unlikely that both q and p (2011: 165).

Suppose that a person believes that p solely for reasons R. If that person acquires a new belief that q, where q entails that reasons R are insufficient for reasonable belief that p, and rejects the belief that p for this reason, then that person's acquisition of the belief that q is an undercutting defeater for their previous belief that p. Again, weaker relationships than entailment may suffice for undercutting defeat: for example, it might be enough that it is very unlikely both that q and that reasons R suffice for belief that p (2011: 165).

Suppose that a person believes that p to degree D solely for reasons R. If that person acquires a new belief that q, where q entails that reasons R are sufficient only for belief that p to degree D', where D'<D, and amends the degree to which the belief that p is held for this reason, then that person's acquisition of the belief that q is an undercutting defeater for that person's confidence in their belief that p. And, yet again, weaker relationships than entailment might suffice for this kind of undercutting defeat (2011: 252).

Rebutting defeaters and undercutting defeaters are *rationality* defeaters: acquired beliefs which, if retained, rationally require adjustments to the stock of beliefs that are held prior to the acquisition of the beliefs in question (2011: 339). By contrast, *warrant* defeaters are features of circumstances that explain why given true beliefs are not knowledge (2011: 166).

Suppose that a person initially believes that p solely for reasons R, but then that person's belief that p suffers undercutting defeat by way of that person's acquisition of the belief that q. Suppose, further, that that person's belief that q is then defeated by the person's acquisition of the belief that s, and that, in consequence, the person's belief that p is reinstated. In these circumstances, that person's acquisition of the belief that s is a *defeater-defeater* for the belief that p: the belief that s is a defeater for the belief that q, where, if undefeated, the belief that q is a defeater for the belief that p (2011: 345).

Suppose that a person initially believes that p solely for reasons R, and that that person's belief that p would suffer undercutting defeat if that person were to acquire the belief that q. Suppose, further, that that person also believes that s, and that that person's belief that s is the sole reason that that person does not take on the belief that q (perhaps, in part, because s entails not q). Then that person's possession of the belief that s is a *defeater-deflector* for the belief that p: in the absence of the belief that s, that person's belief that p would suffer undercutting defeat in virtue of that person's acquisition of the belief that q (2011: 347).

3. 'Superficial conflict'

In response to the claim that evolutionary psychology, and higher Biblical criticism conflict with Christian theism, Plantinga says that, although there is genuine conflict here, the conflict in question is merely superficial, because the existence of evolutionary psychology and higher Biblical criticism does not provide defeaters for Christian belief (2011: xiii).

According to Plantinga, if sciences that produce theories incompatible with Christian belief are characterised by *strong* methodological naturalism – i.e., if those theories assign high prior probabilities to the denials of central Christian beliefs – then those sciences can hardly provide defeaters for Christian belief:

[T]he relevant point is that the evidence base of the inquiry in question includes the denial of central Christian ... beliefs. If so, however, the fact that this inquiry comes to conclusions incompatible with Christian belief would be neither surprising, nor – for Christians – an occasion for consternation or dismay. It would certainly not constitute a defeater for Christian belief.

(2011: 174)

On the other hand, according to Plantinga, if sciences that produce theories incompatible with Christian belief are characterised by *weak* methodological naturalism – i.e., if those theories assign no prior probabilities to central Christian beliefs – then those sciences do not provide the Christian theist with a defeater for Christian beliefs that are incompatible with that science:

> The evidence base for Simonian science (given weak methodological naturalism) is part of the Christian's evidence base, but only part of it. Hence the fact that Simonian science comes to conclusions incompatible with Christian belief doesn't provide the believer with a defeater for her belief.
>
> (2011: 177)

It is not entirely clear what Plantinga is arguing here. Consider the following claims that he makes:

> Though real ... these conflicts are superficial ... because they don't tend to provide defeaters for Christian or theistic belief. ... [T]here theories don't (automatically, at any rate) constitute or provide a defeater for the Christian beliefs with which they conflict.
>
> (2011: xiii)

> [T]he fact that scientists come up with views like Wilson's does not, just as such, offer a defeater for Christian belief.
>
> (2011: 181)

> [T]he fact that competent work from the scientific perspective comes up with claims inconsistent with Christian belief isn't, just as such anyway, a defeater for those beliefs.
>
> (2011: 183)

> Simonian science doesn't (automatically, anyway) constitute a defeater for the Christian beliefs with which it is incompatible. ... The mere existence of Simonian science ... has no tendency to produce a defeater for those tenets. Of course it is theoretically possible ... that a defeater for Christian belief should arise in the course of work at Simonian science; as far as I know, however, this hasn't happened. The conclusion to draw is that

there is indeed conflict between science and Christian belief in this area, but the conflict is merely superficial, of no deep significance.

(2011: 189)

Sure, the *mere* existence of sciences characterised by methodological naturalism – or the *mere* fact that there are such sciences that come to conclusions incompatible with Christian belief – need not be taken by Christians to constitute a strike against Christian belief; sciences characterised by methodological naturalism don't *automatically*, or *as such*, constitute defeaters for Christian belief. But it hardly follows from these observations that *no* such sciences provide defeaters for Christian belief; and Plantinga's assurance, that, as far as he knows, there is no independent reason to suppose that defeaters for Christian belief have arisen in the course of work in such sciences, does nothing to strengthen the case. Moreover, it seems entirely reasonable to suggest that *whether* evolutionary psychology and higher Biblical criticism do provide defeaters for Christian belief depends entirely on the details of those sciences: the data that those sciences have unearthed, the comparative power of the explanations provided by those sciences, the predictive accuracy of those sciences, the comparative simplicity of the theoretical postulates of those sciences, the comparative parsimony of the ontology and ideology of those sciences, the comparative goodness of fit of those sciences with other well-established sciences and background knowledge, and so forth. If those sciences are sufficiently more theoretically virtuous than Christian belief, then it may be that those sciences are defeaters – or, at any rate significant contributors to defeaters – for Christian belief.

I conclude that Plantinga has not established that the conflict between theism and evolutionary psychology and the conflict between theism and higher Biblical criticism are merely superficial. He may be right that evolutionary psychology and higher Biblical criticism do not provide defeaters for Christian belief, but the considerations that he advances in *Where the Conflict Really Lies* are insufficient to establish that this is so.

4. 'Merely apparent conflict'

In response to the claim that there is conflict between theism and evolutionary theory, and between theism and natural science concerning divine action in the world, Plantinga claims that, in fact, there is merely *apparent* conflict. On the one hand, while theism is inconsistent with the claim that natural selection is 'unguided' ('mindless', 'blind', 'ultimately mechanical'), the claim that natural selection is 'unguided' is no part of evolutionary theory, but rather 'a metaphysical or theological addition' (2011: 63). On the other hand: (1) if we think about the universe in classical terms, then, while the claim that there is divine action in the world is inconsistent with the claim that the universe is causally closed, the claim that the universe is causally closed is no part of classical science, but rather 'a metaphysical or theological addition' (2011: 79); and (2) if we think about the universe from the standpoint of quantum mechanics, there is currently nothing that rules out the view that God causes all 'collapse-outcomes' (2011: 116).

I propose to grant without argument that it is *consistent* with the relevant science to suppose that God 'guides' natural selection, causes 'collapse-outcomes', and causally 'intervenes' in the workings of the universe. (Perhaps it would be better to say that I make these concessions for the sake of argument, or for the sake of avoiding argument. I'm not confident that I am in a position to judge that it really is consistent with the relevant science to make these suppositions.)

Even with this concession, it seems to me that it is still a live question whether there is conflict between theism and evolutionary theory, and between theism and natural science concerning divine action in the world. For, even if it is 'metaphysical or theological addition' to suppose that natural selection is 'unguided', and that the universe is causally closed, and that 'collapse-outcomes' are entirely chancy, it is *also* 'metaphysical or theological addition' to suppose that God 'guides' natural selection, and 'intervenes' in the workings of the universe, and causes 'collapse outcomes'. Moreover, while the naturalistic 'metaphysical or theological additions' bring no ontological or ideological costs, the same is manifestly not true for the theistic 'metaphysical or theological additions': Christian belief involves a host of ontological and ideological commitments that naturalism does not incur. Unless those additional commitments are suitably repaid – through better fit with data, or greater explanatory power, or greater predictive accuracy, or better fit with other established science and background knowledge, or the like – it will still be true that the claims that God 'guides' natural selection, and 'intervenes' in the workings of the universe, and causes 'collapse outcomes', are entirely gratuitous from the standpoint of evolutionary theory, physics, and the rest of the sciences.

Perhaps it might be disputed that there is conflict between theism and evolutionary theory – and between theism and natural science concerning divine action in the world – if it turns out that theism makes ontologically and ideologically committing claims about evolutionary theory and divine action in the world that are mere metaphysical and theological additions from the standpoints of evolutionary theory and the rest of the natural and human sciences: even if evolutionary theory and the rest of the natural and human sciences have no need for the hypotheses that God 'guides' natural selection, that God 'intervenes' in the workings of the universe, and that God causes 'collapse outcomes', how does that suffice to show that there is conflict between these theistic claims and those sciences? But what should we suppose are the prior probabilities that evolutionary theory, and the rest of the natural and human sciences, assign to these 'superfluous' hypotheses? Clearly, evolutionary theory and the rest of the natural and human sciences do not assign high prior probability to these hypotheses. But, if they assign low prior probability to these hypotheses, then, by Plantinga's lights, they are characterised by strong methodological naturalism; and if they assign no prior probability to these hypotheses, then, by Plantinga's lights, they are characterised by weak methodological naturalism. Either way, then, it seems that, by Plantinga's lights, the treatment that he makes of evolutionary psychology and higher Biblical criticism should extend to evolutionary theory and the rest of the natural and human sciences. But, since Plantinga does not establish that there is merely superficial conflict between theism and evolutionary psychology, and between theism and higher Biblical criticism, it is then clear that Plantinga also does not establish that there is merely superficial conflict between theism and evolutionary theory, and between theism and the rest of the natural and human sciences. For all that Plantinga argues in the first two parts of *Where the Conflict Really Lies*, it may be that the natural and human sciences do provide defeaters for Christian belief.

5. 'Arguments for theism'

Plantinga claims that the following two arguments offer 'slight support' in favour of theism (2011: 224, 236):

1   Fine-tuning is not at all surprising or impossible on theism.
2   Fine-tuning is exceedingly improbable on the atheistic hypothesis according to which the constants have their values by chance.
3   (Therefore) Theism is to be preferred to atheism.
4   Protein machines are not all surprising or impossible on theism.
5   Protein machines are exceedingly improbable on the atheistic hypothesis of unguided evolution.
6   (Therefore) Theism is to be preferred to atheism.

In Plantinga's view, the chief difficulty that these arguments face is that we don't have good ways to evaluate the conditional probabilities – Pr(F/T), Pr(F/A), Pr(P/T), Pr(P/A) – that figure in their premises. While I agree with Plantinga that it is, indeed, very hard to know how to assess these conditional probabilities, it seems to me that there is another difficulty that these arguments face that renders these arguments entirely useless: namely, that these arguments are plainly invalid.

To compare what theism and naturalism say about the fine-tuning, we need to sketch some of the details of these two (kinds of) big pictures. Of course, in doing this sketching, we should make sure that we develop each sketch to the same level of detail, and that we don't leave details unfilled in one view that are filled in on the other view.

On Plantinga's theism, every possible world contains God. In some possible worlds, God does not create; in other possible worlds, God does create. In many possible worlds, God creates one or more universes. The ensembles of universes that God creates depend upon God's creative intentions. Since there are many different ensembles of universes that God might have created, there are many different creative intentions that God might have had. Moreover, God's creative intentions are fundamental: there is nothing in any possible world that causes God to have the creative intentions that God has in that possible world, and there is nothing in any possible world that explains why God has the particular creative intentions that God has in that possible world rather than other creative intentions that God has in other possible worlds. Furthermore, any possible universe exists in at least one possible world in which God creates that universe and hence in which God has creative intentions appropriate to the creation of that universe.

On a version of naturalism that is appropriately matched to Plantinga's theism, there are many possible worlds that are ensembles of universes. (Perhaps all possible worlds are ensembles of universes; or perhaps there are possible worlds that are 'empty'.) Moreover, any possible universe exists in at least one possible world.

On Plantinga's theism, if our universe is fine-tuned, it will doubtless be true that our universe is fine-tuned because God intended it to be fine-tuned; and it will also be true that the 'fine-tuned values' are as they are because God intended that they should be as they are. But what should we say about God's intention that the 'fine-tuned values' should be as they are? Is it surprising that God had the intention to make a universe in which the 'fine-tuned values' are as they actually are? Recall that, for any possible universe in which the 'fine-tuned values' differ from their actual values, there is a possible world in which God intends to make a universe with those values. If fine-tuned universes are rare in the possible ensembles of universes, then God's intending to create fine-tuned universes will be rare in the space of possible worlds.

On naturalism, if our universe is fine-tuned, there is a question to be faced about why the 'fine-tuned values' are as they are. However, it seems clear that naturalists have no more reason to be surprised by the 'fine-tuning' of the universe than theists have reason to be surprised that God had the intention to create a fine-tuned universe. After all, the extent to which, on naturalism, fine-tuned universes are rare in the total space of possible worlds is exactly matched by the extent to which, on theism, God's intention to create fine-tuned universes is rare in the total space of possible worlds. Hence, while the two views are exactly matched in terms of their 'ultimate' commitments, naturalism actually does better than theism in terms of overall commitments, and the two views are exactly on a par in terms of their ability to provide an 'ultimate' explanation of the fine-tuned values that we observe.

The upshot here is that, so long as we compare like with like, we do not see a relevant difference. On the one hand, the fine-tuning is no more and no less probable on theism than it is on naturalism. On the other hand, the fine-tuning is no more and no less probable on a hypothesis according to which it is a matter of chance that God intended to make a universe in which the 'fine-tuned values' are as they actually are than it is on a hypothesis according to which it is a matter of chance that the 'fine-tuned values' are as they actually are.

Perhaps it might be replied that this argument mistakenly neglects the fact that God could have a preference for fine-tuned universes: while fine-tuned universes are comparatively rare in the space of possible universe ensembles, God's having a preference for fine-tuned universes is not comparatively rare in the space of possible worlds. But that reply is incoherent. On Plantinga's view – setting aside irrelevant complications raised by Plantinga's claim that God's creative activities are constrained by counterfactuals of creaturely freedom – God's creative intentions are a perfect reflection of God's preferences. So it cannot be that God's intending to create fine-tuned universes is rare in the space of possible of worlds even though God's having a preference for fine-tuned universes is not rare in the space of possible worlds.

Perhaps it might be replied that the argument mistakenly supposes that theists and naturalists agree about the space of possible universes: since theists and naturalists actually disagree about which universes are possible, there are no good grounds for supposing that the extent to which, on naturalism, fine-tuned universes are rare in the total space of possible worlds is exactly matched by the extent to which, on theism, God's intention to create fine-tuned universes is rare in the total space of possible worlds. But this reply, even if strictly correct, is ineffective. There just is no reason to accept that God cannot make universes that last only for a tiny fraction of a second or that blow apart so quickly that they only ever consist of empty space. But, if God can make such universes, then God can intend to make such universes, and so, if there is a fine-tuning problem for atheists that is raised by the 'fine-tuned values' being as they actually are, then there will be a fine-tuning problem for theists raised by God's intending the 'fine-tuned values' to be as they actually are.

I conclude that Plantinga's fine-tuning argument is ineffective even against naturalists who accept that there are possible worlds in which the 'fine-tuned values' have values other than the values that they actually take. However, I also note that naturalists are not obliged to accept that there *are* possible worlds in which the 'fine-tuned values' have values other than the values that they actually take. In particular, naturalists may accept a view of (metaphysical or ontological) necessity according to which all (metaphysically or ontologically) possible worlds share laws and initial history with the actual world, and diverge from the actual world only as a result of the outworkings of objective chance. If, on the one hand, the 'fine-tuned values' take the values that they do at all points in the history of the actual world, then those values are themselves (metaphysically or ontologically) necessary, and hence present no problem to the naturalist. If, on the other hand, the 'fine-tuned values' acquire the values that they do at a certain point in history as a result of the outworkings of objective chance, then the naturalist has a perfectly acceptable explanation of the 'fine-tuned values' in terms of the outworkings of objective chance at that time. Moreover, I note that these same considerations apply, with equal force, to Plantinga's protein machine argument. On the one hand, it may be that all (metaphysically or ontologically) possible worlds contain protein machines; on the other hand, it may be that the future existence of protein machines depended upon the outworkings of objective chance at earlier points in the history of the universe. Either way, there is no difficulty for naturalism, on the assumption that all (metaphysically or ontologically) possible worlds share laws and initial history with the actual world, and diverge from the actual world only as a result of the outworkings of objective chance.

Should naturalists accept that all (metaphysically or ontologically) possible worlds share laws and initial history with the actual world, and diverge from the actual world only as a result of the outworkings of objective chance? That's unclear. On the one hand, this assumption yields a parsimonious account of (metaphysical or ontological) possibility; on the other hand, it generates a promiscuous account of (metaphysical or ontological) necessity. While there are those who suppose that 'intuition' tells against parsimonious accounts of (metaphysical or ontological) possibility and promiscuous accounts of (metaphysical or ontological) necessity, proponents of the view can insist that 'intuition' fails to reliably discriminate between (metaphysical or ontological) modality and (epistemic or doxastic) modality. Sure, there's nothing irrational, or incoherent, or inconsistent in, for example, the supposition that the 'fine-tuned values' might have been other than they actually are; but global considerations of theoretical virtue still tell in favour of the claim that the 'fine-tuned values' are (metaphysically or ontologically) necessary.

Even if Plantinga were right that his two arguments offer 'slight support' in favour of theism, that need be of little concern to naturalists, since 'slight support' can clearly be defeated by 'stronger counter-support' elsewhere. However, it seems to me that there is no good reason to suppose that Plantinga's two arguments offer so much as 'slight support' for theism. Even if naturalists are merely undecided whether or not to accept the parsimonious account of (metaphysical or ontological) possibility – and the correlative promiscuous account of (metaphysical or ontological) necessity – they will, all other considerations aside, have no reason to *accept* that Plantinga's two arguments do offer 'slight support' for theism. Moreover, as we noted above, if naturalists do reject the parsimonious account of (metaphysical or ontological) possibility – and the correlative promiscuous account of (metaphysical or ontological) necessity – there are still strong reasons for thinking that, when we look closely at the competing *global* explanations of the 'fine-tuning values' offered by theism and naturalism, there is no reason to suppose that theism offers a superior explanation.

6. 'Support for theism'

Plantinga claims that 'design discourse' – and, in particular, Michael Behe's 'design discourse' – offers some support for theism over naturalism 'although it isn't easy to say how much' (2011: 264).

66 *Does science defeat naturalism?*

As a lead in to his discussion of Behe's 'design discourse', Plantinga discusses the 'design discourse' of William Paley:

> [T]he belief that something or other is a product of design is not formed by way of inference, but in the basic way; what goes on here is to be understood as more like perception than like inference. (245) ... Sometimes [Paley] is calling attention to the sorts of beliefs we do in fact find ourselves forming, or inclined to form. ... Other times what he seems to be doing can perhaps better be described as putting us in the sorts of situations in which design beliefs are in fact formed. (246) ... When you are on the walk with Paley and encounter a watch, you don't make an inference to the thought that this object is designed; instead, upon examining the object, you form the belief in that immediate or basic way.
> (2011: 248)

Plantinga considers the possibility that there might be rebutting defeaters to 'Paley's design beliefs', but insists that such defeaters would need to show that the relevant biological phenomena were produced by 'unguided Darwinian evolution' (2011: 254). Plantinga also considers the possibility that there might be undercutting defeaters to 'Paley's design beliefs', but insists that such defeaters would need to show that 'there is an unguided evolutionary path that is not prohibitively improbable' (2011: 255). Plantinga insists that naturalists have not shown that evolution is unguided, and this rules out rebutting defeaters to 'Paley's design beliefs' (2011: 255); and Plantinga insists that, at best, current evolutionary science provides 'a partial undercutting defeater for those beliefs' (2011: 256).

I think that Plantinga misses an undercutting defeater for 'Paley's design beliefs'. While we can allow that we do 'perceive' design in manufactured objects – e.g., the watch lying on the heath – I think that we should not accept Paley's account of how we 'perceive' design in those objects. Paley thinks that we perceive design in such objects where we perceive 'the precision with which the various parts fit together to accomplish their function, the dependence of each part on others, and the like' (2011: 238). But that's just not so. The truth is that we perceive design in such objects where we perceive materials that we know are the products of human labour: brass, cogwheels, plastics, thin sheets of glass, engraved letters, and the like. On the one hand, we correctly identify objects as designed even when we have no knowledge of their function, or the dependence of their parts, or the like. And, on the other hand, there is plainly no uniform tendency amongst people to discern design in many cases where parts fit together precisely to accomplish function, parts depend upon one another, and so forth. Sure, those who *already* believe that animals and plants are the product of design may profess to perceive design in animals and plants on the basis of precise fitting together of parts to accomplish function, and so forth; but the rest of us make no such professions. The upshot here is (a) that the way that we actually perceive design in manufactured objects has no legitimate extension to the case of plants and animals; and (b) that, given (a), there are obvious grounds for worry about pollution by prior theory in the case of those who profess to perceive design in plants and animals.

Plantinga's discussion of Behe's 'design discourse' goes the same way. According to Plantinga, the 'complex structures' and 'molecular machines' that Behe discusses 'certainly appear to be designed' (2011: 257). But the 'complex structures' and 'molecular machines' that Behe discusses are not composed of materials that we know are the products of human labour; and there is plainly no uniform tendency among people to discern design in these 'complex structures' and 'molecular machines'. Doubtless, Plantinga will suppose that those who lack the tendency to discern design in these 'complex structures' and 'molecular machines' are subject to some kind of cognitive deficit: the outworkings of original sin, or the like. But, as we have already noted, naturalists will suppose that Plantinga – and those who think as he does – are here relying on theory to interpret data: it is only those who already believe that God exists who suppose that the 'complex structures' and 'molecular machines' are properly perceived to be products of design. 'Design discourse' does nothing to favour theism over naturalism: 'appearance of design' tracks prior belief, and so cannot be taken to be any kind of vindication of that belief. Rather than providing 'non-negligible' support for theism (2011: 265), 'design discourse' provides no differential support for either theism or naturalism.

7. 'Deep concord'

According to Plantinga:

> Theistic religion [and, in particular, the doctrine of *imago dei*] gives us reason to expect our cognitive capacities to match the world in such a way as to make modern science possible. Naturalism gives us no reason at all to expect this sort of match: from the point of view of naturalism, it would be an overwhelming piece of cosmic serendipity if there were such a match.
>
> (2011: 303)

According to Plantinga: (1) God has created a universe that is regular and predictable, and has so constituted us that we can recognise those regularities and predictabilities. (2) God has created a universe that obeys laws, and has so constituted us that we can grasp those laws (277); moreover, those laws are necessary or inviolable because no creature has the power to act contrary to omnipotent *fiat* (2011: 281). (3) God has created a universe that is mathematically describable and has also given us the ability to grasp and practice the kind of mathematics that describes that universe (2011: 286); moreover, we can gain knowledge of numbers and sets because they are divine thoughts and we are causally related to them by way of our causal relationships with God (2011: 291). (4) God has created a universe in which inductive reasoning is successful, and has so constituted us that we reason inductively (2011: 296). (5) God has created a universe that exhibits certain kinds of simplicity, and has so constituted us that our intellectual success requires the world to be simple in just those kinds of ways (2011: 299). (6) God's creation of the universe is contingent – both in its nature and its existence – and this explains the empirical character of science (2011: 301).

Some naturalists accept the parsimonious account of (metaphysical and ontological) possibility – and the correlative promiscuous account of (metaphysical and ontological) necessity – mentioned earlier. On that account, it is necessary that our universe is mathematically describable, and necessary that our universe is regular and predictable, and necessary that our universe 'obeys the laws of nature', and necessary that our universe supports inductive reasoning, and necessary that our universe exhibits certain kinds of simplicity, and necessary that any scientific inquiry will have an empirical character. Moreover, on that account, it is necessary that any sufficiently intelligent evolved creatures are so constituted that creatures of their kind can: recognise regularities and predictabilities, reason inductively, develop some grasp of 'laws', use mathematics for description and prediction, discern simplicity underlying complexity, and so forth. For these naturalists, it is plainly not true that it is merely an overwhelming piece of cosmic serendipity that our cognitive capacities match the world in ways that make modern science possible.

Some theists hold that it is both necessary that God exists and necessary that, if God creates universes, then God creates universes that are mathematically describable, regular, predictable, obedient to natural law, supportive of inductive reasoning, relevantly simple, apt for scientific inquiry with an empirical character, and containing intelligent creatures who can recognise regularities and predictabilities, reason inductively, grasp natural law, use mathematics for description and prediction, discern simplicity underlying complexity, and so forth. The explanation that these theists give of the fact that our cognitive capacities match the world in ways that make modern science possible is on all fours with the explanation given by the naturalists mentioned in the previous paragraph: all of the explanatory heavy lifting ultimately adverts to primitive (metaphysical and ontological) necessity. The additional commitments of theism purchase no advantage in connection with any of the considerations currently on the table.

Suppose, instead, that both parties – naturalists and theists – accept that there are possible universes that are not mathematically describable, not regular, not predictable, not 'obedient to natural law', not supportive of inductive reasoning, not relevantly simple, and not investigable by way of scientific inquiry with an empirical character. If there are such possible universes, then – by the lights of theists – it is possible for God to intend to make such universes. Moreover – by the lights of theists – there is then no explanation of why God actually had the intention to make a universe that is mathematically describable, regular, predictable, obedient to natural law, supportive of inductive reasoning, relevantly simple, apt for scientific inquiry with an empirical character *rather than* the intention to make a universe not mathematically describable, not regular, not predictable, not 'obedient to natural law', not supportive of inductive reasoning, not relevantly simple, and not investigable by way of scientific inquiry with an empirical character. So, in this case, there is *ultimately* no difference between naturalism and theism when it comes to the explanation of the fact that the universe is mathematically describable, regular, predictable, obedient to natural law, supportive of inductive reasoning, relevantly simple, apt for scientific inquiry with an empirical character: ultimately, in each case, we have an explanatory surd. Sure, theism has an informative answer to the question: Why is the universe mathematically describable, regular, predictable, obedient to natural law, supportive of inductive reasoning, relevantly simple, and apt for scientific inquiry with an empirical character? And naturalism has no informative answer to that question. But theism has no informative answer to the question: Why did God have the intention to make a universe that is mathematically describable, regular, predictable, obedient to natural law, supportive of inductive reasoning, relevantly simple, and apt for scientific inquiry with an empirical character? And that question does not so much as arise for naturalism. Seen from the proper perspective, there is no advantage for theism here.

What should the parties described in the preceding paragraph say about the fact that our cognitive capacities match the world in ways that make modern science possible? Both parties should say that there can only be a match between our cognitive capacities and the universe if the universe is mathematically describable, regular, predictable, obedient to natural law, supportive of inductive reasoning, relevantly simple, and apt for scientific inquiry with an empirical character. Indeed, more strongly, both parties should say that it is necessary, both for our existence and for our possession of the cognitive capacities that we in fact have, that the universe is mathematically describable, regular, predictable, obedient to natural law, supportive of inductive reasoning, relevantly simple, and apt for scientific inquiry with an empirical character. Moreover, I think, both parties should say that, if the universe is mathematically describable, regular, predictable, obedient to natural law, supportive of inductive reasoning, relevantly simple, and apt for scientific inquiry with an empirical character, then it is more or less inevitable that there is some kind of match between the universe and the cognitive capacities of any kinds of beings in the universe that have cognitive capacities. Finally – though perhaps somewhat more controversially – I think that both parties should say that there is nothing surprising about the fact that our universe contains creatures – including human beings – that make reasonably advanced cognitive performance *given* that it has been witness to 4 billion years of life on the surface of the earth.

We know something about the evolution of our advanced cognitive performance. No more than 5 million years ago, the world was inhabited by creatures that were the common ancestors of contemporary gorillas, chimpanzees, and human beings. The earliest hominids – who had brains the size of contemporary chimpanzees, and who used simple stone tools – appeared around 2.3 million years ago. By the time of the first appearance of *Homo erectus* – around 1.5 million years ago – there had been a doubling in cranial capacity, matched with the use of fire and more complex stone tools. *Homo sapiens* – the forerunner of anatomically modern human beings – appeared around 400,000 years ago; anatomically modern human beings themselves appeared no more than 200,000 years ago, and started to spread from Africa no more than 100,000 years ago.

The appearance of the common ancestors of contemporary gorillas, chimpanzees, and human beings was preceded by a lengthy history. Prokaryotes appeared at least 3.6 billion years ago; eukaryotes appeared at least 2 billion years ago. The simplest animals date back at least 600 million years; the earliest mammals appeared at least 200 million years ago. It is not controversial to claim that rudimentary cognitive capacities appeared in our ancestors at least 500 million years ago. Nor is it controversial to observe that *almost all* of evolutionary history pre-dates the point at which our cognitive capacities evolved in independence from the cognitive capacities of gorillas and chimpanzees.

It hardly needs observing that there are marked differences in cognitive *performance* between human beings and other primates. While some chimpanzees have learned to recognise hundreds of symbols, no other primates have achieved linguistic competence. While chimpanzees and gorillas exhibit some general domain intelligence – consider, for example, the problem-solving behaviour described in Kohler (1925) – they are outclassed by young human children. While groups of primates create and share new customs and behaviours – e.g. macaque monkeys on Koshima developed the practice of washing sweet potatoes in the ocean, to enhance their texture and flavour, on the back of individual innovation (see Whiten *et al.* [1999]) – primates do not engage in institutionalised cultural instruction, or the like. However, despite the obvious differences in performance, it remains unclear exactly how to explain the differences in *performance* between humans and primates.

Significant differences between hominids and chimpanzees began to appear around 2 million years ago. These differences were of three kinds: *biological, social,* and *cultural.* Hominid communities became more complex than chimpanzee communities, cultural bequests across generations became more significant in hominid groups than in chimpanzee groups, and human cognitive performance came to exceed chimpanzee performance. These three kinds of differences accumulated together: on the one hand, biological advances were amplified by social and cultural advances; and, on the other hand, social and cultural advances were facilitated by biological advances. But, given these observations, it seems to me to be a mistake to suppose that cognitive *performance* differences between humans and chimpanzees are to be explained – or even to be primarily explained – in terms of merely biological endowment: it is obvious that social and cultural endowment has an enormous part to play in the explanation of cognitive performance differences between humans and chimpanzees.

At some point – probably more than 5 million years ago – the common ancestors of contemporary gorillas, chimpanzees, and human beings had cognitive capacities that were entirely shaped by their biological endowment. For those creatures, there is no mystery about the fit between their cognitive capacities and the universe in which they lived: it is plausibly an inevitable consequence of biological evolution that basic cognitive capacities shaped entirely by biological endowment 'match' the environments in which they evolve.

More recently – for at least the past 2 million years – the cognitive performance of human beings and their hominid ancestors has not been explicable solely in terms of their biological endowment. The cognitive performance of human beings and their hominid ancestors has also been a matter of social and cultural endowment – and the 'advanced nature' of that cognitive performance is unsurprising given (1) its foundation in the preceding 4 billion years of merely biological evolution, and (2) the advances that are made possible by social and cultural 'evolution'. Moreover, the fit between the cognitive performance of human beings and the universe in which they live is unsurprising given the way that human beings have developed, ranging from excellent in the most basic areas to woeful in the most controversial areas (religion, politics, philosophy, and the like). In particular, that human cognitive performance fits the world in such a way as to make science possible seems entirely unsurprising in the light of the history that we have been reviewing.

8. Interim conclusion

In sum: Plantinga fails to establish that there is much merely alleged conflict between theism and science; and Plantinga fails to establish that there is some superficial conflict but much deep concord between theism and science. For all that Plantinga says in the first three parts of *Where the Conflict Really Lies*, it may be that there is deep conflict between theism and science, and it may be that there is much deeper concord between naturalism and science than there is between theism and science. Of course, to say this is not to say that the large claims for which Plantinga argues in the first three parts of *Where the Conflict Really Lies* are mistaken. Moreover, a final assessment of the standing of those large claims cannot be made without first considering the strength of the case that Plantinga makes for the existence of deep conflict between naturalism and science. Consequently, we now turn to an examination of Plantinga's evolutionary argument against naturalism.

9. EAAN

Plantinga's evolutionary argument against naturalism (EAAN) may be summarised as follows. (Here, I follow the presentation in Plantinga (2011:

307ff.), of which he says: 'The version presented here is the official and final version (I hope)'.)

R: Our cognitive faculties are reliable.
N: Naturalism (is true).
E: We and our cognitive faculties have come to be in the way proposed by contemporary evolutionary theory.

(1) Pr (R/N&E) is low.
(2) Anyone who accepts N&E and sees that Pr (R/N&E) is low has a defeater for R.
(3) Anyone who has a defeater for R has a defeater for any other belief she thinks she has, including N&E itself.
(4) If one who accepts N&E thereby acquires a defeater for N&E, then N&E is self-defeating and can't rationally be accepted.
(5) (Hence) N&E cannot be rationally accepted.

Plantinga also defends a similar argument against naturalism with weaker premises (EAAN*).

R': Our cognitive faculties that produce our metaphysical beliefs are reliable.
N: Naturalism (is true).
E: We and our cognitive faculties have come to be in the way proposed by contemporary evolutionary theory.

(1) Pr (R'/N&E) is low.
(2) Anyone who accepts N&E and sees that Pr (R'/N&E) is low has a defeater for R'.
(3) Anyone who has a defeater for R' has a defeater for any other metaphysical belief she thinks she has, including N&E itself.
(4) If one who accepts N&E thereby acquires a defeater for N&E, then N&E is self-defeating and can't rationally be accepted.
(5) (Hence) N&E cannot be rationally accepted.

Here is an argument for the conclusion that (EAAN*) cannot be a good argument for a theist to make.

Let T be theism. Suppose that Pr (R'/T) is not very low.

Clearly, Pr (R') is *very* low. If the cognitive faculties that produce our metaphysical beliefs were reliable, then – on Plantinga's account of reliability – those cognitive faculties would produce a preponderance of true beliefs over false beliefs. But there is simply no agreement – among philosophical experts or among the broader public – on a wide range of metaphysical beliefs. Indeed, in many cases in which there is division of opinion among the philosophical experts, there is no metaphysical belief that is accepted by anywhere near as much as half of those experts. Moreover, this pattern of division of opinion repeats among those who agree on *some* metaphysical matters: there is enormous division of opinion about metaphysical matters among theists; and there is enormous division of opinion about metaphysical matters among Protestant theists; and there is enormous division of opinion about metaphysical matters among Evangelical Protestant theists; and so on.

However, if Pr (R') is very low, then Pr (R' & T) is very low, because the probability of a conjunction is less than or equal to the probability of either conjunct.

But, since Pr (R'/T) = Pr (R' & T) / Pr (T), Pr (R' & T) = Pr (R'/T) x Pr (T).

Hence, given that Pr (R' & T) is very low, if Pr (R'/T) is not very low, then Pr (T) is very low.

But theists cannot suppose that Pr (T) is very low. So, in fact, theists must suppose that Pr (R'/T) is very low.

But, if theists suppose that Pr (R'/T) is very low, then, by the very same reasoning that Plantinga adopts to show that N&E is self-defeating if Pr (R'/N&E) is very low, it follows that T is self-defeating.

I take this last argument to establish that theists must suppose that there is something wrong with the reasoning in EAAN*; and, since the reasoning in EAAN* is the same as the reasoning in EAAN, I also take this last argument to establish that theists must suppose that there is something wrong with the reasoning in EAAN. Since Plantinga is a theist, he cannot suppose that the reasoning in EAAN* and EAAN is good.

10. Reliability

Plantinga (2011: 326) says that, 'like everyone else' he believes that 'our cognitive faculties are, in fact, mostly reliable'. However, we all know that there are some domains in which our cognitive faculties are not mostly reliable. Sure, across a broad range of domains, our faculties – of perception, memory, *a priori* intuition, sympathy, introspection, testimony, moral sense, and so forth – are reliable: they do yield a preponderance of true belief over false belief. But, wherever there is not independent convergence of opinion, we have good reason to suppose that human faculties are not reliably tracking the truth.

Of course, that human faculties are not reliably tracking the truth in certain domains does not entail that human faculties are incapable of tracking the truth in those domains. In particular, in many cases where there is not independent convergence of opinion, there is independent convergence of *expert* opinion. Thus, for example, where there are people who fail to accept well-established science, we write this off as ignorance, or stupidity, or the like: we do not suppose that the beliefs of the ignorant and the stupid serve to show that well-established scientific belief fails to track the truth.

However, there are some domains in which it seems indisputable that, if there is such a thing as expert opinion in those domains, then even expert opinion fails to track the truth. Philosophy is one such domain. Philosophy is rife with disagreement. For any pair of professional philosophers, there are countless propositions upon which they disagree. Even if the chosen pair are theists, or Protestant theists, or Evangelical Protestant theists, they will disagree about an enormous number of philosophical propositions. (There is currently a flood of books with titles like *God and ......: Seventeen Views*, where the views in question are pairwise contradictory, and where almost all of the contributors are theists.) In these circumstances, it would be unimaginable hubris for any philosopher to suppose that his or her uniquely privileged cognitive faculties produce a preponderance of true philosophical beliefs over false philosophical beliefs.

Perhaps it might be insisted that one cannot rationally continue to hold philosophical beliefs while also failing to believe that most of one's philosophical beliefs are true. If we feel the force of this insistence, then the plain consequence is that we should give up on our philosophical beliefs. (See Feldman [2007].) However, it seems to me that there need be nothing irrational in continuing to hold onto one's philosophical beliefs while nonetheless failing to believe that most of one's philosophical beliefs are true (and, indeed, while believing that most of one's philosophical beliefs are false).

Suppose that my philosophical beliefs can be generated from ten independent axioms. Suppose that I give credence of 51% to each of these axioms. Calculation reveals – I think! – that the credence that I should then give to the claim that at least seven of the axioms is true is around 14%. That is, calculation reveals – I think! – that even though I (rather weakly) believe each of the axioms, I rather more strongly disbelieve the claim that at least two-thirds of my axioms are true. If we suppose that most of my axioms are true only if at least two-thirds of them are true, then – in this toy case – it turns out that I quite reasonably believe that it is not the case that most of my philosophical axioms are true while nonetheless continuing to reasonably believe each of those philosophical axioms.

While the toy case is a *toy case*, it is nonetheless instructive. It is quite clear that, if I hold my philosophical beliefs tentatively, then I may be *required* to also believe that it is not the case that most of my philosophical beliefs are true, so long as I do not set the standards for what counts as 'most' too high. True enough, if I am sufficiently dogmatic about my philosophical beliefs – if I assign a very high credence to all of them – then, on almost any standards for 'most', I may be required to believe that most of my philosophical beliefs are true. But, if that's a problem, it's a problem for *dogmatists*, and not for philosophers who are appropriately tentative in the holding of their philosophical beliefs.

Although the discussion to this point may be taken to suffice to show that Plantinga's evolutionary argument against naturalism fails, it is clear that we have not pinpointed exactly why and where the argument fails. I'm not sure that I know exactly why and where the argument fails. However, I can see that there are many points at which questions can be raised about the argument. I now turn to an examination of some of those points.

11. Cases

Most of Plantinga's discussion is devoted to establishing his first premise: that Pr (R/N&E) is low. His defence of this premise involves two significant steps.

First, he argues that, on N&E, the likelihood that any given axiom is true is 0.5. Second, he argues that if there is just a 50/50 chance that any given axiom delivered up by our cognitive faculties is true, then it is clear that our cognitive faculties are not reliable. If the first step is granted, then the second step seems unproblematic. So I shall focus on the first step.

I begin by considering some cases, all but the first of which are discussed by Plantinga in the course of his defence of the claim that, on N&E, the likelihood that any given axiom is true is 0.5.

Thermostat: A thermostat is a device that regulates temperature in a wider system. We can suppose that a given thermostat has two states: ON ('have most recently turned the heating device on') and OFF ('have most recently turned the heating device off'). The thermostat is connected to sensors which measure the temperature of the wider system. When the thermostat is in the OFF state, and the sensors report that the temperature has fallen below the low cut-off temperature, the thermostat triggers the starting up of the heating device and its state changes to ON. When the thermostat is in the ON state, and the sensors report that the temperature has risen above the high cut-off temperature, the thermostat triggers the shutting down of the heating device and its state changes to OFF. Of course, the thermostat is a purely physical device, and its states are purely physical states – electromechanical states, for example. Moreover, there are no intrinsic physical properties of the thermostat that make ON the state of having most recently turned on the heating device: we could alter wiring external to the thermostat to reverse the roles of the intrinsically characterised states of the thermostat. What makes ON the state of having most recently turned on the device is the role that this state plays in the regulation of the temperature of the wider system to which the thermostat belongs when the wider system is operating.

The account that we have just given of the operation of a thermostat is *causal*: the combination of the thermostat's being in the OFF state and the sensors' reporting that the temperature has fallen below the low cut-off temperature *causes* the starting up of the heating device and the thermostat's transition to the ON state; and the combination of the thermostat's being in the ON state and the sensors' reporting that the temperature has risen above the high cut-off state *causes* the shutting down of the heating device and the thermostat's transition to the OFF state. Of course, if you know nothing more about the thermostat than is given in the foregoing account, then there is much that engineers and physicists might know about the operations of the thermostat and the wider system that you do not know; and, in particular, there is much causal information about the operations of the thermostat and the wider system that engineers and physicists might know that you do not know. And, if you knew nothing more than engineers and physicists might know about the operations of the thermostat and the wider system, then there is much more that an omniscient being could know about the operations of the thermostat and the wider system; and, in particular, there is much causal information about the operations of the thermostat and the wider system that an omniscient being might know that engineers and physicists do not know. But your ignorance about how the causal information that you lack relates to the causal information that you have does nothing to defeat your causal knowledge about the operation of the thermostat: you don't need to be omniscient, or even an engineer or physicist, in order to know that, e.g., the combination of the thermostat's being in the OFF state and the sensors' reporting that the temperature has fallen below the low cut-off temperature *causes* the starting up of the heating device and the thermostat's transition to the ON state. Moreover, your ignorance about how the causal information that you lack relates to the causal information that you have does not give you any reason to deny that the thermostat is a purely physical device, and that the causal states of the thermostat are purely physical states. It would, for example, be just silly for you to suppose that the ON and OFF states are states of the thermostat's soul.

Anaerobic marine bacterium: According to a well-known, but dubious, story, anaerobic marine bacteria contain internal magnets. In the oceans of the northern hemisphere, these magnets point the bacteria away from oxygen-rich surface water and towards the oxygen-free depths in which they flourish. Propulsion devices move the bacteria in the direction in which they face; hence, given the way that these bacteria are oriented by their internal magnets, these bacteria are continuously propelled towards the oxygen-free depths in which they flourish. According to our story, these marine bacteria have an orientational state: they are oriented to point towards magnetic north. In their natural environment – in the northern oceans of the earth with the current direction of the earth's magnetic field – an orientation to point towards magnetic north is also an orientation to point towards the oxygen-free depths in which they flourish. So, in their natural habitat, these bacteria are oriented to point towards the oxygen-free depths in which they flourish (and their propulsion devices keep pushing them in this direction, even as other forces conspire to drive them away from the oxygen-free depths).

I do not think that anyone would be inclined to suppose that the orientational state of these bacteria is a representational state for them. True enough, the orientation of the bacteria is an indication to the right kinds of external observers of the direction of magnetic north; but, for these external observers, the orientation of the bacteria is just like the orientation of a compass (and no one supposes that the orientation of a compass is a state of its soul). On the other hand, we know that these bacteria have neither brains nor nervous systems, and that there is no complex computation over representations that is causally responsible for the behaviour that they exhibit. It's not just that these bacteria do not have beliefs, or belief-like representational states; these bacteria do not have any mental life at all.

Caenorhabditis elegans: *C. elegans* is a small, transparent roundworm. It was the first multicellular organism to have its genome fully sequenced (though there are still some errors in that sequencing that are being corrected). *C. elegans* is one of the simplest organisms with a nervous system.

Does science defeat naturalism? 77

It has a fully-mapped network of around 300 neurons, and we have some understanding of neural mechanisms responsible for some of its behaviour: e.g., locomotion along chemical gradients (towards nutrition and away from toxins), locomotion along temperature gradients, and conversion of mechanical signals into electrochemical signals.

Unlike anaerobic marine bacteria which push themselves towards magnetic north come what may, *C. elegans* follows different gradients in its environment. While there is clearly room to argue about exactly what contents we should attribute to the cognitive states of the roundworm, it seems appropriate to suppose that it has states with contents something like these: 'Hotter that way', 'More toxic this way', 'More food over there', 'Get food!', 'Find mate!', 'Away from toxin!', and so forth. Moreover, it also seems appropriate to suppose that the content of these states explains the behaviour that *C. elegans* exhibits: neural computation involving the states just mentioned directs the path that *C. elegans* takes through its environment and the kind of behaviours in which it engages.

Frog: Imagine a frog sitting on a lily pad. A fly buzzes by. The frog flicks out its tongue and captures the fly. Clearly, the frog must have some way of tracking the trajectory of the fly, and of bringing it about – with at least some degree of success – that its tongue gets to be where the fly is, so that it captures the fly. As a first approximation, we may suppose that the frog has states with the following kinds of contents: 'Hungry!', 'Food within reach', 'Not too hot', 'Shadow moved', 'Find mate!', and so forth. Moreover, we may suppose that the content of some of these states explains the behaviour of the frog: on this particular occasion, 'Hungry!' and 'Food within reach' are the contents of the states that conspire to cause the flicking out of the tongue.

Of course, there are various disputes to be had, even at this level of approximation. Perhaps one content is 'Fly within reach', or 'Small, dark, moving object within reach', rather than 'Food within reach'. Perhaps another content is 'Hungry for fly!' or 'Hungry for meat!' rather than 'Hungry!' More information about the full set of behaviours of the frog, its environment, and perhaps even its evolutionary history might provide reasons to prefer one content attribution above another. However, it is clear that there is a reasonably narrow range of contents that it would be appropriate to attribute to the frog in connection with the fly-capturing use of its tongue. It would, for example, be just plain silly to suppose that 'Arithmetic is undecidable' is a relevant content.

Zebra: A zebra is grazing on the veldt; a lion approaches. The zebra notices the lion. Perhaps – depending upon the 'estimated' age and state of the lion – the zebra takes flight, or readies itself to take flight. Perhaps the zebra begins anxiously scanning the horizon – particularly downwind – to see whether it seems safe to flee in that direction. Perhaps, if the lion is female, the zebra starts making a 360 degree search to see whether there are other members of the pride that are also stalking it. Perhaps the zebra moves closer to the centre of the herd. Perhaps, if the lion is old and male, the zebra 'estimates' that it will have no difficulty outrunning this particular lion, and so it returns to its grazing unconcerned. As in the previous case involving the frog, it seems appropriate to attribute a range of contentful states to the zebra: 'Hungry!', 'Danger over there!', 'Tasty grass here', 'Sore foot', 'Lion getting closer', and so forth. As before, there will be disputes to have about the precise content of the states. Nonetheless, it is clear that there is a reasonably narrow range of contents that it would be appropriate to attribute to the zebra in connection with its registration of the presence of the lion. It would be just plain silly to suppose that 'Naturalism is vastly overrated' is a relevant content.

12. Analysis

Plantinga's argument for the claim that, on N&E, the likelihood that any given axiom is true is 0.5 has two parts. First, he argues that, on N&E, there is no reason to suppose that any particular belief content is true. Then, second, he argues that, if there is no reason to suppose that any particular belief content is true, the likelihood that any given axiom is true is 0.5. We shall be focusing our attention on the first part of the argument.

Plantinga's argument begins like this:

> According to naturalists, beliefs are neural structures with two different kinds of properties: electrochemical/neurophysiological ('physical') properties and content ('mental') properties.
>
> (2011: 321)

> As we go up the evolutionary scale, we find neural structures with greater and greater complexity. Near one end, there are bacteria, which have no beliefs. At the other end are human beings, with rich and varied beliefs. Somewhere between, at a certain level of complexity, neural structures start to display belief content. Perhaps it starts with *C. elegans*.
>
> (2011: 324f.)

> Suppose *C. elegans* has beliefs. Given that *C. elegans* has survived for millions of years, its behaviour is adaptive. That behaviour is caused by the neurological structures in the *C. elegans* nervous system. (326f.) ... The underlying neurology causes adaptive behaviour and also determines belief content. But there is no reason, on N&E, why that belief content should be true. All that's required for survival and fitness is that the neurology causes adaptive behaviour; this neurology also determines belief content but whether or not that content is true makes no difference to fitness.
>
> (2011: 327)

Anticipating the objection that the frog must have reliable cognitive mechanisms if it is to catch the fly, and that the zebra must have reliable cognitive mechanisms if it is to evade the lion, Plantinga goes on to add that, of course, the frog has 'indicators' – neural structures that receive input from the frog's sense organs, are correlated with the path of the insect as it flies past, and are connected with the frog's muscles in such a way that it flicks out its tongue – and, in just the same way, the zebra also has 'indicators' – neural structures that monitor the environment, are correlated with the presence of predators, and are connected with its muscles in such a way as to cause it to flee when a predator threatens. But the important point to see, according to Plantinga, is that

> Indication does not require belief. In particular, it does not require belief having to do with the state of affairs indicated; indeed it is entirely compatible with belief inconsistent with that state of affairs. (328) ... Indication is one thing, belief content is something else altogether, and we know of no reason (given materialism) why the one should follow the other. Content simply arises upon the appearance of neural structures of sufficient complexity; there is no reason why that content need be related to what the structures indicate, if anything. The proposition constituting the content need not be so much as about that which is indicated; it certainly need not be true.
>
> (2011: 331)

In support of the claim that indication does not require content, Plantinga asks us to consider the (likely counterfactual) case of anaerobic marine organisms. However, while I agree with Plantinga that there are no contentful states in this case, I insist that, *in the relevant sense*, there is no indication either. Insofar as we are taking account only of putative contentful properties, anaerobic marine organisms are much closer to thermostats then they are to zebras, or frogs, or even *C. elegans*.

Why does Plantinga suppose otherwise? Well, I think that Plantinga describes zebras and frogs in a way which makes them sound much more like anaerobic marine organisms than they really are. There is no neural structure in the frog that ties perception of flying insects directly to tongue flicking muscles; and there is no neural structure in the zebra that ties perception of lions directly to the muscles involved in urgent flight. If the frog is sated, then the frog will not flick out its tongue at flying insects; if the frog is engaged in mating, then the frog will not flick out its tongue at flying insects; if the frog is fleeing from a swooping bird, then the frog will not flick out its tongue at flying insects. If the zebra is in the middle of the herd, then the zebra will not take flight when it sees the lion; if the zebra is downwind from the lion, then it will not take flight without evidence that the lion has detected it; if the zebra has young, then the zebra will not immediately take flight without making some effort to ensure the safety of its young. Plantinga's accounts of zebras and frogs stand to the truth in much the same kind of way that behaviourist accounts of human beings stand to the truth: they fail to do justice to the complex internal processing that is involved in the production of behaviour.

As my account of the cases involving zebras, frogs, and *C. elegans* suggests, what Plantinga calls 'indicator' states in these cases are actually content-bearing states. In order to avoid the age-old dispute about whether there are any non-language using animals that are properly said to have *beliefs*, I shall not take a stance on the question whether zebras, frogs, and *C. elegans* have beliefs. However, I do say that zebras, frogs, and *C. elegans* all have belief-like, content-bearing states – and, moreover, these belief-like, content-bearing states just are certain kinds of neural states. Creatures with neural structures have belief-like, content-bearing neural states with contents that are something like the following: 'that's a potential mate', 'that's potential food', 'that's toxic', 'that's a serious foe', 'that's an annoying parasite', and so forth. Moreover, for undamaged creatures whose evolutionary history has fitted them for the environment in which they are presently located, their belief-like, content-bearing states of these kinds will mostly be true.

13. Contra

Even if it is accepted that Plantinga fails to establish the strong claim that, on N&E, there is no reason to suppose that any belief is true, it might well be objected that it could still be true, on N&E, that the likelihood that most of our beliefs are true is very low. After all, we have beliefs about all kinds of things that played no role in the evolutionary history of our cognitive faculties. Given that our 'central processor' is the product of evolutionary pressure – in large part from the complex social environments that human groups produced – what reason is there to think that it would yield a preponderance of true beliefs about, for example, complex scientific matters?

Short answer: The demands of living in complex social environments produced, in us, a sufficiently competent all-purpose 'central processor' whose possession allowed us to be moulded into creatures that, over a very wide range, do have a preponderance of true beliefs: education provides a corrective to many of the errors in belief to which we would otherwise be prone. In particular, while many – perhaps even most – of our 'intuitive' beliefs about complex scientific matters are mistaken, we have developed social institutions and ways of living that allow us to correct the shortcomings of those 'intuitive' beliefs. Of course, as I have already emphasised, there are areas – philosophy, religion, politics, etc. – where our cognitive faculties are visibly and demonstrably unreliable. Moreover, there are also various ways in which our (uncorrected) cognitive faculties are prone to error: we systematically ignore base rates, overestimate our own abilities, and so forth. But there are many areas where – at least collectively, and at our best – we are quite good at discovering the truth. Moreover, this is exactly what we should expect to say, whether or not we accept N&E.

14. Truth

The question whether our cognitive faculties deliver a preponderance of true beliefs requires that we have a method for estimating what fraction of our beliefs are true. Our having a method for estimating what fraction of our beliefs are true likely depends upon our having a method for counting our beliefs. But do we have a method for counting our beliefs?

Suppose that we are deemed to believe anything entailed by things that we believe. Even if our beliefs are consistent, it seems that we all then have infinitely many true beliefs and infinitely many false beliefs. After all, if I believe that p, then what I believe entails that it is true that p, that it is true that it is true that p, and so on. But we all have *some* true beliefs and *some* false beliefs.

Perhaps it might seem too much to say that one counts as believing anything that is entailed by things that one believes, even if 'entailment' is understood in formal terms. However, we get to the same conclusion even if we suppose merely that we count as believing all sufficiently obvious consequences of things that we believe. For example, it seems plausible to suppose that I believe that (A&B) if I believe that A and I believe that B. (Similarly, it seems plausible that I believe that it is true that it is true that A if I believe that it is true that A.) But suppose that I have a false belief that B. Then, for any true belief A that I have, I also have the false belief that (A&B). So, it seems, if I have even one false belief, then I have just as many false beliefs as true beliefs.

In order to avoid these difficulties, we might suppose that, for the purposes of estimating what fraction of our beliefs are true, we should start with an axiomatisation of our beliefs. On the assumption that our beliefs are consistent, we suppose that our beliefs are represented by a set of mutually independent propositions which somehow 'yield' all of our beliefs. While we may once again be committed to the claim that one counts as believing anything that is entailed by one's beliefs, we set any worries that this might prompt to one side. On the plausible assumption that there is a *finite* axiomatisation of our beliefs, we now have a straightforward procedure for estimating the fraction of our beliefs that are true: we simply look to the proportion of our axioms that are true.

Of course, there are still problems. First, it is not obvious that all axiomatisations will yield the same answer – and, if different axiomatisations yield different answers, then we do not (yet) have a satisfactory procedure. Second, and more importantly, we can't actually axiomatise anyone's beliefs; so we can't actually use the procedure that we have outlined. Even if, in principle, we could estimate what fraction of our beliefs are true by estimating the proportion of our axioms that are true, it is unclear how to get from there to the claim that the preponderance of our axioms are true.

Perhaps it might be said – in the style of Wittgenstein, Davidson, and many others – that we don't actually need to examine our axioms in order to be justified in thinking that the preponderance of our axioms are true: for, in fact, we can only attribute axioms to others on the assumption that the preponderance of their axioms are true. But to proceed in this way would simply be to assume the main point at issue. Sure, we can grant to Wittgenstein, Davidson, and the rest, that we need to presuppose a body of true axioms in order to make attributions of axioms: it can't be that all – or nearly all – of the axioms of a given agent are false. In particular, if we are to make sense of someone as a believing agent, then we shall need to suppose that their cognitive faculties – of perception, memory, *a priori* intuition, sympathy, introspection, testimony, moral sense, and so forth – deliver bodies of true axioms across a range of domains. But it is consistent with the delivery of bodies of true axioms across a range of domains that those same cognitive faculties deliver bodies of entirely false axioms across other domains; and, moreover, it is also consistent to suppose that some agents have more axioms that belong to the second set of domains than to the first.

Consider Paul. Paul is a philosophical obsessive. He spends almost all of his waking time engaged in developing his own philosophical system. Alas, as it happens, Paul's philosophical system is completely misbegotten: none of the axioms that belong to his philosophical system are true. Moreover, Paul's philosophical system involves a vast number of axioms: his system is comprehensive in its ambition, and extraordinarily detailed in its development. While Paul's cognitive faculties deliver plenty of true axioms in other domains, it simply isn't true that, overall, his cognitive faculties deliver a majority – let alone a preponderance – of true axioms, because Paul's cognitive faculties spend so much time churning out false philosophical axioms.

Perhaps it might be replied that the story of Paul doesn't ring true. For any person – even a philosophical obsessive – the vast bulk of their axioms concern mundane matters: their own immediate environment, their own comfort, and so forth. And, in those kinds of domains – on Wittgensteinian and Davidsonian grounds – it must be that their cognitive faculties deliver a preponderance of true axioms.

However, if this objection wins the battle, it loses the war. For – as we have seen in our earlier discussion – we can expect the cognitive faculties of evolved creatures to deliver true axioms about their own immediate environments, their own comfort, and so forth. If our cognitive faculties are primarily concerned with the delivery of axioms concerning our immediate environments, our own comfort, and so forth, that Pr (R/N&E) is high, and the first premise of Plantinga's argument is false. However, if our cognitive faculties are primarily concerned with the delivery of highly theoretical axioms of philosophy, politics, religion, and so forth, then it is a mistake to suppose that our cognitive faculties are reliable, and it is actually a point in favour of N&E that Pr (R/N&E) is low.

15. Premise 2

Suppose that Pr (R/N&E) is low. Does the rest of Plantinga's argument go through?

The second premise of Plantinga's argument is that no one who accepts N&E and recognises that Pr (R/N&E) is low can accept R. So, on the assumption that Pr (R/N&E) is low, naturalists who accept that we and our cognitive faculties have come to be in the way proposed by contemporary evolutionary theory cannot reasonably suppose that our cognitive faculties are reliable, i.e., that our cognitive faculties deliver a preponderance of true beliefs.

We have that Pr (R/N&E) = Pr (R&N&E) / Pr (N&E). That is: Pr (R&N&E) = Pr (R/N&E). Pr (N&E).

Someone who accepts N&E supposes that Pr (N&E) is not low. Someone who also accepts R supposes that Pr (R&N&E) is not low. But if neither Pr (R&N&E) nor Pr (N&E) is low, then – contrary to our hypothesis – Pr (R/N&E) cannot be low. So, I think, the second premise of Plantinga's argument is correct.

16. Premise 3

The third premise of Plantinga's argument is that no one who denies or fails to accept that our cognitive faculties are reliable can rationally believe anything at all. In other words: if someone denies or fails to accept that her cognitive faculties produce a preponderance of true beliefs, then that one is not rationally entitled to believe anything at all.

This premise seems evidently mistaken. Recall our earlier story about Paul, and add to it the assumption that Paul recognises that it is very unlikely that he has a preponderance of true philosophical beliefs. Just because Paul is a philosophical obsessive who recognises that he very likely has a preponderance of false philosophical beliefs, it certainly does not follow that Paul is not rationally entitled to beliefs about his own immediate environment, his own comfort, and so forth. Indeed, so long as Paul thinks it rather likely that his cognitive faculties produce a preponderance of true beliefs concerning his own immediate environment, his own comfort, and so forth, there is not even a *prima facie* problem that arises for him.

Doubtless it will be replied that, if Paul believes that N&E, then, since it is clearly a philosophical belief that N&E, his belief that his cognitive faculties produce mostly false philosophical beliefs does undermine his rational entitlement to believe that N&E. Of course, Paul's brother, Saul – a political obsessive who has, and who recognises that he very likely has, a preponderance of false political beliefs, but who further supposes that his cognitive faculties produce a preponderance of true philosophical beliefs on those rare occasions when he forms philosophical beliefs – does not have his rational entitlement to believe that N&E undermined in the same way. But if Paul believes that N&E, and accepts that N&E is a philosophical belief, then there is at least a *prima facie* challenge that arises for him if he supposes that his cognitive faculties mostly produce false philosophical beliefs.

Before we consider the merit of this reply, it is worth noting that it effectively abandons EAAN in favour of EAAN*. Since this reply tacitly concedes that the third premise of EAAN is false, this reply cannot make a contribution to a defence of EAAN. We shall return to consider the merits of this reply after we finish our examination of EAAN.

17. Premise 4

The fourth premise of Plantinga's argument is that, if anyone who believes N&E is unable to rationally believe anything at all, then belief in N&E is self-defeating and N&E cannot be rationally believed. I do not propose to challenge this premise.

18. Upshot

EAAN fails. There are serious problems involved in even making sense of claims about ratios of truth to non-truth in systems of beliefs. However, to the extent that we can make sense of such claims, it seems that, on E&N, we should expect evolved creatures' cognitive faculties to deliver a healthy preponderance of true beliefs concerning their immediate environments, their own comfort, and so forth. On the one hand, if we suppose that most of a creature's beliefs concern its immediate environment, own comfort, and so forth, then Plantinga's first premise is just false: Pr (R/N&E) is high. On the other hand, if we suppose that most of a creature's beliefs concern things other than its immediate environment, own comfort, and so forth, then, while Plantinga's first premise may be true, his third premise will then be false: for, in that case, a creature's cognitive faculties will deliver a preponderance of true beliefs over the smaller domain of its beliefs concerning its immediate environment, own comfort, and so forth, while failing to deliver a preponderance of true beliefs over the domain of all of its beliefs.

19. EAAN*

Of course, if this analysis is right, it immediately directs our attention to EAAN*. However, given the preceding discussion of EAAN, our discussion of EAAN* can be mercifully brief. We can simply grant the first two premises: Pr (R'/N&E) is low, and no one who accepts N&E and recognises that Pr (R/N&E) is low can accept R'. However, we should not accept the third premise: it is perfectly possible to rationally accept N&E even though one rejects R'. As we noted at the beginning of our discussion, there is nothing inconsistent in (1) accepting a bunch of axioms while (2) supposing that it is unlikely that any conjunction of most of those axioms is true. True enough, by these lights, rationality requires that you don't give *too much* credence to your philosophical axioms – but, given the state of expert philosophical opinion, it seems eminently sensible not to give *too much* credence to your philosophical axioms.

Does it then follow that naturalists cannot rationally give very high credence to naturalism? Not at all! The credence that one gives to one's axioms can be moderate even if the credence given to some axioms is very high. Suppose that I have ten axioms, one of which is N. Suppose, further, that I give credence 1.0 to N, and credence 0.51 to my other nine axioms.

Calculation reveals (I think) that the credence that I should give to the claim that more than two-thirds of my axioms are true is about 0.27. So, it seems, I can consistently hold that I am not reliable in my philosophical believing while nonetheless being *certain* of my naturalism. (Of course, there are independent reasons for thinking that it would not be rational to give credence 1 to N. But if we choose a more sensible credence – say 0.999999999 – then that simply drives down the credence that I should give to the claim that more than two-thirds of my axioms are true.)

20. Disclaimer

There are some topics that arise in the course of Plantinga's exposition and defence of EAAN that I have not broached. For example, Plantinga takes controversial stances on (a) the interpretation of probability claims (2011: 332); (b) the semantics for counterfactuals (2011: 338); and (c) 'the conditionalization problem' (2011: 347). However, it is beyond the scope of the present chapter to examine what Plantinga has to say about these matters. Moreover, it is also beyond the scope of the present chapter to compare the argument of Plantinga (2011) with the arguments of Plantinga (1991) (1993) (1994) (2002).

21. Concluding remarks

The conclusion of our discussion of Plantinga (2011) is that it fails to show that there is any conflict between science and naturalism. While it is an open question whether there is conflict between science and Plantinga's theism, there is nothing in Plantinga (2011) that supports the claim that naturalism is defeated by science.

6 Does religion defeat naturalism?

It might seem odd to suppose that religion could defeat naturalism. After all, it seems pretty clear that the commitments of best religious big pictures properly include the commitments of best naturalistic big pictures. Whereas naturalists take the scientific method as their touchstone for identifying the denizens of causal reality, proponents of religious big pictures suppose that scientific method requires supplementation with religious methods that identify additional denizens of causal reality. While it may be rationally permissible to suppose that the additional commitments are justified – e.g., by the additional explanatory breadth and depth that they permit – it is not even remotely *prima facie* plausible to suppose that there is any prospect of convergence of expert opinion on what those additional commitments are and what benefits they bring.

Despite the *prima facie* implausibility of the claim that religion defeats naturalism, there are many contemporary philosophers eager to take up the challenge of showing that religion does defeat naturalism. In this chapter, I propose to examine two of these challenges in detail. The first of these challenges is provided by the work of Michael Rea, and, in particular, by Rea (2002). The second is a more generic challenge provided by contemporary Thomism. I shall consider these challenges in turn.

1. Rea's argument against naturalism

Rea (2002) argues for something like the following set of claims:

Inquiry is a process in which we try to revise our beliefs on the basis of what we take to be evidence.
In order to engage in inquiry, we must have methodological dispositions: dispositions to treat at least some of our cognitive faculties as sources of evidence, and dispositions to take certain kinds of experiences and arguments as evidence.
Anyone who has methodological dispositions has an individual research program: a maximal set of methodological dispositions.
Naturalism cannot be a substantive philosophical position.

Since naturalism cannot be a substantive philosophical position, naturalism is most charitably interpreted to be a research program.

Commitment to the naturalistic research program precludes one from accepting realism about material objects, materialism, and realism about other minds.

1.1 Initial quibbles

I'm inclined to quibble with Rea's account of inquiry. I think that it would be more accurate to say that inquiry is a process in which we aim to review our beliefs where, and only where, we have good reason to do so. Pressure to revise beliefs can have two sources. On the one hand, there are the 'internal' demands of consistency, coherence, and the like. On the other hand, there are the 'external' demands of data or evidence. Even in the absence of new data or evidence, we may have good reason to revise our beliefs, given that we've detected *prima facie* inconsistency, or incoherence, or the like.

I'm also inclined to quibble with Rea's account of methodological dispositions. I think that it would be more accurate to say that, in order to engage in inquiry, we employ our cognitive faculties, and rely upon their (collective) deliverances.

While I concede that we have dispositions to treat certain kinds of experiences as reasons to revise some of our beliefs, it seems to me to be trivially true that *any* experience is evidence that bears on some of our beliefs (and hence trivially true that I ought to be disposed to treat all of my experience as evidence). Suppose, for example, that I had Cotard delusion. My having of any experience at all would be evidence that I am not dead, and hence would be a reason for me to revise the belief that is constitutive of the delusion. It seems to me to be trivially true that much of our evidence confirms what we already know; this fact is plainly consonant with the claim that *any* experience is evidence that bears on some of our beliefs.

I think that we should at least quibble with the claim that we have dispositions to take certain kinds of arguments as evidence. True enough, there are times when our being presented with arguments gives us reason to revise our beliefs. In particular, as I noted above, receipt of an argument may bring us to recognise inconsistency, or incoherence, or the like. However, it seems more natural to me to say that, in this kind of case, the argument *exhibits* the inconsistency, or incoherence, or the like, rather than that the argument – or perhaps the receipt of the argument – is *evidence* for inconsistency, or incoherence, or whatever.

I also think that we should at least quibble with the suggestion that we have dispositions to treat our cognitive faculties as sources of evidence. If I thought that what is in my memory *originated* there, then I would have no reason at all to suppose that my memories are veridical. Similarly, if I thought that what is presented to me in perception *originated* with my perceptual faculties, then I would have no reason at all to suppose that my perceptions are veridical. My cognitive faculties are almost never *sources* of evidence. When I rely upon the deliverances of my cognitive faculties, what I rely upon – by

88 *Does religion defeat naturalism?*

and large – is that my employment of my cognitive faculties generates true beliefs.

1.2 Dispositions, experience, and evidence

Rea's argument for the claim that we all have individual research programs is based on the following assertion (which he claims 'just seems obvious'):

> For any kind of experience or argument, anyone who is disposed to treat *some* experiences or arguments as evidence either will be disposed to treat *that* kind of experience or argument as evidence or will be disposed not to treat *that* kind of experience or argument as evidence.
>
> (2002: 4)

However, given the various quibbles above, we can see that there are two ways of interpreting this assertion. On the one hand, it could be taken to collapse into the (trivial) claim that one is (properly) disposed to treat any kind of experience as evidence that has some bearing on some beliefs that one has. On the other hand, it could be taken to be an expression of something like the following claim:

> For any kinds of experiences and any kinds of beliefs, anyone who is disposed to treat some experiences as evidence that bears on some beliefs will either be disposed to treat *those* kinds of experiences as evidence that bears on *those* kinds of beliefs, or else will be disposed not to treat *those* kinds of experiences as evidence that bears on *those* kinds of beliefs.

Rea says:

> If ... a person lacked a disposition to trust tabloids, she would not be able to acquire that disposition without losing a disposition not to trust them.
>
> (2002: 4)

But this claim depends upon a controversial assumption about the connection between *lacking a disposition to trust tabloids* and *possessing a disposition not to trust tabloids*. Suppose that I have no conception of what a tabloid might be. Given that I do not so much as possess the concept of a tabloid, I am in no condition to be disposed to have any attitudes towards them; hence, in particular, I am in no condition to be disposed not to trust them. So, I think, the controversial assumption that Rea makes is false: I could perfectly well acquire the disposition to trust tabloids even though I had no previous dispositions of any kind concerning them. Moreover, this point generalises. Given that there are countless concepts that I do not possess, there are countless beliefs whose content I am currently unable to frame. Consequently, there are many pairs of kinds of experiences and kinds of beliefs for which I am neither disposed to treat those kinds of experiences as evidence that bears on those kinds of beliefs nor disposed not to treat those kinds of experiences as evidence that bears on those kinds of beliefs. It is neither the case that Socrates was disposed to treat data from bubble chambers as evidence for certain physical theories nor that Socrates was disposed not to treat data from bubble chambers as evidence for certain physical theories.

Rea says:

> [O]ur research program is something we bring to the table of inquiry. Method is therefore prior to theory; and so ... our research program is not something that we intentionally adopt as a result of inquiry.
>
> (2002: 4)

But, as we have just seen, it is simply *not* true that we bring a maximal set of methodological dispositions to the table of inquiry. In the sense that Rea gives to his remarks, it is not true that method is prior to theory. Moreover, in the sense that Rea gives to his remarks, it is not true that we have research programs, and so, *a fortiori*, it is not true that our research programs are things that we do not intentionally adopt as the result of inquiry.

1.3 Methodological dispositions

We noted earlier that Rea gives a disjunctive account of methodological dispositions: some methodological dispositions are dispositions concerning the reliability of our cognitive faculties, and some methodological dispositions are dispositions to treat certain kinds of experiences as reasons to revise some of our beliefs. However, it seems to me that the combining of these two classes under a single label obscures the many significant differences between them.

It seems to me that we do have *some* 'dispositions concerning the reliability of our cognitive faculties' that we bring to the table of inquiry and that are prior to theory. If I am to engage in any kind of inquiry, I need to draw upon the resources of perception, memory, and inference. Moreover, while I ought to give due recognition to the fallibility of all of these resources, I could not be a functioning inquirer unless I correctly supposed that these resources are reliable across significant ranges of application. Sure, when I am sufficiently tired, or upset, or intoxicated – or when the subject matter of my inquiry is sufficiently complex or difficult – my perceptions, memories, and inferences are less than fully reliable. But, when I'm in good shape, and conditions are friendly, and the subject matter is not too demanding, then, across a wide range of topics, my perception, memory, and inference is highly reliable.

Furthermore, I think, we have *some* 'dispositions concerning the reliability of the cognitive faculties of others' that we also bring to the table of inquiry and that are prior to theory. If I am to engage in any (but the most basic) kind of inquiry, I need to draw upon the resources of other people's perception, memory, and inference. While, again, I must give due recognition to the fallibility of these resources, I could not be a functioning inquirer unless I correctly supposed that these resources are reliable across significant ranges of application. Sure, there is variation in the basic reliability of the perceptions, memories, and inferences of other people – even at their best, some people are less reliable informants than others – and there are the same complicating factors that apply in my own case. But, when they're in good shape, and conditions are friendly, and the subject matter is not too demanding, and they're not trying to deceive me, then, across a wide range of topics, the testimony of other people is highly reliable.

Of course, we constantly revise our views about exactly where we and other people are highly reliable in our perception, memory, and inference. We have very different expectations for different kinds of other people – e.g. infants, children, enemies, liars, the depressed, the deluded, the demented, and so forth. Moreover, we are – at least sometimes – cognisant of changes in our own cognitive powers: perhaps, for example, we notice deterioration in memories, or eyesight, or ability to perform complex reasoning tasks. In the course of our lives, we come to recognise that there are many large subject areas – likely including religion, politics, and philosophy – where there is no universal convergence of informed opinion, and hence concerning which it would be absurd to suppose that our cognitive faculties are reliable. And, if we follow developments in psychology and related disciplines, we may also be aware of various more or less universal pitfalls to which we are collectively prone: ignoring base rates, failing to recognise framing effects, overconfidence, overlooking regression to the mean, and so on.

In sum, then, while we *do* bring to inquiry a *general disposition* concerning the reliability of the cognitive faculties of ourselves and others, we do *not* bring to inquiry *highly specific dispositions* concerning the reliability of the cognitive faculties of ourselves and others. On the contrary, our highly specific dispositions concerning the reliability of the cognitive faculties of ourselves and others are – and must be – *informed* by inquiry, and are – and must be – *constantly updated* on the basis of inquiry. Moreover, while our general disposition concerning the reliability of the cognitive faculties of ourselves and others is not intentionally adopted as a result of inquiry, our highly specific dispositions concerning the reliability of the cognitive faculties of ourselves and others very often are intentionally adopted as a result of inquiry.

Given these claims about dispositions concerning the reliability of the cognitive faculties of ourselves and others, what should we say about dispositions to treat certain kinds of experiences as reasons to revise particular beliefs? I'm inclined to think – though I admit to being rather uncertain about this – that we may only have a general disposition to treat certain kinds of experiences as reasons for belief revision, and that we may not have any particular dispositions to treat certain specified kinds of experiences as reasons to revise specified beliefs.

Some theorists suppose that our cognitive faculties collectively work to predict future experiences, and that we have a general disposition only to make further use of our cognitive faculties where there is a mismatch between predicted experience and actual experience. On this view, it is true that we have a general disposition to treat unpredicted future experiences as reasons to engage in belief revision. However, on this view, it remains a further question whether we should also suppose that we have particular dispositions to treat particular possible unpredicted future experiences as reasons to engage in particular possible revisions of belief. And, given the sheer range of possible unpredicted future experiences and the sheer range of possible revisions of current total belief state, it seems improbable that we actually do have particular dispositions in respect of all of those possible unpredicted future experiences and all of those possible revisions of current total belief state.

Even if it is a mistake to suppose that our cognitive faculties collectively work to predict future experiences, it seems that the conclusion that we reached at the end of the preceding paragraph should still stand. It is simply not credible to suppose that we have particular dispositions in respect of all possible future experiences and all possible revisions of current total belief state. At any point in my life, it is true that there are certain beliefs that I might take on if I were to acquire certain concepts that I do not yet possess. But, given that I do not possess those concepts, I am in no position to be disposed to take on those beliefs given specified possible future experiences. Socrates simply had *no* dispositions concerning electroweak theories and data from bubble chambers.

1.4 Sources of basic beliefs

Rea writes:

> [M]ethodological dispositions differ from person to person. ... Furthermore, people differ with respect to what they take to be basic sources of evidence – sources that are to be trusted even in the absence of positive evidence in favour of their reliability. For some (maybe most), sense perception, reason, memory, rational intuition, and religious experience all count as basic sources. For others, at least some of these sources are derivative – they are to be trusted only after their reliability has been verified by evidence from other basic sources.
>
> (2002: 2)

Much of this seems to me to be open to question. Subject to the qualifications mentioned in the preceding discussion, *every inquirer* has a general disposition to treat perception, memory, and inference as reliable that does not depend upon the prior acquisition of evidence for reliability, and properly so. If one is to engage in inquiry, then it must be that one's perception, memory, and inference is reliable across a wide range of domains (when one is in good shape, conditions are friendly, the subject matter is not too demanding, and so forth); and, moreover, if one considers the matter, one must take one's perception, memory, and inference to be reliable across that wide range of domains (when one is in good shape, conditions are friendly, the subject matter is not too demanding, and so forth).

However, there are no similar requirements that apply in the case of religious experience and rational intuition. On the one hand, it is manifestly not true that every inquirer has a general disposition to treat rational intuition and religious experience as reliable; and still less is it so that every inquirer has a general disposition to treat rational intuition and religious experience as reliable that does not depend upon a prior acquisition of evidence for their reliability. On the other hand, it is manifestly proper that not all inquirers have a general disposition to treat rational intuition and religious experience as reliable; and it is also manifestly proper that not all inquirers have a general disposition to treat rational intuition and religious experience as reliable that does not depend upon a prior acquisition of evidence for their reliability. In particular, it is obvious to all that religious experience is claimed to support a wide range of mutually incompatible beliefs by those who claim to have religious experiences; and it is not less obvious to all that rational intuition is claimed to support a wide range of mutually incompatible beliefs by those who claim to have rational intuitions. It is hardly any less obvious that, while there could not be inquiry in the absence of a general disposition to treat perception, memory, and inference as reliable (that does not depend upon the prior acquisition of evidence for reliability), there certainly can be inquiry in the absence of a general disposition to treat rational intuition and religious experience as reliable, and, even more certainly, there can be inquiry in the absence of a general disposition to treat rational intuition and religious experience as reliable that does not depend upon a prior acquisition of evidence for their reliability.

Perhaps the preceding remarks about rational intuition require some qualification. On Rea's view, some quintessentially metaphysical claims – e.g., that it is possible that God exists, that there cannot be an infinite regress of causes, that there are absolute moral values, that there cannot be absolute moral values unless God exists – are justifiable, if at all, only by rational intuition (2002: 219). It is clear that there can be inquiry in the absence of a general disposition to suppose that we have a faculty that is reliable with respect to *these* kinds of claims; and it is even more clear that there can be inquiry in the absence of a general disposition to suppose that we have a faculty that is reliable with respect to these kinds of claims that does not depend upon a prior acquisition of evidence of the reliability of such a faculty. However, it is not so clear that there can be inquiry in the absence of a general disposition to suppose that we have a faculty that is reliable with respect to a more or less basic range of mathematical, logical, statistical, and methodological claims. Perhaps we might suppose that reliability with respect to a more or less basic range of mathematical, logical, statistical, and methodological claims is built into central processing, rather than housed in a relatively autonomous faculty; or perhaps we might suppose that the faculty of inference is reliable with respect to that more or less basic range of mathematical, logical, statistical, and methodological claims. But an alternative to these views that perhaps should not be immediately dismissed is that there is a further faculty – 'rational intuition' – which is reliable with respect to a more or less basic range of mathematical, logical, statistical, and methodological claims. (Of course, we might also think that talk about 'faculties' is too imprecise to support the kinds of distinctions being adverted to here.)

1.5 Big picture conflict

Rea (2002) is primarily about a conflict between big pictures. On the one hand, there is the theistic big picture that Rea endorses: a big picture according to which there is a supernatural, omnipotent, omniscient, perfectly good, sole creator *ex nihilo* of everything else, including the universe in which we live. On the other hand, there are the naturalistic big pictures that Rea rejects: big pictures according to which there is only the universe in which we live (and no supernatural, omnipotent, omniscient, perfectly good, sole creator *ex nihilo* of that universe and perhaps other things besides). According to Rea's theistic big picture, there are many reliable basic sources of information: perception, introspection, inference, rational intuition, and religious experience. However, according to the naturalistic big pictures that Rea rejects, there are fewer reliable basic sources of information: just perception, introspection, and inference. According to Rea's theistic big picture, there are many reliable methods to be used in obtaining information: methods of commonsense, methods of science, and religious methods (prayer, reading scripture, seeking revelation, etc.) However, according to the naturalistic big pictures that Rea rejects, there are fewer reliable methods to be used in obtaining information: just the methods of commonsense and science. Although it is perhaps not exactly right, it is at least approximately correct to say that, in all respects, naturalistic big pictures are trimmed down versions of theistic big pictures: naturalistic big pictures add nothing to theistic big pictures, but they do throw a great deal away.

When we consider things in the light of the preceding paragraph, we see that it is plausible to suppose that, in any well-ordered big picture, there will be a concordance between metaphysics, epistemology, and method: the additional commitments that the theist has over the naturalist under each of these three heads are both distinctive and connected. However, there is no reason to suppose that the commitments under one head are somehow prior to the commitments under the other heads; rather, we should see the three kinds of commitments as a package deal. Moreover, when we seek to compare the virtues of theistic big pictures with the virtues of naturalistic big pictures, we should see the commitments of both big pictures as package deals. Or so I say.

But Rea disagrees. In his view, we are required to suppose that there is and can be no substantive characterisation of naturalism: the basic commitments of naturalism cannot be taken to be metaphysical, or epistemological, or methodological, or some combination of these three. Rather, as we noted above, he claims that naturalism can only be a research program, i.e. a maximal set of dispositions to trust cognitive faculties as sources of evidence and to take certain kinds of experiences and arguments as evidence. I think that the preceding discussion more than suffices to show that naturalism cannot be a research program: whatever naturalism may be, it most certainly is *not* a maximal set of dispositions to trust cognitive faculties as sources of evidence and to take certain kinds of experiences and arguments as evidence. Perhaps, then, Rea is also mistaken in claiming that the basic commitments of naturalism cannot be taken to be metaphysical, or epistemological, or methodological, or some combination of these three?

1.6 Metaphysical commitments of naturalism

An obvious first thought is that the principle *metaphysical* commitment of naturalism is to the non-existence of anything supernatural. Against this, Rea objects that this claim is uninformative because naturalists disagree about how to classify things as either natural or supernatural.

> There are common paradigms: men, beasts, plants, atoms and electrons are natural; God, angels, ghosts, and immaterial souls are supernatural. But even these paradigms are controversial; and, in any case, it is not clear what the items on each list have in common with their other list-mates that makes them examples of natural or supernatural entities.
>
> (2002: 54–55)

I think that Rea exaggerates the difficulties raised by the paradigms that he cites. On the one hand, it is uncontroversial (by the lights of naturalists) that men, beasts, plants, atoms, and electrons are natural. On the other hand, it is uncontroversial (by the lights of naturalists) that God, ghosts, and immaterial (human) souls are supernatural (and, if angels are essentially messengers from God, then it may also be uncontroversial that angels are supernatural). Moreover, there is no problem explaining why these things are classified as they are. On the one hand, men, beasts, plants, atoms, and electrons are all entities recognised in well-established science: for example, school and university science textbooks authorised by national academies of science commit themselves to the existence of these kinds of things. On the other hand, God, ghosts, and immaterial (human) souls are entities recognised by no well-established science: for example, no national academies of science authorise school and university science textbooks that commit themselves to the existence of these kinds of things.

Suppose that Rea were right that naturalism requires a supplementary account of the distinction between the natural and the supernatural. Rea offers the following argument in defence of the claim that no version of naturalism can include any such supplementary account:

1   Naturalists respect the natural sciences as absolutely authoritative; naturalism demands that we follow science wherever it leads (and it will lead somewhere).
2   (Therefore) Naturalism must be compatible with anything science might tell us about the natural and the supernatural.

3 (Therefore) No version of naturalism can include any supplementary account of the natural and the supernatural.

The premise of this argument is one that Rea insists on repeatedly; indeed, he goes so far as to say that it is 'uncontroversial' (2002: 55). Nonetheless, it seems to me to be evidently false. On the one hand, it is obviously not true that naturalists regard *current natural science* as absolutely authoritative: a simple historical induction tells naturalists that it is very likely that some significant parts of current natural science are false; and it is obvious on its face that most areas of current natural science are incomplete. On the other hand, there is no way that naturalists of the early twenty-first century can follow *ideal or completed natural science* wherever it leads, since those naturalists have no current access to ideal or completed natural science. Moreover, there is nothing in naturalism that requires commitment to the claim that our descendants will one day be in possession of ideal or completed natural science; indeed, I would expect almost all naturalists to suppose that it is extremely unlikely that we shall have descendants who are in possession of ideal or completed natural science.

Of course, naturalists do accord a special place to *current established* natural science. According to naturalists, current established natural science is by far the most reliable source of information that we have concerning the subject matters treated by current natural science. Consequently, when we are engaged in philosophical speculation and the subject matters treated by current established natural science are relevant, our best bet, by far, is to build on the foundations of current established natural science. Sure, some parts of current established natural science will be reconfigured by theories that are not currently available to us; but almost all of current established natural science will survive in some form. Moreover, choosing other foundations for philosophical speculation, based on less reliable sources of information currently in our possession, would clearly be an inferior option. Of course, by naturalist lights, we may not have very good reason to be confident that philosophical speculation based on current established natural science is true; but, by naturalist lights, we do have very good reason to be confident that we would do worse if we based our speculation on anything other than current established natural science.

That naturalists accord a special place to current established natural science does not entail that those naturalists will continue to accord a special place to current established natural science no matter what tomorrow brings. If there were an 'intelligence explosion' that saw the development of ultra-intelligent machines with capacities that far surpass those of any possible human being (see Chalmers [2010]), and if the ultra-intelligent machines were suitably disposed towards human beings, then the most reliable sources of information for human beings would be the ultra-intelligent machines. If what the ultra-intelligent machines said disagreed in some places with the doctrines of our current established natural science, then it would be our current established natural science that went by the board. Moreover, this would be so even if human beings were incapable of understanding how the ultra-intelligent machines acquired the information in their possession. (Similar conclusions might be reached by consideration of ultra-intelligent aliens, or other conceivable supra-human sources of information.)

Perhaps it might be replied that, even if the argument that Rea actually gives fails, there is a way in which his argument can be repaired. Suppose that there will be no Singularity, and that there are no intelligent aliens or other supra-human sources of information. Suppose, indeed, that there are no sources of information for us other than those with which we are already familiar: perception, introspection, inference, and so forth. On these assumptions, surely it is true that naturalists suppose that our established natural science will always be authoritative for us, and it is also true that naturalism demands that we follow our science wherever it leads. And then Rea's argument can proceed as before.

Suppose that we grant that if established natural science is authoritative, then established natural science must be compatible with anything science might tell us about the natural and the supernatural. Does it follow that no version of naturalism can include any supplementary account of the natural and the supernatural?

I don't think so. At the very least, we need to think about what established natural science *could* tell us concerning the natural and the supernatural. Suppose that all ontologically or metaphysically possible worlds share both laws and initial history with the actual world, and depart from the actual world only as a result of the outworkings of objective chance. Suppose, too, that it is ontologically and metaphysically impossible for there to be gods, ghosts, immaterial souls, and the like. On these assumptions, it seems that established natural science *could not* tell us that there are gods, ghosts, or immaterial souls. Perhaps there are weaker assumptions on which it would also turn out that established natural science could not tell us that there are gods, ghosts, or immaterial souls – but, in any case, it seems to me that naturalists ought to find the above assumptions plausible.

Even if it is accepted that naturalists might reasonably suppose that it is ontologically and metaphysically impossible that established science tells us things that are incompatible with naturalism, it might be insisted that it is surely conceivable – 'epistemically' or doxastically possible – that established science tells us things that are incompatible with naturalism. Surely even the most diehard naturalists must concede that it is conceivable that established natural science tells us things about the natural and the supernatural that are incompatible with naturalism.

Agreed! Even the most diehard naturalist accepts that it is *conceivable* or *imaginable* that established natural science tells us things about the natural and the supernatural that are incompatible with naturalism. But the naturalist insists that conception and imagination of the ontologically or metaphysically impossible is commonplace, and imposes no constraints upon 'supplementary accounts of the natural and the supernatural'. While it is true that naturalism must be compatible with anything that – according to naturalism – it is ontologically or metaphysically possible that established science tell us about the natural and supernatural, it is not true that naturalism must be compatible with anything that – according to naturalism – it is 'epistemically' or doxastically possible that established science tell us about the natural and the supernatural. So the proposed repair to Rea's argument is to no avail.

1.7 Armstrong

Consider Armstrong's claim that naturalism is the doctrine that [causal] reality consists of nothing but a single, all-embracing spatio-temporal system. According to Rea:

> [This claim is] at the mercy of scientific research and so not compatible with every possible development in science ... [It is not the sort of thesis] that one could unconditionally endorse while at the same time following scientific investigation wherever it might lead.
>
> (2002: 56)

I think that matters here are worse than Rea supposes. Even given current natural science, it seems doubtful that causal reality consists of nothing but a single, all-embracing, spatio-temporal system. On the one hand, if our universe is a bubble in a background de Sitter space, then it is not true that causal reality involves a *single*, all-embracing, *spatio-temporal* system. On the other hand, if string theory is correct, then there is *more* to causal reality than a *single*, all-embracing, *spatio-temporal* system.

However, it seems plausible that Armstrong's claim is not beyond repair. Suppose that we suggest that naturalism entails the doctrine that causal reality is limned by a single, all-embracing manifold with an entirely natural constitution. This claim is falsified neither by the claim that our universe is a bubble in a background de Sitter space, nor by the claim that string theory is correct. On the one hand, if our universe is a bubble in a background de Sitter space, then the background de Sitter space is the single, all-embracing manifold with the entirely natural constitution. On the other hand, if string theory is true, then the single, all-embracing manifold is constituted from strings, and those strings are entirely natural entities. I see no reason why naturalists should allow that it is ontologically or metaphysically possible that scientific investigation will lead to the rejection of the claim that causal reality is limned by a single, all-embracing manifold with an entirely natural constitution.

1.8 Pettit

Pettit (1992: 245–247) claims that:

> Naturalism imposes a constraint on what there can be, stipulating that there are no non-natural or unnatural, preternatural or supernatural

98   *Does religion defeat naturalism?*

> entities. ... Nature comprises those entities and constructs made of those entities that the ideal physics, realistically interpreted, posits.

Rea objects:

> [T]here is no such thing as the ideal physics or the best physics. ... But if there is no ideal physics, then there is no ontology of the ideal physics. [Pettit's definition] implies that no ontology is correct. But that is obviously false. Of course, the idea probably is that the correct ontology is whatever ontology would be implied by an ideal physical theory if such a one were to exist. But, if that's right then [Pettit's definition] is not so much a metaphysical thesis as an affirmation of the ability of physics to tell us the whole truth about the world. In other words, it is a disguised epistemological thesis.
>
> (2002: 57–58)

I think that it is plainly wrong to claim that Pettit's definition is an affirmation of the ability of physics to tell us the whole truth about the world. Pettit himself tells us that he is committed to the claim that physics cannot tell us the whole truth about the world. ('The approach leaves room for entities that are quite alien to the posits of physics and the other sciences.' [Pettit 1992: 248]) I suspect that Rea has been misled by an ambiguity in Pettit's formulation. What Pettit means is that nature comprises (1) entities that the ideal physics, realistically interpreted, posits, together with (2) constructs made of the entities mentioned in (1). But Rea interprets Pettit to mean that nature comprises (1) entities that the ideal physics, realistically interpreted, posits, together with (2) constructs made of entities mentioned in (1) that the ideal physics, realistically interpreted, also posits.

Might it nonetheless be the case that 'the idea' that Pettit strives to capture is that the correct ontology is whatever ontology would be *implied* by an ideal physical theory if such a one were to exist? The quoted remark from Pettit suggests otherwise: if there can be 'constructs made of the entities of ideal physics' that are 'quite alien' to the posits of ideal physics and other ideal sciences, then it seems unlikely that the existence of those constructed entities is implied by the posits of ideal physics and other ideal sciences.

Should we conclude that Pettit's definition is empty, because it is not properly subject to reinterpretation, and yet it has no content? I don't think so. While it is true that we don't know exactly what an ideal physics would posit, we do know something about what an ideal physics would say. In particular, we know that an ideal physics would identify the fundamental constituents of the single, all-embracing manifold that limns causal reality. Moreover, while we don't know exactly what those fundamental constituents will be, we do have some currently live hunches – e.g., they might be strings. And, while we don't know exactly what the single, all-embracing manifold that limns causal reality is, we do have some currently live hunches – e.g., the background de Sitter space of multiverse theories.

Furthermore, there has not been particularly wide variation in our live hunches about either of these matters. On the one hand, candidates for fundamental constituents have not extended much beyond: fundamental particles, fundamental fields, and strings. On the other hand, candidates for the single, all-embracing manifold that limns causal reality have not extended much beyond: truncated Euclidean space, infinite Euclidean space, general relativistic spacetime, and background de Sitter space. While we do not have any reason to say that we know exactly what ideal physics would posit, we do have good reason to say that we are not completely in the dark about the kinds of things that ideal physics would posit.

Drawing together the threads of this discussion of metaphysical naturalism, we have the following conclusions. First, Rea exaggerates the difficulties involved in classification by paradigms. Second, Rea's argument for the claim that no version of naturalism can include a supplementary account of the natural and the supernatural fails. Third, Rea's objections to the metaphysical characterisations of naturalism provided by Armstrong and Pettit are unconvincing. While it is perhaps not a straightforward task to provide a metaphysical characterisation of naturalism, Rea does not provide us with any good reason to suppose that all attempted characterisations of this kind will be 'vacuous, obviously false, or incompatible with possible developments in the natural sciences' (2002: 59).

1.9 Epistemological commitments of naturalism

We turn, next, to a consideration of the *epistemological* commitments of naturalism. Rea cites examples such as the following:

> It is within science itself, and not in some prior philosophy, that reality is to be identified and described.
>
> Quine (1981: 21)

> There is only one way of knowing: the empirical way that is the basis of science (whatever that way may be).
>
> Devitt (1998: 45)

In Rea's opinion:

> It is hard to see how epistemological theses like these could be presented as versions of naturalism without being either self-defeating or otherwise unacceptable from a naturalistic point of view. ... [For] suppose one of [these theses] is proposed as a version of naturalism. As such, it would have to be consistent with the methodological dispositions distinctive of naturalism. But then it must not be an empirical thesis. For ... theses

refutable by science cannot plausibly count as versions of naturalism because naturalism involves, first and foremost, a commitment to follow science wherever it leads. Thus [these theses] would have to be taken as theses justified, if at all, by methods other than the methods of science. But now they truly are self-defeating. For ... by their own lights they are precisely the sorts of theses that must be justified by scientific methods if at all.

(2002: 60–63)

The argument here is somewhat slippery. I think that it can be properly rendered as follows:

1   Any thesis that characterises naturalism is consistent with the methodological dispositions distinctive of naturalism.
2   The first and foremost methodological disposition distinctive of naturalism is to follow science wherever it leads.
3   No thesis that is consistent with the methodological disposition to follow science wherever it leads is capable of refutation by science.
4   (Therefore) No thesis that characterises naturalism is capable of refutation by science.
5   Only theses capable of refutation by science are capable of justification by the methods of science.
6   Any epistemological thesis that characterises naturalism entails that only theses capable of justification by the methods of science are capable of justification.
7   (Therefore) Any epistemological thesis that characterises naturalism entails that it is not itself capable of justification.
8   (Therefore) Any epistemological thesis that characterises naturalism is self-defeating.

An immediate difficulty with this argument is that it is not clear what it means to say that a thesis is consistent with a methodological disposition. While theses are truth-bearers, and hence the kinds of things that can be jointly inconsistent, methodological dispositions are not truth-bearers, and hence, at least *prima facie*, not the kinds of things that could be inconsistent with theses. I think – though I admit to some uncertainty about this – that the right way to understand the first premise in our reconstruction of Rea's argument is something like this: *any thesis that characterises naturalism is consistent with any claim that might issue from conformity to the methodological dispositions distinctive of naturalism*. Given the understanding, we can reconstruct the argument as follows:

1   Any thesis that characterises naturalism is consistent with any claim that might issue from conformity to the methodological dispositions characteristic of naturalism.

2   The first and foremost methodological disposition distinctive of naturalism is to follow science wherever it leads.
3   No thesis that is consistent with any claim that might issue from conformity to the methodological disposition to follow science wherever it leads is capable of refutation by science.
4   (Therefore) No thesis that characterises naturalism is capable of refutation by science.
5   Only theses capable of refutation by science are capable of justification by the methods of science.
6   Any epistemological thesis that characterises naturalism entails that only theses capable of justification by the methods of science are capable of justification.
7   (Therefore) Any epistemological thesis that characterises naturalism entails that it is not itself capable of justification.
8   (Therefore) Any epistemological thesis that characterises naturalism is self-defeating.

In order to further assess this argument, we need to know more about the methods of science. Rea says:

> The present methods of science are those methods regularly employed and respected in contemporary biology, chemistry and physics departments. Reliance on memory and testimony is included ... as well as reliance on judgments about apparent mathematical, logical and conceptual truths.
> (2002: 97)

While, as Rea claims, it is hard to say exactly what methods are supposed to count as the methods of science, we can surely improve upon what Rea has to say here. Most importantly, we should emphasise that, while they 'include' perception and inference, the methods of science are primarily concerned with extensions of, or improvements upon, 'pre-scientific' observation and reasoning. Among other things, science involves refined techniques for collection of data – precision instruments, controlled experiments, uniform sampling from populations, and so forth – and refined techniques for mining of data in order to test theories – statistical analysis, mathematical modelling, computer simulation, and the like. While there are some domains where the methods of science correct 'pre-scientific' methods of inquiry, there are many domains where the methods of science are merely extensions of those 'pre-scientific' methods, and take those 'pre-scientific' methods as foundations. For example, a certain amount of accurate astronomy can be done by the naked eye and the unaided brain – at least if you live in an appropriate location – but much astronomy requires precision instruments, computer-based data analysis, and the like. Consequently, there is a potential ambiguity in talk about the methods of science that requires attention. On the one hand, 'scientific method' might be taken to include the 'pre-scientific methods' upon which science is founded; on the other hand, 'scientific method' might be taken to exclude the 'pre-scientific' methods upon which science is founded.

If 'scientific method' is taken to exclude the 'pre-scientific' methods upon which science is founded, then it is not true that any epistemological thesis that characterises naturalism entails that only theses capable of justification by the methods of science are capable of justification. No sensible naturalism eschews justification by the 'pre-scientific' methods upon which science is founded: all sensible naturalists suppose that, in a wide range of circumstances, their perceptual and inferential faculties are reliable without any further supplementation from science. Hence, if Rea's argument is to have any hope of succeeding, it must be that 'scientific method' is taken to include the 'pre-scientific' methods upon which science is founded.

But, if 'scientific method' is taken to include the 'pre-scientific' methods upon which science is founded, then it is certainly not true that only theses capable of refutation by science are capable of justification by the methods of science. The claim that there are stars is capable of justification by the methods of science, but – on my favoured account of the metaphysics of modality – there is no ontologically or metaphysically possible world in which the claim that there are stars is refuted by the methods of science. Mathematical truths are capable of justification by the methods of science, but – on any account of the metaphysics of modality – there are no ontologically or metaphysically possible worlds in which the claims of mathematics are refuted by the methods of science.

I conclude that Rea's argument against epistemological characterisations of naturalism is unsuccessful: his argument does not establish that the kinds of characterisations given by Quine and Devitt are self-defeating. I note, further, that even if Rea had been correct in arguing that Pettit's characterisation of naturalism is a disguised epistemological thesis, he would not have succeeded in establishing that Pettit's characterisation of naturalism is deficient, since he gives no other reasons for supposing that epistemological characterisations of naturalism are deficient. Finally, I note that there are other features of Rea's account of scientific method that should not be allowed to pass without comment. In particular, it is surely a mistake to suppose that the methods of biology, chemistry, and physics are also the methods of neuroscience, geology, archaeology, econometrics, and so forth. While there doubtless are some scientific methods that are common to all of the sciences, there are also scientific methods that are proper to only some of the sciences: and, in particular, there are methods that are proper to neuroscience, geology, archaeology, econometrics, and so forth that are not proper to physics, chemistry, or biology.

1.10 Methodological commitments of naturalism

Rea's critique of *methodological* characterisations of naturalism is very brief. He begins by citing the following examples:

Does religion defeat naturalism? 103

[Methodological naturalism claims] that philosophical theorising should be continuous with empirical inquiry in the sciences.

(Leiter 1998: 81)

Methodological naturalism holds that the best methods of inquiry in the social sciences and philosophy are, or are to be modelled on, those of the natural sciences.

(Schmitt 1995: 343)

Methodological naturalism is the view that philosophy ... must pursue knowledge via empirical methods exemplified by the sciences, and not by a priori or non-empirical methods.

(Hampton 1998: 20)

He then observes that:

[M]ethodological assumptions [such as these] are either background presuppositions about what the world is like that guide and constrain the process of inquiry, views about how inquiry should be conducted, or views about what sorts of inquiry are likely to be fruitful. In other words, methodological assumptions [such as these] are either metaphysical theses about how inquiry in a particular discipline ought to be conducted, or theses about knowledge or justified belief. But we have already seen that it is a mistake to take any such theses as characterising a version of naturalism.

(2002: 64–65)

While we might quibble about the extent to which the examples conform to the subsequent descriptions that Rea gives, the main point to note is that, even if it is true that characterisations of methodological naturalism have the features that he claims, his prior critiques of metaphysical naturalism and epistemological naturalism fail, and so do not provide adequate foundations for criticisms of methodological naturalism.

1.11 Combined characterisations of naturalism

Rea's critique of 'combined' characterisations of naturalism – i.e., characterisations of naturalism that involve some combination of metaphysical and epistemological theses – is equally brief. Apart from the assertion that 'it seems equally clear' that the problems that he has identified separately for metaphysical and epistemological characterisations will also defeat 'combined' combinations, he offers some brief comments on a 'doubly defective' characterisation in Rosenberg (1996: 4).

Rosenberg says that naturalism is characterised by the following three claims: (1) epistemology is not a propaedeutic to the acquisition of further knowledge; (2) the sciences are the guides to epistemology and metaphysics; and (3) Darwinian theory is the model of scientific theorising and the guide to philosophical theory because it maximally combines relevance to human affairs and well-foundedness.

Against Rosenberg, Rea objects (a) that Darwinian theory is surely at the mercy of further developments in science; and (b) that the conjunction of (1) and (2), construed as substantive epistemological or methodological theses, is self-defeating.

While I'm inclined to think it doubtful that there are ontologically or metaphysically possible worlds in which Darwinian theory (broadly construed) is false, I accept that, for all we know, there are hitherto undiscovered theories that are models for scientific theorising – and guides for philosophical theory – that combine relevance to human affairs and well-foundedness better than Darwinian theory. What Rosenberg ought to have said, I think, is that those current scientific theories that best combine relevance to human affairs and well-foundedness are our best current guides to philosophical theorising – and, of course, Darwinian theory is one such current scientific theory. (Perhaps he might also have added that (3) is not so much an independent part of the characterisation of naturalism as it is a consequence – or a more comprehensive articulation – of (2).)

As noted above, Rea does not make a convincing claim for the case that epistemological characterisations of naturalism are self-defeating, and he provides no additional reason for supposing that the conjunction of (1) and (2) is self-defeating. So, at the very least, this part of his case against Rosenberg's characterisation of naturalism remains unproven.

1.12 Substantive conclusions

Drawing together all of the preceding discussion of Rea (2002), I conclude that not only does he fail to establish that naturalism can only be a research program – i.e., a maximal set of dispositions to trust cognitive faculties as sources of evidence and to take certain kinds of experiences and arguments as evidence – he also fails to establish that the basic commitments of naturalism cannot be taken to be metaphysical, or epistemological, or methodological, or some combination of these three. While it is undeniable that it is difficult to give a short, precise, analytical characterisation of 'naturalism', it is worth remembering that there are very few interesting philosophical terms for which we have short, precise, analytical definitions. Moreover – even setting other considerations aside – it is worth recalling that we have not abandoned talk of causation, knowledge, art, virtue, and so forth merely because we have been unable to find short, precise, analytical definitions of 'cause', 'knows', 'work of art', 'virtue', and so on. And, as we noted way back, it is independently plausible to suppose that naturalistic big pictures are characterised by distinctive metaphysical, epistemological, and methodological commitments that distinguish naturalistic big pictures from theistic big pictures and the like.

Does religion defeat naturalism? 105

1.13 Charity

Rea (2002: 53f.) insists that his account of naturalism is 'charitable'. But, if charity is not dead in Rea's discussion, at the very least it ain't half sick. Rea maintains that, while naturalism has 'close conceptual connections' with the 'doctrines' of empiricism, materialism, physicalism and scientism, it is simply a confusion to suppose that naturalism is also a 'doctrine'. While these other 'doctrines' are 'imprecise', it is adequate to say that *empiricism* says that 'beliefs about the world cannot be justified independently of sense perception' (2002: 39); and that *materialism* says that all phenomena of experience are reducible to facts about material objects and their material properties (2002: 39); and that *physicalism* says that all phenomena of experience are reducible to facts about physical objects and their physical properties (2002: 69); and that *scientism* says that what cannot be known by science cannot be known at all (2002: 69).

But, bizarre linguistic stipulation aside, it is obvious that naturalism, physicalism, and materialism have exactly the same kind of *metaphysical* status: materialism is a doctrine about the material; physicalism is an exactly analogous doctrine about the physical; and naturalism is an exactly analogous doctrine about the natural. Whatever difficulties of formulation there may be for naturalism, there are precisely the same difficulties of formulation for physicalism and materialism. If materialism says that all else supervenes on the material, and physicalism says that all else supervenes on the physical, then naturalism says that all else supervenes on the natural. If materialism says that all else has an exclusively material constitution, and physicalism says that all else has an exclusively physical constitution, then naturalism says that all else has an exclusively natural constitution. If materialism says that material regularities govern all, and physicalism says that physical regularities govern all, then naturalism says that natural regularities govern all. And – as Rae himself tacitly admits (e.g., at 2002: 8, 57n5) – whatever difficulties may confront accounts of 'the natural', there are precisely parallel difficulties that confront accounts of 'the material' and 'the physical'.

Moreover, bizarre linguistic stipulation aside, it is obvious that naturalism, empiricism, and scientism have exactly the same kind of *epistemological* status: scientism is a doctrine about the scientific; empiricism is a doctrine about the empirical; and naturalism is a doctrine about the natural. Whatever difficulties of formulation there may be for naturalism, there are precisely the same difficulties of formulation for scientism and empiricism. If empiricism says that justified belief about the world requires empirical justification, and scientism says that justified belief about the world requires scientific justification, then naturalism says that justified belief about the world requires natural justification. If empiricism says that there can only be empirical knowledge of the world, and scientism says that there can only be scientific knowledge of the world, then naturalism says that there can only be natural knowledge of the world. And – as Rae himself tacitly concedes (e.g., at 2002: 39, 42) – whatever difficulties may confront accounts of 'the natural', there are precisely parallel difficulties that confront accounts of 'the scientific' and 'the empirical'.

Of course, in response to these observations, Rea could insist that – like naturalism – materialism, physicalism, empiricism, and scientism are only research programs, and not big pictures involving substantive metaphysical, epistemological, and methodological theories. However, it seems peculiarly *immodest* to suppose that, while you have a big picture characterised by substantive metaphysical, epistemological, and methodological theses, your philosophical opponents fail to have big pictures characterised by substantive metaphysical, epistemological, and methodological theses. Much of philosophy is concerned with the development and comparison of big pictures; it is surely just incredible to suppose that naturalists, materialists, physicalists, empiricists and the like do not have distinctive big pictures.

1.14 Rational intuition

Rea divides research programs into three kinds: naturalistic, intuitionistic, and supernaturalistic. Naturalism 'treats the methods of science alone as basic sources of evidence' (2002: 173). Intuitionism 'treats rational intuitions and the methods of natural science alone as basic sources of evidence' (2002: 173). Supernaturalism 'takes at least the methods of science and religious experience as basic sources of evidence' (2002: 174).

Rea's distinction between naturalism and intuitionism relies upon an understanding of 'rational intuition'. Rea makes it clear that naturalists are entitled to some claims concerning 'rational intuition': they can appeal to some basic mathematical, logical, statistical, and methodological beliefs. Moreover, Rea insists that the reason why naturalists are entitled to these claims concerning 'rational intuition' is that natural scientists rely upon basic appeals to mathematical, logical, statistical, and methodological beliefs: physicists, chemists, and biologists rely upon basic appeals to mathematical, logical, statistical, and methodological beliefs in plying their trades. However, Rea also makes it clear that he thinks that there are certain kinds of 'rational intuitions' to which naturalists have no similar entitlement: for example, naturalists cannot properly appeal to basic beliefs about the modal properties of material objects.

But, by Rea's own lights, whether naturalists can properly appeal to basic beliefs about the modal properties of material objects depends upon whether physicists, chemists, and biologists rely upon basic appeals to beliefs about the modal properties of material objects in plying their trades. And yet it seems obvious that physicists, chemists, and biologists *do* rely upon basic appeals to beliefs about the modal properties of material objects in plying their trades. Biologists do not need some further dispensation in order to be able to rely on the belief that rabbits cannot survive being flattened by a steamroller (2002: 105); chemists do not need some further dispensation in order to be able to rely on the belief that the particular water molecules before them could not be atoms of gold (2002: 97); physicists do not need some further dispensation in order to be able to rely on the belief that a sugar cube cannot survive its own dissolution in a cup of tea (2002: 82). If it is insisted that these kinds of basic 'metaphysical' beliefs issue from a faculty of 'rational intuition', then, by his own lights, Rea should allow that naturalistically acceptable 'rational intuitions' include *some* basic mathematical, logical, statistical, methodological, *and* 'metaphysical' beliefs. But, of course, he should still continue to deny that a naturalistically acceptable faculty of 'rational intuition' delivers basic 'metaphysical' belief in such claims as that it is possible that God exists, that there cannot be an infinite regress of causes, that there are absolute moral values, and that there cannot be absolute moral values unless God exists.

The considerations just rehearsed seem to me to be fatal to Rea's claims about the ontological consequences of naturalism. Rea's case for the claim, that the naturalistic research program precludes one from accepting realism about material objects, materialism and realism about other minds, depends upon his contention that naturalists cannot coherently suppose that they 'rationally intuit' basic beliefs about the modal properties of material objects. But, in fact, naturalists can coherently – and, indeed, plausibly – suppose that they 'rationally intuit' basic beliefs about the modal properties of material objects, just as they can coherently – and, indeed, plausibly – suppose that they 'rationally intuit' basic mathematical, logical, statistical, and methodological beliefs.

Perhaps it might be objected that Rea says:

> [W]e have quite convincing evidence that our intuitions are not reliable [when it comes to the modal properties, including the intrinsic modal properties, of material objects]. ... There is much disagreement about the truth of IMP-propositions, split not only along realist-antirealist lines, but also along the lines of different intuitions about what properties are essential to what kinds of objects.
>
> (2002: 210)

But the claims that Rea makes here miss the mark: there is no disagreement about – and no evidence of unreliability concerning – the kinds of beliefs mentioned a couple of paragraphs back. We all know that rabbits cannot survive being flattened by a steamroller, and we all know that sugar cubes cannot survive dissolution in cups of tea. Moreover, this kind of common knowledge is plainly of a piece with our basic mathematical, logical, statistical, and methodological knowledge. Our knowledge of the intrinsic modal properties of material objects is no more challenging to naturalists than our knowledge of mathematics, logic, statistics, and methodology.

1.15 Tradition

Rea describes naturalism as a 'tradition' and a 'movement'. While he sees the modern origins of the 'tradition' in German materialism (Feuerbach, Vogt, Moleschott, Büchner, Czolbe), French positivism (Comte), British philosophy of science (Herschel, Mill, Whewell), and Darwinian evolutionary theory, he identifies Dewey and Quine as the 'twin pillars of the tradition' in the twentieth century.

> No one will deny that the methodological dispositions shared by Quine and Dewey – high regard for science and scientific method, a disposition to employ scientific methods and results in all domains of inquiry as much as possible to the exclusion of *a priori* speculative methods, opposition to theories, particularly religious ones, that are untestable and do not play any significant role in filling out interstices of scientific theory – are the crucial identifying dispositions of naturalism.
> (2002: 49)

Before we turn to more substantive matters, it is perhaps worth noting that the dispositions that Rea mentions in the above passage are *not* unique to naturalists. Everyone should have *a high regard* for science and scientific method. (Having a high regard for science and scientific method is perfectly consistent with having a high – or higher – regard for other methods of inquiry.) Everyone should have a disposition to employ scientific methods and results in all domains of inquiry *as much as possible to the exclusion of* a priori *speculative methods*. (Having a disposition to employ scientific methods and results in all domains of inquiry as much as possible to the exclusion of *a priori* speculative methods is perfectly consistent with supposing that scientific methods and results have no bearing on many domains of inquiry.) Everyone should be opposed to *untestable* theories that play no significant role in filling out interstices of scientific theory. (Opposition to untestable theories is perfectly consistent with acceptance of theories that do not belong to science and that do not merely fill out interstices of scientific theory.) If naturalism were a 'tradition' or a 'movement', then the methodological dispositions cited in the previous paragraph would be insufficient to characterise it.

Rea's account of the history of naturalism, and his identification of Dewey and Quine as the prime exemplars of the 'tradition' revealed by the history is nicely consonant with his view that naturalists cannot coherently suppose that they 'rationally intuit' basic beliefs about the modal properties of material objects. For, plausibly enough, Dewey and Quine, and their 'precursors' amongst the German materialists and French positivists wanted no truck with 'rational intuition' of basic beliefs about the modal properties of material objects. However, it is just a mistake to suppose that contemporary naturalists inherit a commitment, to rejection of 'rational intuition' of basic beliefs about the modal properties of material objects, from the 'prime exemplars' of 'the naturalistic tradition'. If 'naturalism' is a tradition or a movement, it is not so in the same kind of way that 'Christian theism' is a tradition or a movement. While Christian theists take themselves to be constrained by the pronouncements of scripture, authority and tradition, naturalists do not take themselves to be similarly constrained by the pronouncements of previous generations of naturalists. One can perfectly well be a naturalist while rejecting the attitudes that Dewey and Quine had towards 'rational intuition' of basic beliefs about the modal properties of material objects.

1.16 Concluding remarks

Rea (2002) contains much interesting material that has not been discussed here. Nonetheless, I think that the preceding discussion suffices to establish that Rea has not demonstrated that naturalism has the untoward consequences that Rea claims it has. For all that Rea argues, naturalists can be realists about material objects and the mindedness of others, and they can suppose that naturalistic big pictures are characterised by substantive metaphysical, epistemological, and methodological commitments.

2. The Thomist challenge to naturalism

Some Thomists suppose that Aquinas' work contains proofs that defeat naturalism. In particular, some Thomists suppose: (a) that Aquinas' work contains proofs of the existence of God; and (b) that the powers of God are non-natural causal powers.

2.1 Summa Theologiae

In the *Summa Theologiae*, in the text that is commonly called 'The Five Ways' (I, q.2, a.3), Aquinas presents five proofs (*probationem*) of the existence of God. There is almost nothing about these proofs that is uncontroversial. In particular, it is controversial how to interpret the text that records the conclusions of these arguments.

Consider the conclusion of the First Way: *Ergo necesse est devenire ad aliquod primum movens, quod a nullo movetur, et hoc omnes intelligent deum.* There are many translations – see, for example, Wippel (2002) – that are minor variants of:

(1) Therefore it is necessary to arrive at a first mover, put in motion by no other; and this everyone understands to be God.

But there are also more recent translations – see, for example, Freddoso (2016) – that are minor variants of:

(2) Therefore it is necessary to suppose some first mover, not itself moved, and this all understand to be a God.

There are two related differences between these translations. In (1), the quantifier 'a' – in 'a first mover' – might be read in a way that imputes uniqueness – 'exactly one' – and, as a result, the text after the semi-colon

110   *Does religion defeat naturalism?*

might be taken to identify the unique first mover with God. In (2), the quantifier 'some' – in 'some first mover' – might be read in a way that does not impute uniqueness – 'at least one' – and, as a result, the text after the semi-colon might be taken to suggest no more than that all first movers are divine.

If we go with (1), then we will end up with something like the following renditions of the 'outer shell' of the Five Ways:

The First Way

1 Some things are moved. (Premise.)
2 Whatever is moved is moved by another (i.e., nothing moves itself). (Premise.)
3 There cannot be an infinite regress of movers. (Premise.)
4 (Therefore) There is exactly one first mover (and that first mover is God). (From 1, 2, and 3.)

The Second Way

1 Essentially ordered efficient causes are ordered in series. (Premise.)
2 Nothing can be its own efficient cause. (Premise.)
3 There cannot be an infinite regress of essentially ordered efficient causes. (Premise.)
4 (Therefore) There is exactly one uncaused first efficient cause (and that uncaused first efficient cause is God). (From 1, 2, and 3.)

The Third Way

1 Some contingent things exist. (Premise.)
2 For any contingent thing that exists, there was a time at which it did not exist. (Premise.)
3 If everything that exists is contingent, then there was a time at which nothing existed. (Premise.)
4 If there was a time at which nothing existed, then nothing exists now. (Premise.)
5 (Therefore) There are necessary things. (From 1, 2, 3, and 4)
6 Any necessary being either depends on something else for its necessity or it does not. (Premise.)
7 There cannot be an infinite regress of necessary beings each of which owes its necessity to another. (Premise.)
8 (Therefore) There is exactly one necessary being that does not owe its necessity to other necessary beings (and this necessary being is God). (From 5, 6, and 7.)

The Fourth Way

1 Things are more or less good, more or less true, more or less noble, etc. (Premise.)

2   Things are more or less good, more or less true, more or less noble, etc., depending upon how closely they approach something that is maximally good, maximally true, maximally noble, etc. (Premise.)
3   (Therefore) There is exactly one thing that is truest, best, noblest, and in being to the maximal degree. (From 1 and 2.)
4   Whatever is supreme in a given genus is the cause of all other things that belong to that genus. (Premise.)
5   (Therefore) There is exactly one cause of being – and goodness, and truth, and nobility, etc. – for all other beings (and this cause is God). (From 3 and 4.)

The Fifth Way

1   Natural bodies always, or frequently, act in the same way in order to attain that which is best. (Premise.)
2   (Therefore) Natural bodies reach their ends by intention rather than by chance. (From 1.)
3   (Therefore) Natural bodies act for the sake of an end. (From 2.)
4   Natural bodies lack knowledge. (Premise.)
5   Things which lack knowledge do not tend to an end unless they are directed to it by some knowing and intelligent being. (Premise.)
6   (Therefore) There is exactly one intelligent being by which all natural things are ordered to their end (and this intelligent being is God). (From 3, 4, and 5.)

One immediate difficulty with all of the Five Ways, on this way of understanding them, is that they are plainly invalid. If we run with this kind of interpretation of the Five Ways, either we impute serious logical errors to Aquinas, or we need to provide an account of what Aquinas is doing in the Five Ways that is consistent with his knowingly presenting arguments that are invalid. Perhaps, for example, what we are given in the Five Ways is only intended to be something like 'pointers to' or 'reminders of' proofs of the existence of God that are fully presented elsewhere in Aquinas' writing, for example, in the *Summa contra Gentiles*. (We shall return to discussion of this proposal anon.)

If we go with (2), then we end up with something like the following renditions of the 'outer shell' of the Five Ways:

The First Way

1   Some things are moved. (Premise.)
2   Whatever is moved is moved by another (i.e., nothing moves itself). (Premise.)
3   There cannot be an infinite regress of movers. (Premise.)
4   (Therefore) There are unmoved first movers (and these unmoved first movers are divine). (From 1, 2, and 3.)

The Second Way

1. Essentially ordered efficient causes are ordered in series. (Premise.)
2. Nothing can be its own efficient cause. (Premise.)
3. There cannot be an infinite regress of essentially ordered efficient causes. (Premise.)
4. (Therefore) There are uncaused first efficient causes (and these uncaused first efficient causes are divine). (From 1, 2, and 3.)

The Third Way

1. Some contingent things exist. (Premise.)
2. For any contingent thing that exists, there was a time at which it did not exist. (Premise.)
3. If everything that exists is contingent, then there was a time at which nothing existed. (Premise.)
4. If there was a time at which nothing existed, then nothing exists now. (Premise.)
5. (Therefore) There are necessary things. (From 1, 2, 3, and 4.)
6. Any necessary being either depends on something else for its necessity or it does not. (Premise.)
7. There cannot be an infinite regress of necessary beings each of which owes its necessity to another. (Premise.)
8. (Therefore) There are necessary beings that do not owe their necessity to other necessary beings (and these necessary beings that do not own their necessity to other necessary beings are divine). (From 5, 6, and 7.)

The Fourth Way

1. Things are more or less good, more or less true, more or less noble, etc. (Premise.)
2. Things are more or less good, more or less true, more or less noble, etc., depending upon how closely they approach something that is maximally good, maximally true, maximally noble, etc. (Premise.)
3. (Therefore) There are things that are truest, best, noblest, and in being to the maximal degree. (From 1 and 2.)
4. Whatever is supreme in a given genus is the cause of all other things that belong to that genus. (Premise.)
5. (Therefore) There are causes of being – and goodness, and truth, and nobility, etc. – for all other beings (and these causes are divine). (From 3 and 4.)

The Fifth Way

1. Natural bodies always, or frequently, act in the same way in order to attain that which is best. (Premise.)

Does religion defeat naturalism? 113

2   (Therefore) Natural bodies reach their ends by intention rather than by chance. (From 1.)
3   (Therefore) Natural bodies act for the sake of an end. (From 2.)
4   Natural bodies lack knowledge. (Premise.)
5   Things which lack knowledge do not tend to an end unless they are directed to it by some knowing and intelligent being. (Premise.)
6   (Therefore) There are intelligent beings by which all natural things are ordered to their ends (and these intelligent beings are divine) (From 3, 4, and 5.)

One immediate difficulty with the Five Ways, on this way of understanding them, is that they are incomplete: they do not take us all the way to the existence of God. If we run with this kind of interpretation of the Five Ways, then, at the very least, we should wonder whether, in the following sections of the *Summa Theologiae*, Aquinas provides for the completion of the incomplete arguments of the Five Ways. Before we investigate this suggestion, we shall consider what can be said on behalf of the proposal that what we are given in the Five Ways is only intended to be something like 'pointers to' or 'reminders of' proofs of the existence of God that are fully presented elsewhere in Aquinas' writing, for example, in the *Summa contra Gentiles*.

2.2 Summa contra Gentiles

In the *Summa contra Gentiles*, Chapter 13, Aquinas gives four demonstrations of the existence of God that he finds in the works of Aristotle, and one demonstration of the existence of God that he finds in the works of Damascene. (In Chapter 15, in his demonstration of God's eternity, he provides a sub-demonstration that bears close affinity to the Third Way. Setting this sub-demonstration aside has no significant effect on the outcome of the following discussion.)

The 'outer shell' for the first demonstration (Ch. 13, Para 3–16) runs like this:

1   Some things are moved. (Premise.)
2   Whatever is moved is moved by another (i.e., nothing moves itself). (Premise.)
3   There cannot be an infinite regress of movers. (Premise.)
4   (Therefore) There is an unmoved first mover (and this unmoved first mover is God.) (From 1, 2, and 3.)

The 'outer shell' for the second demonstration (Ch.13, Para 17–28) runs more or less like this:

1   If the proposition that every mover is moved is true, then this proposition is either true by itself or true by accident. (Premise.)

2 If the proposition that every mover is moved is true by accident, then it is possible that no mover is moved. (Premise.)
3 (Therefore) If the proposition that every mover is moved is true by accident, then it is possible that there is no motion. (From 2.)
4 It is impossible that there is no motion. (Premise.)
5 (Therefore) The proposition that every mover is moved is not true by accident. (From 3 and 4.)
6 If the proposition that every mover is moved is true by itself, then either the mover is moved by the same species of motion as that by which it moves, or the mover is moved by a different species of motion from that by which it moves. (Premise.)
7 If the proposition that every mover is moved is true by itself, then, if the mover is moved by the same species of motion as that by which it moves, then it could both have and lack that species of motion. (Premise.)
8 It is impossible for anything to both have and lack the same species of motion. (Premise.)
9 (Therefore) If the proposition that every mover is moved is true by itself, the mover is not moved by the same species of motion as that by which it moves.
10 If the proposition that every mover is moved is true by itself, then, if the mover is moved by a different species of motion from that by which is moves, then, since the genera and species of motion are finite in number, there cannot be an infinite regress.
11 (Therefore) If the proposition that every mover is moved is true by itself, then, if the mover is moved by a different species of motion from that by which is moves, then there is a first mover that is not moved by any exterior moving cause.
12 If the proposition that every mover is moved is true by itself, then it is not the case that there is a first mover that is not moved by any exterior moving cause. (Premise.)
13 (Therefore) If the proposition that every mover is moved is true by itself, the mover is not moved by a different species of motion from that by which it moves. (From 10, 11, and 12.)
14 (Therefore) The proposition that every mover is moved is not true by itself. (From 6, 9, and 13)
15 (Therefore) The proposition that every mover is moved is not true. (From 1, 5, and 14.)
16 (Therefore) There is a first mover that is not moved by any exterior cause. (From 15.)
17 (Therefore) there is an unmoved first mover (and this unmoved first mover is God). (From 15, with further steps of the derivation suppressed.)

The 'outer shell' for the third demonstration (Ch.13, Para 33) – left largely tacit in the text – runs like this:

Does religion defeat naturalism? 115

1 Essentially ordered efficient causes are ordered in series. (Premise.)
2 Nothing can be its own efficient cause. (Premise.)
3 There cannot be an infinite regress of essentially ordered efficient causes. (Premise.)
4 (Therefore) There is an uncaused first efficient cause. (From 1, 2, and 3.)

The 'outer shell' for the fourth demonstration (Ch.13, Para 34) – somewhat more fully rendered in the text – runs like this:

1 Some false things are more false than other false things. (Premise.)
2 Things are more or less false insofar as they approach more or less closely to that which is absolutely and supremely true. (Premise.)
3 (Therefore) There is something that is supremely true. (From 1 and 2.)
4 What is most true is most fully in being. (Premise.)
5 (Therefore) There is something that is supremely being (and this is God). (From 3 and 4.)

The 'outer shell' for the fifth demonstration (Ch.13, Para 35) runs like this:

1 Contrary and discordant things cannot always, or for the most part, belong to one order, except under governance that enables all and each to tend to a definite end. (Premise.)
2 Things with diverse natures do come together under one order, not rarely or by chance, but always or for the most part. (Premise.)
3 (Therefore) There is a being by whose providence the world is governed (and this is God). (From 1 and 2.)

There are various things to note about these arguments. First, while in Ch.13, Aquinas merely attributes them to Aristotle and Damascene, he begins Ch.14 with the assertion that 'we have shown that there is a first being whom we call God'. This makes it clear that Aquinas means to endorse these arguments (whatever exactly that endorsement amounts to). Second, the conclusions of these arguments are subject to exactly the same question of interpretation that arises in connection with the interpretation of the conclusions in the Five Ways. Third, while it is true that the first demonstration receives more extended discussion in the *Summa contra Gentiles* than in the *Summa Theologiae* – there being three 'proofs' for each of the second and third premises in the *Summa contra Gentiles*, but only one 'proof' for each of these premises in the *Summa Theologiae* – the final three demonstrations are actually given more careful expression in the *Summa Theologiae*. It is clearly not plausible to suppose that what we are given in the Five Ways is only intended to be something like 'pointers to' or 'reminders of' proofs of the existence of God that are fully presented in the *Summa contra Gentiles*. Perhaps, though, what we are given in the Five Ways is intended to be something like 'pointers to' or 'reminders of' proofs of the existence of God that are fully presented in some *other* work in the Thomistic corpus.

116 *Does religion defeat naturalism?*

2.3 De Ente et Essentia

In *De Ente et Essentia* (Para. 80), in his discussion of the essences of intelligences, Aquinas gives us the materials to construct a rather different argument for the existence of God:

> Whatever belongs to a thing is either caused by the principles of its nature, as the ability to laugh in man, or comes to it from some extrinsic principle, as light in the air from the influence of the sun. But it cannot be that the existence of a thing is caused by the form or quiddity of that thing – I say caused as by an efficient cause – because then something would be its own cause, and bring itself into existence, which is impossible. It is therefore necessary that every such thing, the existence of which is other than its nature, have its existence from some other thing. And because every thing which exists by virtue of another is led back, as to its first cause, to that which exists by virtue of itself, it is necessary that there be some thing which is the cause of the existence of all things because of its existence alone. Otherwise, there would be an infinite regress among causes, since every thing which is not existence alone has a cause of its existence, as has been said. It is clear, therefore, that an intelligence is form and existence, and that it has existence from the First Being, which is existence alone. And this is the First Cause, which is God.

We can represent the 'outer shell' of the constructible argument as follows:

1. Necessarily, whatever belongs to a thing is either caused by the principles of its nature or comes to it from some extrinsic principle. (Premise.)
2. It is impossible that the existence of a thing is caused by the form or quiddity of that thing, i.e., by the principles of its nature. (Premise.)
3. (Therefore) Necessarily, for any thing in which its existence is other than its own nature, there is some other thing – some extrinsic principle – from which it has its existence. (From 1 and 2.)
4. There are things that have their existence from other things. (Premise.)
5. It is impossible for there to be an infinite regress of things, each of which has its existence from another. (Premise.)
6. (Therefore) There is a First Being which is existence alone, which is the cause of existence in all other things (and this First Being is God) (From 3, 4, and 5.)

Perhaps we can 'reconfigure' this constructible argument so that it looks more like one of the arguments from the Five Ways:

1. Some things have their existence from other things. (Premise.)
2. Nothing can have its existence from itself. (Premise.)

3   There cannot be an infinite regress of things each of which has its existence from another. (Premise.)
4   (Therefore) There is a first existent thing that does not have its existence from anything else. (From 1, 2, and 3.)
5   Only that in which its existence is its nature – i.e., only that which is existence alone – can be a first existent thing that does not have its existence from anything else. (Premise.)
6   (Therefore) There is a First Being that is existence alone (and this First Being is God). (From 4 and 5.)

The claim that the arguments in the Five Ways text are intended to be 'pointers to' or 'reminders of' this argument is not at all plausible. Why would we need *five* arguments to 'point to' or 'remind us' of this one? More importantly, why wouldn't we just *give* this argument? After all, it's no harder to state than the arguments that are actually given in the Five Ways texts. And, finally, we do have the same questions about the interpretation of the conclusion of this argument that arise in connection with the arguments that are contained in the Five Ways text. Although there are works by Aquinas that I have not discussed here, I take it that I've done enough to make it clear that the claim, that what we are given in the Five Ways is only intended to be something like 'pointers to' or 'reminders of' proofs of the existence of God that are fully presented elsewhere in Aquinas' writing, is not particularly attractive.

2.4 Summa Theologiae *revisited*

Suppose, then, that we adopt the second of the proposed interpretations of the text of the Five Ways. On this interpretation, we are to suppose that the text of the Five Ways deliberately leaves the formulation of the arguments incomplete. Moreover, we are to suppose that the materials that are required in order to complete the arguments are to be found in the following sections of the work.

One immediate question is: What more do we need? We suppose that we have arguments for the following five claims: (1) there is at least one unmoved first mover; (2) there is at least one uncaused first cause; (3) there is at least one necessary being that does not owe its necessity to anything else; (4) there is at least one cause of being – and goodness, and truth, and nobility, and so forth – for all other beings; and (5) there is at least one intelligent being by which all natural things are ordered to their ends. Moreover, we have the claim, in each case, that the mentioned things are divine.

It seems to me that there are two things to be done. One is to show that there is exactly one of each of these things: exactly one unmoved first mover; exactly one uncaused first cause; exactly one necessary being that does not owe its necessity to anything else; exactly one cause of being – and goodness, and truth, and nobility, and so forth – for all other beings; and exactly one intelligent being by which all natural things are ordered to their ends. The other is to show that whatever falls into one of these classes of beings falls into all of them: unmoved first movers are uncaused first causes; uncaused first causes are necessary beings that do not owe their necessity to anything else; necessary beings that do not owe their necessity to anything else are causes of being – and goodness, and truth, and nobility, and so forth – for all other beings; causes of being – and goodness, and truth, and nobility, and so forth – for all other beings are intelligent beings by which all natural things are ordered to their ends; and intelligent beings by which all natural things are ordered to their ends are unmoved first movers.

One commonly encountered claim is that the work that is needed here is done in *Summa Theologiae* I, q.11, and/or in other places in which Aquinas discusses the uniqueness of God. We start by presenting the 'outer shells' for the three arguments that are offered in *Summa Theologiae* I, q.11, along with 'outer shells' for relevant supporting arguments, as appropriate. My renderings of the arguments follow Freddoso (2016). Bear in mind that, on the interpretative hypothesis now in play, you should read the word 'God' in a way that does not entail that there is just one 'God'.

First argument for uniqueness

1 For any haecceity ('thisness'), it is impossible that two distinct individuals have that haecceity. (Premise.)
2 (Therefore) For any haecceity, for any nature ('suchness'), if the haecceity is identical to the nature, then it is impossible for two individuals to have that same nature. (From 1.)
3 God's haecceity is identical to God's nature. (Lemma 1.)
4 (Therefore) There cannot be more than one God. (From 3.)

Lemma 1 (q.3 a.3)

1 In things that are not composed of matter and form, the nature or essence must be identical to the suppositum. (Premise.)
2 God is not composed of matter and form. (Lemma 2.)
3 (Therefore) God is identical to God's nature (God's divinity, God's life, etc.) (From 1 and 2.)

Lemma 2 (q.3 a.2)

1 Matter is that which is in potentiality. (Premise.)
2 God is pure actuality. (Premise.)
3 (Therefore) God is not composed of matter and form. (From 1 and 2.)

Lemma 3 (q.3 a.1)

1 What is in potentiality is led into actuality only by a being that is in actuality in a relevant respect. (Premise.)
2 God is the first being. (Premise.)

3   (Therefore) In God, there is no potentiality, i.e., God is pure actuality. (From 1 and 2.)

Second argument for uniqueness

1   God has total perfection of being. (Lemma 1.)
2   If there were two Gods, they would differ in some respect. (Premise.)
3   If this respect is a privation, then one of the Gods is not totally perfect. (Premise.)
4   If this respect is a perfection, then one of the Gods is not totally perfect. (Premise.)
5   (Therefore) It is impossible for there to be more than one God. (From 1, 2, 3, and 4.)

Lemma 1 (q.4 a.2)

1   God is esse itself. (Lemma 2(a) and/or 2(b), and/or 2(c).)
2   (Therefore) Necessarily, God has all of the perfections of esse. (From 1.)
3   Possession of the perfections of esse entails possession of all of the perfections of being. (Premise.)
4   (Therefore) God has total perfection of being. (From 2 and 3.)

Lemma 2 (a) (q.3 a.4)

1   Necessarily, whatever there is in a thing beyond its essence cannot be caused either (a) by the principles of its essence, or (b) by some cause outside itself. (Premise.)
2   (Therefore) Necessarily, if a thing's esse is distinct from its essence, then the esse of the thing is caused either (a) by the principles of its essence, or (b) by something outside of itself. (From 1.)
3   Nothing is sufficient to be a cause of its own esse if it has esse that is caused. (Premise.)
4   (Therefore) It is impossible for the esse to be caused solely by the principles of the essence of a thing. (From 3.)
5   Necessarily if a thing's esse is distinct from its existence, then the esse of the thing is caused by something outside itself. (From 2 and 4.)
6   God is the first efficient cause. (Second Way.)
7   (Therefore) God's esse is not caused by another. (From 6.)
8   (Therefore) God's esse is not distinct from God's essence. (From 5 and 7.)

Lemma 2 (b) (q.3 a.4)

1   Esse is the actuality of any form or nature. (Premise.)
2   (Therefore) A thing's esse is related to an essence that is distinct from it in the way that actuality is related to potentiality. (From 1.)
3   There is no potentiality in God. (Premise; see Lemma 3, q.3 a.1 on pages 118–19.)
4   (Therefore) God's esse is not distinct from God's essence. (From 2 and 3.)

Lemma 2 (c) (q.3 a.4)

1. That which has esse and is not itself esse is a being through participation. (Premise.)
2. God is God's own essence. (Premise; see Lemma 1, q.3 a.3 on page 118.)
3. (Therefore) If God is not God's own esse, then God is a being through participation rather than through God's essence. (From 1 and 2.)
4. Nothing that is a being through participation is a first being. (Premise.)
5. God is the first being (*ens*). (Premise.)
6. (Therefore) God is God's esse as well as God's essence. (From 3, 4, and 5.)

Third argument for uniqueness

1. All things that exist are ordered to one another. (Premise.)
2. One thing can be a cause *per se* of one thing. (Premise.)
3. Many things can only be only a cause *per accidens* of one thing. (Premise)
4. Therefore, it is better that many things are brought into a single ordering by one thing than by many.
5. That which is first is the most perfect.
6. That which is first is a *per se* – not *per accidens* – principle.
7. (Therefore) There is just one first being that brings all things into a single ordering.

If the second argument for uniqueness is taken to appeal to Lemma 2(a), then the second argument for uniqueness takes, as a premise, the conclusion of the Second Way. So it is obvious that we then cannot use the second argument for uniqueness to 'complete' the argument of the Second Way: using the conclusion of an argument as a premise of that argument may secure validity, but only at the cost of utterly vicious circularity. Moreover, it is not less obvious that we cannot use this version of the second argument for uniqueness to 'complete' the arguments of the other Ways. There is, for example, nothing in this argument that helps us to show that there is just one necessary being that does not owe its necessity to other necessary beings.

If we trace back through the Lemmas, we see that the first argument for uniqueness and the two versions of the second argument for uniqueness that makes use of Lemma 2(b) and Lemma 2(c) rely upon claims like the following: *God is pure act, God is esse itself*, and *God's esse is identical to God's existence*. But, if we have derivations of these claims that are independent of the 'incomplete' arguments that are under consideration, then interest in those 'incomplete' arguments lapses: as we saw in our discussion of *De Ente et Essentia*, there is then no work left to be done by the premises in those 'incomplete' arguments. A 'completion' of any of the 'incomplete' arguments that renders one or more of the premises of the argument redundant simply does not 'complete' it in the right kind of way.

Whereas the first two arguments for uniqueness are, indeed, arguments for uniqueness, the third argument for uniqueness is actually an *existence* argument: the conclusion of the argument is that *there is* exactly one thing that brings all things into a single ordering. So, in this case, too, we are being offered a 'completion' of the 'incomplete' arguments that would simply render the premises in those arguments redundant. For example, from the claim that there is just one first being that brings all things into a single ordering, we can immediately conclude that that being is the one and only first efficient cause and the one and only unmoved mover. If we add the premises of this argument to either the First Way or the Second Way, we no longer need the rest of the premises of those arguments in order to 'complete' them.

The upshot here is that it is pretty clearly not the case that the discussion in *Summa Theologiae* I, q.11 provides what is needed to 'complete' the allegedly 'incomplete' arguments that are presented in *Summa Theologiae* I, q.3. Moreover – though I shall not try to defend this claim here – I think that it is pretty clear that there is no other part of the *Summa Theologiae* that provides what is needed to 'complete' the allegedly 'incomplete' arguments of *Summa Theologiae* I, q.3.

If it is accepted that the Five Ways are either logically flawed or incomplete as they stand, and if it is also accepted that there is nothing in the writings of Aquinas that shows how to rectify those flaws, then it might be supposed that we should 'write off' the Five Ways as something in which Aquinas had no deep investment. Perhaps, for example, the intended purpose of the Five Ways is merely to direct readers towards, and to encourage them to examine, the work of others – e.g., Aristotle and Avicenna – who develop these kinds of arguments in much greater details and with much greater precision. Moreover, even if the textual evidence in support of this claim seems slight, it is hard to see that much is to be gained by trying to mount further, strenuous argument against it.

2.5 De Ente et Essentia *revisited*

Even if it is agreed that the best thing to say about the Five Ways is that they are not to be taken too seriously, nothing much follows for the claim that Thomism defeats naturalism. After all, as we have already noted, at least *inter alia*, it is pretty clear that Aquinas himself did not rely upon the Five Ways in his theorising about God. The beating heart of Thomism is the metaphysical framework that is first developed in *De Ente et Essentia*. If we are looking for Thomistic arguments against naturalism, we should be looking to arguments that are developed in the context of that metaphysical framework.

I noted earlier that, in *De Ente et Essentia*, we are given more or less the following argument:

1   Necessarily, whatever belongs to a thing is either caused by the principles of its nature or comes to it from some extrinsic principle. (Premise.)

2   It is impossible that the existence of a thing is caused by the form or quiddity of that thing, i.e., by the principles of its nature. (Premise.)
3   (Therefore) Necessarily, for any thing in which its existence is other than its own nature, there is some other thing – some extrinsic principle – from which it has its existence. (From 1 and 2.)
4   There are things that have their existence from other things. (Premise.)
5   It is impossible for there to be an infinite regress of things, each of which has its existence from another. (Premise.)
6   (Therefore) There is a First Being which is existence alone, which is the cause of existence in all other things (and this First Being is God) (From 3, 4, and 5.)

And I noted that we can give 'reconfigured' versions of this argument that has many similarities with the Five Ways of the *Summa Theologiae*. Consider, for example, the following 'reconfigured' version of the argument:

1   Some things have their existence from other things. (Premise.)
2   Nothing can have its existence from itself. (Premise.)
3   There cannot be an infinite regress of things each of which has its existence from another. (Premise.)
4   (Therefore) There are first existent things that do not have their existence from other things. (From 1, 2, and 3.)
5   Only that in which its existence is its nature – i.e., only that which is existence alone – can be a first existent thing that does not have its existence from anything else. (Premise.)
6   There can only be one thing that is existence alone. (Premise.)
7   (Therefore) There is a First Being that is existence alone (and this First Being is God). (From 4 and 5.)

What might a naturalist say in response to this reconfigured version of the argument?

Before we turn to consider the premises of this argument, we note that naturalists might countenance any of the following three kinds of beings: (1) contingent beings that have their existence from other things; (2) brutely contingent beings that do not have their existence from other things; and (3) necessary beings that cannot have their existence from other things.

Naturalists who suppose that there are contingent beings accept Premise 1. Some naturalists deny that there are contingent beings; however, in this discussion, we shall set this minority opinion aside. From here on, we pretend that naturalists agree that there are contingent beings, and that some contingent beings have their existence from other contingent beings.

Naturalists accept Premise 2, given that this is understood to be the claim that nothing is the efficient cause of its own existence. There are other ways to interpret the claim that nothing has its existence from itself; we postpone discussion of this matter.

Naturalists divide in their attitude towards Premise 3. Some naturalists think that there might be an historical infinite regress of things, each of which owes its existence to the next. Some naturalists think that there might be a mereological infinite regress of things, each of which owes its existence to the wholes to which it belongs, even though there is no maximal whole to which all things belong. From here on, for the purposes of this discussion, I shall pretend that naturalists agree that there is no infinite regress of things each of which has its existence from another.

Given that they accept the first three premises of this argument, naturalists accept that there are first existent things that do not have their existence from other things. However, naturalists disagree about the identity of these first existent things. Naturalists who suppose that there are necessary things suppose that necessary things are first existent things that do not have their existence from other things. Naturalists who suppose that there are brutely contingent things suppose that brutely contingent things are first existent things that do not have their existence from other things. Naturalists who suppose that there are necessary things might suppose that initial things and/or abstract things are first existent things that do not have their existence from other things. Naturalists who suppose that there are brutely contingent things might suppose that initial things are first existent things that do not have their existence from other things.

The key premise in the argument is the claim that only that in which its existence is its nature – i.e., only that which is existence alone – can be a first existent thing that does not have its existence from anything else. Very few – if any – naturalists accept that there could be a thing whose nature is its existence, or a thing that is existence, or a thing that is identical to its existence, or a thing that is identical to its attributes, or a thing in which there is no potentiality, and so forth. Indeed, many naturalists – and not a few theists – deny that it even *makes sense* to claim that there is a thing whose nature is its existence, or a thing that is existence, of a thing that is identical to its existence, or a thing that is identical to its attributes, or a thing in which there is no potentiality, and so forth.

Metaphysical disagreement between Aquinas and contemporary naturalists can be very broad and very deep.

In *De Ente et Essentia*, Aquinas follows Aristotle in supposing that: (a) the Aristotelian categories exhaust the familiar first-class things that can be subjects or predicates in propositions; (b) the category of familiar substances divides into primary substances ('particulars') and secondary substances ('universals'); (c) familiar substances are informed matter: roughly speaking, 'composites' of form and matter; (d) the essences of familiar substances are that in virtue of which those substances have *esse*, i.e., that which makes a familiar substance the kind of familiar substance that it is; (e) familiar particular substances have essences but not definitions, but familiar secondary substances are defined by their essences; (f) a genus is a concept that applies to a familiar substance in virtue of its matter; a differentia is a concept that applies to a familiar substance in virtue of its form; a species is a concept that applies to a familiar substance in virtue of its essence or composition; (g) there are four kinds of causes or explanations of change in familiar particular substances: material, formal, efficient, and final; and (h) final causes are ubiquitous – though not universal – in complete explanations of changes in familiar particular substances.

All of this is controversial. The vast majority of contemporary naturalists do not accept all of (a)–(f). Moreover, and more importantly, more or less no contemporary naturalists accept (g) and (h). If we are looking for considerations to decide against naturalism in favour of Thomism, we cannot simply appeal to, or rely upon, (a)–(h). Rather, reliance upon or rejection of (a)–(h) will be spoils to the victor in the decision between Thomism and naturalism.

Beyond the broadly Aristotelian background, there are further, particular, claims to which Aquinas commits himself in *De Ente et Essentia*. Aquinas thinks that, in addition to the familiar particular substances, there are *souls* – disembodied dead people who will be brought back to life when the Kingdom of God is established – and *intelligences* – immaterial agents who drive the motions of the stars and planets, and angels – and there is *God*. According to Aquinas, the souls and intelligences are composites of *esse* and form: their essence is pure form, without any 'admixture' of matter. Moreover, according to Aquinas, God is pure *esse*: unlike the souls and intelligences, God is utterly simple and uncompounded.

These views about souls, intelligences, and God are problematic from the standpoint of broadly Aristotelian metaphysics. As we hinted above, the distinction between form and matter is motivated by considerations about predication: Aristotle's metaphysics begins with the subject/predicate analysis of propositions. The predicate in the sentence 'Aristotle is erudite' is the linguistic shadow of Aristotle's erudition: we cannot separate our reason to believe that there is such a form from our willingness to assent to the proposition expressed by the sentence. But, in the sentence 'Aristotle is erudite', the subject term is a linguistic shadow of Aristotle: the predicate in the sentence 'Aristotle is erudite' can only be a linguistic shadow of Aristotle's erudition if there is some particular informed matter that is Aristotle. In the nature of the case, we can have no similar reason to believe in pure forms: obviously enough, there are no sentences in which there are expressions that are linguistic shadows of pure forms. (As Kenny [2002: 30]) says: 'A pure form would be something that corresponded to a predicate in a sentence that had no subject; but this seems close to an absurdity.')

The doctrine that God is pure *esse* – pure existence – is, if anything, even more problematic than the doctrine that souls and intelligences are pure form. In the case of a familiar particular, it seems that existence is part of essence. As we noted earlier, an essence is that which makes a thing the kind of thing that it is. But no familiar particular would be the kind of thing that it is if it did not exist. These points are reflected in the claims that we can make about the existence of familiar particulars. I can intelligibly say that Barack Obama exists. And I can intelligibly say that it was once the case that Bertrand

Russell existed. In the former instance, the proposition is true because 'Barack Obama' refers to a particular whose essence includes existence. In the latter instance, the proposition is true because it was once true – though it is no longer – that 'Bertrand Russell' referred to a particular whose essence included existence. But how are we to think about the proposition expressed by the sentence 'God exists'? If God is pure existence, then this proposition entails the claim that pure existence – just as such – exists. But pure existence is not of the right ontological category for it to be true that – just as such – it exists.

Given the breadth and depth of metaphysical disagreement between Thomists and naturalists, it is not credible to suppose that there is a relatively compact set of considerations that suffice to resolve their differences. It may well be that Thomists suppose that the argument that we have found in *De Ente et Essentia* is sound; i.e., it may well be that Thomists suppose (a) that the conclusion of the argument is a logical consequence of its premises; and (b) that all of the premises of the argument are true. But it is obvious that naturalists disagree with Thomists about the truth of at least some of those premises. Moreover, it is not at all plausible that this disagreement is readily resolved. There is no reason for naturalists to suppose that there are Thomistic *arguments* that defeat their naturalism.

2.6 Disclaimer

It is important not to misunderstand the conclusion for which I have been arguing. I do not claim that the considerations that have been advanced towards the end of the last section are sufficient to persuade Thomists to change their big pictures. My purpose has not been to argue against Thomistic big pictures. Rather, my purpose here has been to argue that there is no knockdown argument against naturalism that has been advanced by proponents of Thomistic big pictures.

I claim that, when we look at the writings of Aquinas, we do not find arguments that are required to give naturalists pause; and I also claim that, when we examine the Thomistic big picture, it is not plausible to suppose that it yields materials that compel assent to the conclusion that Thomism defeats naturalism.

3. Concluding remarks

In this chapter, I have considered two attempted demonstrations that religion defeats naturalism. I have argued that naturalism survives the case made against it by Rea (2002) and that naturalism is not threatened by any of the arguments found in the works of Aquinas.

Of course, I have not here considered every attempted demonstration that religion defeats naturalism. It clearly is – and will always remain – an open theoretical possibility that there are religious arguments that defeat naturalism. However, I think that all *extant* attempts to show that religion defeats naturalism go the way of the two cases to which I have given detailed attention.

7 Does science defeat religion?

It might seem odd to suppose that science could defeat religion. After all, science has developed and flourished against a background of near universal religious belief. If it were the case that science defeats religion, then it seems very puzzling that religion survived the rise of science. True enough, you might invoke some kind of conspiracy theory to explain why religion persists even though it is defeated by science – but, in general, it is a bad policy to put your trust in such large-scale conspiracy theories.

This chapter begins with a rough characterisation of science, a taxonomy of the sciences, a very brief history of the development of the sciences and scientific institutions, and a discussion of in-built mechanisms that protect the integrity of the sciences from predictable threats.

In the second section of this chapter, I investigate the claim – popular in some quarters – that science is a religion. I argue that it follows immediately from my definitions of religion and science that science is not a religion; I add that there are some important similarities between religion and science.

In the third section of this chapter, we take up the question whether scientists are religious. I begin with demographic data which shows that, in many – but not all – places, scientists are less religious than their compatriots. I then consider – and argue against – the proposal that these discrepancies might be well-explained by appeal to bias against, or internalisation of negative societal stereotypes by, religious people.

In the fourth section of this chapter, I turn my attention to 'models' that some have proposed for 'the relationship between science and religion'. I argue that it is obvious that religious commitment *can* and *does* come into conflict with science; I also argue that religious commitment *need not* come into conflict with science. In closing this section, I note that scientists themselves are often confused about 'the relationship between science and religion'.

In the fifth section of this chapter, I look at the claims that religions make about science. I distinguish between (a) the official general pronouncements that religions make about science; and (b) the attitudes that religions take towards particular well-established scientific claims. I argue that there are many different types of relationships between branches of religions and science. Most controversially, I argue that there are some branches of some religions that are in no conflict with science. This chapter is rounded out with a critical discussion of contemporary proponents of the view that there is a state of 'war' between religion and science.

In the sixth section of this chapter, I give some consideration to the claim that contemporary science actually makes about religion. I begin by identifying some of the sciences that take religion as an object of study, and I say something about the claims that these sciences make about religion. I conclude with some brief discussion of a range of studies in the psychology of religion, none of which suggests that humanity has compelling reason to give up on religion.

1. What is science?

Science is, roughly speaking, a collective enterprise of data-driven description, prediction, and understanding in which universal expert agreement functions as regulative ideal. The role of universal expert agreement as regulative ideal entails that (1) reproducibility, parsimony, and consilience are fundamental scientific values; (2) there are strict protocols governing the conduct of experiments and the collection and analysis of data; and (3) there are significant institutions devoted to protecting the integrity of scientific investigation, publication, recognition, and reward.

At least in a rough and ready way, some divide sciences into theoretical sciences and applied sciences. According to this rough and ready taxonomy, applied sciences are disciplines in which theoretical sciences are given practical application: for example, engineering sciences use theoretical sciences to develop and maintain technologies; and health sciences use theoretical sciences to diagnose, treat, and prevent ill-health. It is not clear that the division between theoretical sciences and applied sciences will withstand scrutiny; however, we shall suppose that it is in good enough shape for the limited use that we shall make of it.

The theoretical sciences divide, broadly, into the formal sciences, the natural sciences, and the social sciences.

Formal sciences study formal systems including, in particular, formal systems that are used in the natural sciences and the social sciences. Formal sciences include: (theoretical) computer science, decision theory, game theory, information theory, (theoretical) linguistics, logic, mathematics, (theoretical) statistics, and systems theory. Formal sciences are distinguished from natural sciences and social sciences in at least the following three respects: (1) formal sciences often function as auxiliaries to the natural sciences and the social sciences, providing them with key analytical tools; (2) formal sciences do not depend upon experimental design and collection of replicable data: at least in principle, formal sciences could be conducted from the armchair; and (3) some of the formal sciences – notably, logic and mathematics – made significant advances long before the methods of the natural sciences and the social sciences were understood; and the other formal sciences had later origins either because they depended upon sophisticated mathematics – e.g., theories of probability and measure – that was not developed until the scientific revolution was already under way, or because their primary interest depends upon technology that was spawned by the scientific revolution.

Natural sciences study all those aspects of natural causal reality that are not studied in the social sciences. Natural sciences divide, broadly, into physical sciences and life sciences. Physical science comprises: astronomy, chemistry, geoscience – which includes environmental science, geology, geo-informatics, physical geography, and scientific study of, e.g., the earth's atmosphere, glaciers, oceans, soils, etc. – and physics. Life sciences divide, broadly, into biological sciences and medical sciences, but also include food science, sports science, and the like.

Social sciences study human society and relationships among individuals in human society, using both quantitative and qualitative methods. Social sciences include anthropology, archaeology, communications and media studies, demography, economics, education, history, human geography, jurisprudence, (applied) linguistics, political science, social psychology, and sociology. Some social sciences rely heavily on natural sciences. For example, much contemporary archaeology depends upon the application of techniques and technologies developed in the physical, chemical, and earth sciences. Some social sciences rely heavily on the humanities. For example, history draws on ancient languages, classics, cultural studies, literature, modern languages, musicology, philosophy, and religious studies.

The natural and social sciences, as we now know them, are a relatively recent invention in the history of humanity. However, the seeds for their development belong to our distant pre-history. Prior to the rise of philosophy, human beings acquired extensive knowledge in a vast range of practical domains: cooking, toolmaking, timekeeping, musical instrumentation, animal husbandry, cropping, pottery, weaving, spinning, ploughing, smelting, trading, boatbuilding, counting, writing, sailing, brickmaking, masonry, currency, birth control, codified laws, and so forth. As astronomy, mathematics, and philosophy developed – in India, China, Greece, and elsewhere – questions began to be asked about the prospects for systematic theoretical understanding, explanation, and prediction of natural and social phenomena, but without any serious attention being given to experimental design and the collection of replicable data. During the following centuries – up until the European scientific revolution – there were many further advancements in practical domains, including making instruments to assist with calculation, navigation, timekeeping, printing, and so forth. However, while there were methodological advances – e.g., in Alhazen's thoughts about reproducible experimental results, and in the works of those, such as Roger Bacon and Francis Bacon, who followed his lead – natural science really became a going concern only after the contributions of Galileo and Descartes, and the establishment of national academies of science. And social science did not begin to emerge until several decades into the nineteenth century.

Given that universal expert agreement functions as a regulative scientific ideal, 'scientific opinion' – i.e., opinion that properly belongs to the domain of a given formal science, or natural science, or social science, and that secures universal or near-universal agreement among those working in that formal science, or natural science, or social science – has, and ought to have, significant *authority*. Moreover, given that scientific opinion has, and ought to have, significant authority, being a 'scientific expert' – i.e., being an expert in a particular formal science, or natural science, or social science – is, and ought to be, a matter of significant *prestige*. However, these facts – that scientific opinion has, and ought to have, significant authority, and that being a scientific expert is, and ought to be, a matter of significant prestige – create various kinds of difficulties.

Because being a scientific expert is a matter of significant prestige, there is strong incentive for people to pass themselves off as scientific experts – and for institutions to pass themselves off as collectives of scientific experts – even though they do not have the relevant scientific expertise. Moreover, because there is strong incentive for people to pass themselves off as scientific experts – and for institutions to pass themselves off as collectives of scientific experts – there is also strong incentive for other people to act as enablers for those people who wish to pass themselves off as scientific experts and for those institutions that wish to pass themselves off as collectives of scientific experts. Some people – and some institutions – simply lie about their scientific credentials; other people – and other institutions – have fake credentials and false testimonials that merely appear to justify their claims to scientific expertise.

Because scientific opinion is authoritative, there is significant incentive for people and institutions to pass themselves off as reliable sources of scientific opinion, when, in fact, they are not reliable sources of scientific opinion. Moreover, because there is significant incentive for people and institutions to pass themselves as reliable sources of scientific opinion, there is also significant incentive for other people and institutions to act as enablers for those who wish to pass themselves off as reliable sources of scientific opinion. Some people and institutions deliberately lie when giving their purportedly scientific opinions; some people and institutions engage in bullshit when giving their purportedly scientific opinions; and some people and institutions honestly fail to recognise that what they claim are scientific opinions are not, in fact, scientific opinions.

Because some people and some institutions that claim scientific expertise and reliability with respect to scientific opinion have neither scientific expertise nor reliability with respect to scientific opinion, those who – quite properly – wish to believe in accordance with scientific opinion need to have ways of discriminating between those people and institutions that really do have scientific expertise and that really are reliable with respect to scientific opinion, and those people and institutions that merely purport to have scientific expertise and to be reliable with respect to scientific opinion. Moreover, because some people and some institutions claim scientific expertise and reliability with respect to scientific opinion in domains other than those in which they genuinely have scientific expertise and reliability, those who – quite properly – wish to believe in accordance with scientific opinion also need to have ways of discriminating between those people and institutions that really do have scientific expertise and that really are reliable with respect to scientific opinion in the current domain of interest, and those people and institutions that really do have scientific expertise and that really are reliable with respect to scientific opinion in some domains, but who do not have scientific expertise and are really not reliable with respect to scientific opinion in the current domain of interest.

Peak scientific bodies – e.g., national academies of science – provide assistance with some of these difficulties. There is *credentialing*: those who possess doctorates in relevant fields typically have some expertise in those fields. (Of course, establishing that someone has a doctorate in a relevant field is not entirely unproblematic. Some people lie. Some people cheat. Some institutions offer fake PhDs. Some institutions that confer PhDs ought not to be in the business of conferring PhDs. Not everyone is honest about the field of their PhD.) There is *affiliation*: those who hold appointments in relevant fields at elite universities typically have some expertise in those fields. (Of course, establishing that someone has an appropriate affiliation is not always straightforward. Some people lie. Some people cheat. Some institutions merely purport to be the kind of institutions at which affiliation is some guarantee of expertise.) There is *education*: where there are peak scientific bodies staffed with scientific experts that vet the content of the national science curriculum, there is a good chance that science education will help to give people the ability to identify people and institutions that really do have scientific expertise and that really are reliable with respect to scientific opinion in a given domain of interest. But, even given the various kinds of assistance that are available, it can still be very difficult for those who – quite properly – wish to believe in accordance with scientific opinion to determine what scientific opinion is in given domains.

In response to the difficulties that we all face in identifying people and institutions that really do have scientific expertise and that really are reliable with respect to scientific opinion in given domains, some theorists have supposed that we need to be supplied with a checklist of features that will equip us to distinguish between (a) people and institutions that really do have scientific expertise and that really are reliable with respect to scientific opinion in given domains – those who support and promulgate *science*; and (b) people and institutions that do not have scientific expertise and that are not reliable with respect to scientific opinion in given domains – those who support and promulgate *pseudoscience*, or *fake science*, or *junk science*.

Given that science is, roughly speaking, a collective enterprise of data-driven description, prediction, and understanding in which universal expert agreement functions as a regulative ideal, there are various ways in which people and institutions that do not have scientific expertise and that are not reliable with respect to scientific opinion in given domains might fall from grace. Some have said that pseudoscience is characteristically irrefutable, or untestable, or unfalsifiable. Some have said that pseudoscience is not progressive, not updated in the light of new data, and not increasing in explanatory power. Some have said that pseudoscience ignores theoretical difficulties and recalcitrant data. Some have said that pseudoscience ignores the virtues of directly competing theories. Some have said that pseudoscience is uninterested in genuine critical evaluation, particularly in connection with neighbouring theoretical domains. Some have said that pseudoscience is characterised by use of vague, or misleading, or exaggerated claims. Some have said that pseudoscience typically abandons explanations without replacing them, etc.

There are two serious difficulties that confront those who make these kinds of claims. First, while it is no doubt true that, for each of these claims, there are *some* people and institutions that do not have scientific expertise and that are not reliable with respect to scientific opinion in given domains to which the claim in question can be legitimately applied, there are *many* people and institutions that do not have scientific expertise and that are not reliable with respect to scientific opinion in given domains whose claims are not vulnerable to that criticism; and, moreover, there are *many* people and institutions that do not have scientific expertise and that are not reliable with respect to scientific opinion in given domains whose claims are not vulnerable to any of these criticisms. Second, while it is no doubt true that, in some cases, people and institutions that really do have scientific expertise and that really are reliable with respect to scientific opinion in given domains *are* properly able to make some of these kinds of criticisms of people and institutions that do not have scientific expertise and that are not reliable with respect to scientific opinion in those domains, there is no way that people and institutions that do not have scientific expertise in those domains will be able to judge for themselves that these criticisms properly apply. While, given my earlier account, it is plainly true that people and institutions that do not have scientific expertise and that are not reliable with respect to scientific opinion in given domains may be open to criticism on grounds of failure of reproducibility, or theoretical profligacy, or lack of consilience, or violation of protocols governing the conduct of experiments and the collection and analysis of data, or behaving in ways that threaten the integrity of scientific investigation, there is no reason to expect that anyone other than people and institutions that really do have scientific expertise and that really are reliable with respect to scientific opinion in given domains will be in a position to properly make that criticism.

Those who – quite properly – wish to believe in accordance with scientific opinion do have reasonably secure ways of determining the state of expert opinion in given domains. However, there is no *cost free* method for determining the state of expert opinion in given domains. Given that you are not, yourself, an expert in a given domain – and given that you do not have the resources to make yourself an expert in that domain – you will likely need to conduct some research, in order to determine who, among those contributing to public discussion on a given topic, is genuinely an expert in that domain. In particular, you will be looking for evidence of their standing, across a range of national academies of science and elite research institutions, in the domain in question. Moreover, in order to determine what is expert opinion in the domain in question, you will want to check considered declarations by a range of the people that you have identified as experts. Where the declarations of these people yield the same verdict about the unanimous (or near unanimous) agreement of experts on a given claim, you can be pretty sure that you have identified a claim that is worthy of your belief.

Of course, in a wide range of cases, there are slightly less secure, but nonetheless perfectly acceptable, shortcuts. A recent scientific textbook, from a suitably credentialed publisher, with the approval of a range of people that you have identified as experts, is a very highly reliable source of claims that are worthy of your belief. Similarly, a current encyclopedia that is appropriately keyed to the views of a wide range of genuine experts is a highly reliable source of claims that are worthy of your belief. Even *Wikipedia*, when read with suitable care, is an excellent guide to expert *scientific* opinion that is worthy of your belief.

Unfortunately, there are other shortcuts that are not in the least bit secure. Media reports of the state of expert scientific opinion are notoriously unreliable. ('Balancing' expert opinion with inexpert opinion generates the kind of heated debate that moves product; but that kind of 'balancing' carries highly misleading implicatures about the true state of expert opinion. And translation of perfectly acceptable 'science communication' – i.e. 'science communication' that has not already been corrupted – into saleable journalism often misrepresents the genuine content of that 'science communication'.) Inexpert commentary on the state of expert scientific opinion is also notoriously unreliable, particularly when it is driven by partisan political, financial, and religious interests. And if you pay attention to nothing other than Internet debates, you have next to no chance of identifying expert scientific opinion concerning, for example, astrology, channelling, chiropractic, Christian science, climate change, cryptozoology, dianetics, dowsing, ESP, feng shui, flat earthism, flood geology, geocentrism, Holocaust denial, hollow earthism, homeopathy, iridology, moon landing conspiracies, naturopathy, 9/11 conspiracies, numerology, orgone, palmistry, parapsychology, polywater, primal therapy, psychokinesis, reiki, rolfing, and ufology.

Thomas Young (1773–1829) has been described as the last man who knew everything. Since Young's time, the fraction of total science of which one person can have genuine expertise has continually declined, to the point that any given person's scientific expertise is now a mere drop in an ocean of lack of scientific expertise. The consequences of this explosion of merely collective scientific expertise are profound. Obviously enough, there are co-ordination difficulties: it is a challenge to assemble teams with the right collective expertise to solve the hard problems that we face. Slightly less obviously, there are the prior challenges that I have been discussing: (a) enabling the ready identification of those with genuine expertise; (b) enabling the ready identification of those with merely purported expertise; and (c) protecting genuine scientific institutions from the corrupting influence of partisan non-scientific interests.

2. Is science a religion?

A quick Google search turns up a vast number of webpages on which people affirm – and, often enough, argue – that science is a religion. Almost always, the reasons given in support of this claim are that science and religion are *alike* in certain respects. But, of course, what really matters is whether science and religion *differ* in important respects. It is readily established that this is, in fact, the case.

Begin by recalling the accounts of religion and science that I have defended.

At least approximately, religions are passionate, communal displays, of costly commitments to the satisfaction of non-natural causal beings – e.g., gods and/or ancestor spirits – and/or the overcoming of non-natural causal regulative structures – e.g., cycles of reincarnation, reward and punishment – resulting from evolutionary canalisation and convergence of:

1 widespread belief in non-natural causal agents and/or non-natural causal regulative structures;
2 hard to fake public expressions of costly material commitments – offerings and/or sacrifices of goods, property, time, and/or life – to the satisfaction of those non-natural causal agents and/or the overcoming of, or escape from, those non-natural causal regulative structures;
3 mastering of people's existential anxieties – death, deception, disease, catastrophe, pain, loneliness, injustice, want, and loss – by those costly commitments to the satisfaction of those non-natural causal agents and/ or the overcoming of, or escape from, non-natural causal regulative structures; and
4 ritualised, rhythmic, sensory co-ordination of (1), (2), and (3) in communion, congregation, intimate fellowship, or the like.

And, at least approximately, science is a collective enterprise of data-driven description, prediction, and understanding in which universal expert agreement functions as regulative ideal, and hence in which (a) reproducibility, parsimony, and consilience are fundamental scientific values; (b) there are strict protocols governing the conduct of experiments and the collection and analysis of data; and (c) there are significant institutions devoted to protecting the integrity of scientific investigation, publication, recognition, and reward.

In science, unlike in religion, there is no commitment to non-natural causal agents and non-natural causal regulative structures; no hard to fake public expressions of costly material commitments to the satisfaction of non-natural causal agents and the overcoming of, or escaping from, non-natural causal regulative structures; no mastery of existential anxiety through [the public expression of] costly material commitments; and no ritualised, rhythmic, sensory coordination of commitment, public expression and mastery of anxiety in communion, congregation, and intimate fellowship. And, in religion, unlike in science, there is no collective enterprise of data-driven description, prediction, and understanding in which universal expert agreement functions as regulative ideal.

Although religion and science are plainly distinct – and even though it is perfectly obvious that science is not a religion and religion is not a science – it is true that there are some important similarities between religion and science. In particular, it is worth observing that both religion and science demand commitment from those who participate in them. To be a scientist is to be committed to the values and imperatives generated by the regulative ideal of universal expert agreement. To belong to a particular religion is to take on, and to give public expression to, the costly commitments that the religion requires. The important grain of truth in the affirmations of those who say that science is a religion is the recognition that the institutions of science are grounded in commitments to certain values and imperatives.

3. Are scientists religious?

There have been many social scientific studies that have attempted to gain insight into levels of religious belief among scientists.

We shall begin by looking at studies that have been conducted on populations of natural scientists and social scientists in the United States. In order to have a rough baseline for the population of the United States at large, we shall rely upon Gallup poll results, which show a steady decline the percentage of theists in the United States, from 97% in 1944 to 86% in 2014. While there are some suggestions that the given current estimate is too high, it lines up reasonably well with other recent demographic studies; for example, a Pew Research Centre survey reported in Masci and Smith (2016) suggests that 89% of the US general public are theists.

On the basis of survey data, Leuba (1916) claimed to have shown that, in the US, natural scientists exhibit a much lower level of belief in God compared to the general public. Larson and Witham (1997) replicated Leuba's study, and obtained more or less the same results. It is not clear that much significance can be attached to Leuba's study because the questions posed in his survey are so poorly framed. (Larson and Witham note that Leuba himself experienced a 10% rejection rate for his questions among those who responded to the survey.)

Larson and Witham (1998) found that, among natural scientists in the US National Academy of Science, only 7% believed in God. Larson and Witham also found that belief was unevenly distributed across the sciences, with 14.3% of mathematicians, 7.5% of physicists and astronomers, and just 5.5% of biological scientists believing in God. It is perhaps worth noting that the response rate for this survey was just over 50%.

Ecklund and Scheitle (2007) found that, among social scientists and natural scientists in elite universities in the US, no more than 30% believed in God, or a higher power, with some degree of conviction, at least some of the time. Moreover, Ecklund and Scheitle found that, unlike in the public at large, the percentage of believers was higher for younger members of the surveyed cohort.

Gross and Simmons (2009) found that, among academics from a broad range of higher education institutions – elite doctoral granting universities, non-elite four-year state schools, small liberal arts colleges, and community colleges – 75% believed in God, or a higher power, with some degree of conviction, at least some of the time. Gross and Simmons also found that belief decreased as the prestige of schools increased, and that belief was lower in the physical and biological sciences than in the social sciences and humanities.

Kohut et al. (2009) found that, among members of the American Association for the Advancement of Science, no more than 51% believed in God, or a higher power, with some degree of conviction, at least some of the time. Like Ecklund and Scheitle, Kohut *et al.* reported that younger natural scientists are significantly more likely to believe. Like Gross and Simmons, Kohut *et al.* reported on levels of belief across the different natural sciences: 59% in biological and medical sciences; 61% in chemical sciences; 53% in geosciences; and 54% in physical and astronomical sciences.

Curlin et al. (2005) found that, in comparison to the general population, physicians are more likely to be affiliated with minority religions, much more likely to claim to be 'spiritual but not religious', and much more likely to cope with major life problems without 'relying on God'. I failed to find any studies of the religious beliefs of engineers. Perhaps there is *some* indication in the study by Curlin *et al.* that, in the US, a reduced level of belief and conviction is seen in those who work in applied sciences.

While it is hard to assess the strength of the support provided, it seems to me that studies in the US clearly offer some support for all the following claims: (1) levels of unbelief and irreligiosity run higher among academics than they do in the general population; (2) levels of unbelief and irreligiosity run higher among natural scientists than among social scientists and scholars in the humanities; (3) levels of unbelief and irreligiosity run higher among scientists in more elite institutions than among scientists in less elite institutions; (4) levels of unbelief and irreligiosity run higher among scientists in the biological and physical sciences than among scientists in other natural sciences; and (5) levels of unbelief and irreligiosity run higher among at least some kinds of applied scientists than among the general population.

Stirrat and Cornwell (2013) surveyed the Fellows of the Royal Society of London; the cohort of respondents was roughly evenly divided between those working in physical sciences and those working in biological sciences. The results of this study are very similar to the results of Larson and Witham (1998). Stirrat and Cornwell found that about 8% of their respondents believed in God, about 7% believed in a personal God, and about 9% believed in life after death. Moreover, they found, in each case, that these

136 *Does science defeat religion?*

percentages were higher for those in the physical sciences than for those in the biological sciences; that is, they found that there were lower levels of belief in God and an afterlife for those working in biological sciences than for those working in physical sciences. Interestingly, the overall cohort of respondents was evenly divided on the question of the possible peaceful coexistence of science and religion, though the level of negative response was higher for the biological sciences than for the physical sciences.

Ecklund *et al.* (2016) conducted a very large-scale study of the religious beliefs of scientists in eight countries: France, Hong Kong, India, Italy, Taiwan, Turkey, the UK, and the US. Interestingly, they found that in two of these countries, the percentage of people who claim to be at least slightly religious is higher among scientists than it is among the general population: Hong Kong (39% against 20%) and Taiwan (54% against 44%). In the other six countries, the results were: France (16% against 46%), India (59% against 77%), Italy (52% against 85%), Turkey (57% against 84%), the UK (27% against 47%), and the US (30% against 67%). The pool of the study was drawn from both elite and non-elite universities in each of the eight countries. The findings of Ecklund *et al.* show that it is not universally true that scientists exhibit lower levels of religiosity than is exhibited by the wider communities to which they belong. However, it would be good to have more data points; it is not clear whether Hong Kong and Taiwan are simply unusual special cases.

When we cast a wider net, it seems that we lack sufficient data to draw robust conclusions. Ecklund *et al.* (2016: 6) claim that it is significant that their study shows that more than half of the scientists in four of the regions identify as at least slightly religious. But our examination of US studies shows that, depending upon what you take the pool of scientists to be, the percentage who identify as at least slightly religious is somewhere between 7% and 75%. The study of Ecklund *et al.* simply does not tell us, for example, about levels of religiosity among natural scientists who belong to national academies of science, or about levels of religiosity among natural scientists who work in elite research institutions.

Despite the need for caution, it does seem that the often wide discrepancies between the religious beliefs of scientists and the religious beliefs of the wider populations to which they belong, calls for explanation. De Cruz (2017) suggests that the discrepancy in the US might be explained by (a) bias against theists in academia; and (b) internalisation of negative societal stereotypes by theists.

In support of the claim that there is bias against theists in academia, De Cruz cites Yancey (2012). This citation is curious. Yancey argues that there is bias against cultural and religious conservatives in academia. But Yancey also suggests that there are very few cultural and religious conservatives in academia, and that bias against cultural and religious conservatives is much worse in the humanities and social sciences than it is in the natural sciences. Yet our earlier examination of the religiosity of natural scientists in the US shows that the representation of any kinds of religious belief are at their lowest ebb in the National Academy of Science and in *natural science* departments in elite universities. Even if there is bias against cultural and religious conservatives in academia, that bias cannot explain the under-representation of religious liberals in academia, and nor can it explain the differential under-representation of religious adherents across the natural sciences, social sciences, and humanities.

The suggestion that we might explain the under-representation of religious adherents in academia by appeal to theistic internalisation of negative societal stereotypes is interesting. De Cruz cites Rios *et al.* (2015), which argues that, along with lower intelligence and habitual employment of intuitive – as opposed to analytical – modes of thought, internalisation of negative societal stereotypes is a factor that contributes to the under-representation of religious adherents in academia. The study had five different sets of participants, each of which was allocated to a different study.

In the first study, a questionnaire, all participants recognised that Christians are stereotyped as less competent and trusting in science, while just the non-Christian participants believed that Christians are less competent and trusting in science.

In the second study, Christians who had just read that Christians are stereotyped as bad at science, and Christians who had received no priming about stereotypes concerning Christian scientific expertise, identified less with science than Christians who had just read that Christians are stereotyped as good at science.

In the third study, Christians who had just read that Christians are worse at science than non-Christians, and Christians who had received no priming about relative scientific abilities of Christians and non-Christians, performed worse on a reasoning task than both Christians and non-Christians who had just read that there is no difference in the scientific abilities of Christians and non-Christians.

The fourth study was just like the third, except that the reasoning task had 'easy' and 'hard' components, and the under-performance was present even on the 'easy' components, suggesting that the under-performance was due to disengagement rather than to performance anxiety.

One week prior to the fifth study, participants completed a demographic survey that included five religiosity questions. Participants who undertook the 'test' in the divinity building were read a mission statement that affirmed that religion is compatible with disciplines in the humanities and social sciences. Participants who undertook the 'test' in the physical sciences building were read a mission statement that did not mention any non-scientific disciplines. For Christian participants, religiosity correlated negatively with performance in the physical sciences building, but not in the divinity building.

Because Rios *et al.* do not give the details of the five religiosity questions that they used in the final study, it is unclear whether the test would distinguish between 'conservative' and 'liberal' religious adherents. We are told that all of the participants were US citizens. So there is at least some room for

138 *Does science defeat religion?*

wondering whether we would get the same results if we applied all of the tests to an exclusively 'liberal' religious cohort. If there are countries in which the religious are primarily 'liberal' and yet nonetheless poorly represented in the upper reaches of the scientific academy, then we may need to cast around elsewhere for an explanation of that under-representation.

Whatever statistical correlations hold between scientists and religiosity, it is clear – both from the historical record and from contemporary observation – that there have been, and are, very distinguished scientists who exhibit high degrees of religiosity. For a historical example, we might point to Blaise Pascal; for a contemporary example, we might point to Francis Collins. Whatever statistical correlations hold between scientists and religiosity, it is clear – both from the historical record and from contemporary observation – that there have been, and are, scientists distributed all the way across the spectrum of religiosity.

4. How is science related to religion?

Many discussions of 'the relationship between science and religion' launch into considerations of 'models' for 'the relationship' – 'conflict', 'independence', 'dialogue', 'integration' – without adequately considering exactly what the proper focus of attention is in those discussions. In particular, many of those discussions proceed from very woolly understandings of 'religion' and 'science'.

Recall that, at least roughly, science is a collective enterprise of data-driven description, prediction, and interpretation in which universal expert agreement functions as regulative ideal.

At any time, *established* science is the sum of what is established in any of the sciences: formal, natural, social, and applied. At any time, for a claim to be *established* in a particular science, that claim must have universal – or near-universal – expert agreement: it must be, for example, a claim that is not controversial among the relevant members of national academies of science and elite research institutions. Among the claims that are established in a particular science, there are claims about the territory, or domain, that belongs to that science: that is, there are established claims that identify a body of not yet established claims that belong to the science in question. Of course, at any time, expert scientists will be investigating – and developing opinions about – claims that are not established science, and about which there may well be disagreement among expert scientists; and, at any time, expert scientists may have opinions, not yet established in the science, about further not yet established claims that they suppose belong to the science in question.

Recall that, at least roughly, religions are passionate, communal displays, of costly commitments to the satisfaction of non-natural causal beings – e.g., gods and/or ancestor spirits – and/or the overcoming of non-natural causal regulative structures – e.g., cycles of reincarnation, reward and punishment – resulting from evolutionary canalisation and convergence of:

1   widespread belief in non-natural causal agents and/or non-natural causal regulative structures;
2   hard to fake public expressions of costly material commitments – offerings and/or sacrifices of goods, property, time, and/or life – to the satisfaction of those non-natural causal agents and/or the overcoming of, or escape from, those non-natural causal regulative structures;
3   mastering of people's existential anxieties – death, deception, disease, catastrophe, pain, loneliness, injustice, want, and loss – by those costly commitments to the satisfaction of those non-natural causal agents and/or the overcoming of, or escape from, non-natural causal regulative structures; and
4   ritualised, rhythmic, sensory co-ordination of (1), (2), and (3) in communion, congregation, intimate fellowship, or the like.

Given this definition of religion, at any time, for any person who belongs to a religion, there are claims about non-natural causal agents and/or non-natural causal regulative structures to which they have commitment, and there are claims about what is required in order to satisfy those non-natural causal agents and/or to escape from those non-natural causal regulative structures to which they also have commitment. But these claims – about non-natural causal agents and/or non-natural causal regulative structures and what is required in order to satisfy those non-natural causal agents and/or to escape from those non-natural causal regulative structures – may, and often enough, do, carry entailments about domains that are the proper purview of the sciences. And, in particular, these claims – about non-natural causal agents and/or non-natural causal regulative structures and what is required in order to satisfy those non-natural causal agents and/or to escape from those non-natural causal regulative structures – may, and often enough, do, carry entailments that contradict established scientific claims.

Consider, for example, young earth creationism. There are people whose religious commitments to claims, about non-natural causal agents and/or non-natural causal regulative structures and what is required in order to satisfy those non-natural causal agents and/or to escape from those non-natural causal regulative structures, bring with them commitment to young earth creationism, e.g., commitment to the claim that the universe is less than 10,000 years old. But there is universal expert scientific agreement that the universe is approximately 13.8 billion years old. (Here, 'approximately' means ± 0.1 billion years.) For people whose religious commitments to claims, about non-natural causal agents and/or non-natural causal regulative structures and what is required in order to satisfy those non-natural causal agents and/or to escape from those non-natural causal regulative structures, bring with them a commitment to young earth creationism, there is a conflict between their religion and established science.

Consider, for example, the belief that chimpanzees and humans do not have a common ancestor. There are people whose religious commitments to claims, about non-natural causal agents and/or non-natural causal regulative structures and what is required in order to satisfy those non-natural causal agents and/or to escape from those non-natural causal regulative structures, bring with them a commitment to the claim that chimpanzees and humans do not have a common ancestor. But there is universal expert scientific agreement that chimpanzees and humans do have common ancestors. For people whose religious commitments to claims, about non-natural causal agents and/or non-natural causal regulative structures and what is required in order to satisfy those non-natural causal agents and/or to escape from those non-natural causal regulative structures, bring with them a commitment to the claim that chimpanzees and humans do not have a common ancestor, there is a conflict between their religion and established science.

Since it is obvious that religious commitments *can* – and *do* – come into conflict with science, the remaining question of interest is whether they *must*. Could there be people who have commitments to claims, about non-natural causal agents and/or non-natural causal regulative structures and what is required in order to satisfy those non-natural causal agents and/or to escape from those non-natural causal regulative structures, that do not contradict any established science? Are there people who have commitments to claims, about non-natural causal agents and/or non-natural causal regulative structures and what is required in order to satisfy those non-natural causal agents and/or to escape from those non-natural causal regulative structures, that do not contradict established science?

There is nothing in established science that entails commitment to non-natural causal agents and/or non-natural causal regulative structures. But there is also nothing in established science that says that there are no non-natural causal agents and/or non-natural causal regulative structures. It is true that, if you open any standard properly scientific textbook, you will find nothing in its pages that entails commitment to non-natural causal agents and/or non-natural causal regulative structures. But, equally, it is true that, if you open any standard properly scientific textbook, you will find nothing in its pages that entails commitment to there being no non-natural causal agents and/or non-natural causal regulative structures. Moreover, these same points apply to requirements for satisfaction of non-natural causal agents and/or escape from non-natural causal regulative structures: nothing in the pages of standard properly scientific textbooks entails either that there are, or that there are not, such requirements.

I argued, earlier, that religion is in conflict with naturalism. If you suppose that natural reality exhausts causal reality, and you suppose that we have no reason to believe in any causal entities beyond those vouchsafed by science, then you will suppose that there are no non-natural causal agents and/or non-natural causal regulative structures. Moreover, it may be – for all that has been argued so far – that there is compelling reason to be a naturalist. But, even if there is compelling reason to be a naturalist, it is not just science that provides that compelling reason. There is no science that adjudicates big pictures; there is no science that says that naturalistic big pictures are the best big pictures.

Clearly enough, there is no reason to suppose that it *could not be* that there are people who have commitments to claims, about non-natural causal agents and/or non-natural causal regulative structures and what is required in order to satisfy those non-natural causal agents and/or to escape from those non-natural causal regulative structures, that do not contradict any established science. Moreover, I think, there *are* people who have commitments to claims, about non-natural causal agents and/or non-natural causal regulative structures and what is required in order to satisfy those non-natural causal agents and/or to escape from those non-natural causal regulative structures, that do not contradict any established science. There are adherents of all of the major world religions whose commitments to non-natural causal agents and/or non-natural causal regulative structures, and to what is required in order to satisfy those non-natural causal agents and/or to escape from those non-natural causal regulative structures, are not contradicted by any established science.

The upshot of the discussion to this point is that 'the relationship between science and religion' takes different forms for different versions of religion. For some versions of religion, the relationship is one of *conflict*; for other versions of religion, the relationship is one of *independence*. Those who suppose that the relationship is always one of conflict typically conflate science with naturalism; those who suppose that the relationship is always one of independence typically fail to pay serious attention to the defining properties of religion.

Consider Gould (2002). Famously, Gould claims that science and religion are non-overlapping magisteria that deal with fundamentally separate aspects of human experience. Gould's basic idea can be filled out in various ways. Some say that science is descriptive and religion is prescriptive. Some say that scientific explanations appeal only to natural forces and entities, whereas religious explanations appeal to non-natural forces and non-natural entities, etc. But there is no good way of filling out Gould's claim. There is no human experience that cannot be investigated by science. There is no good reason to agree that the normative reduces to the religious. It is just a mistake to suppose that religious explanation appeals only to non-natural forces and non-natural entities, etc.

What should we say to those who suppose that 'the relationship between science and religion' is one of 'dialogue' or 'integration'? Most obviously, that any 'dialogue' or 'integration' can only proceed *from* science *to* religion. Religions postulate a vast panoply of non-natural causal agents and/or non-natural causal regulative structures and requirements for satisfaction of those non-natural causal agents and/or escape from those non-natural causal regulative structures; there is no agreement – and no prospect of agreement – among the proponents of different religions about these postulates. However, in the sciences, expert agreement is a regulative ideal: established science requires universal – or near-universal – expert agreement. There is no prospect – and no reason to suppose – that religions offer any useful resources to any of the formal, natural, social, or applied sciences. Of course, no adequate big picture contains nothing but science; every one of us has beliefs that are not mandated by science. But these further beliefs make no contribution *to* the content of the pronouncements of science.

Perhaps it will be said that there is another question to address, concerning 'the relationship between science and theology'. Perhaps it will be added that 'science' and 'religion' share concepts, presuppositions, and methods; that, for example, both exhibit model-dependence, use metaphors, and value coherence, comprehensiveness, and fruitfulness. To this, the most apt response is Goodmanian: since everything is like everything else in ever so many ways, it is, *of course*, true that there are similarities between science and theology. But, given what science and religion actually are, recounting similarities between science and theology is not an activity that promises to deliver useful results to *science*.

Before we close this section, it is perhaps worth noting that scientists are often confused about the relationship between science and religion. Ecklund et al. (2016) asked those scientists whom they surveyed whether science and religion are in conflict, independent, or in collaboration. The reported results were as follows. France: 27% Conflict; 58% Independent; 7% Collaborative; 8% Don't Know. Hong Kong: 18% Conflict; 44% Independent; 24% Collaborative; 14% Don't Know. India: 20% Conflict; 44% Independent; 29% Collaborative; 7% Don't Know. Italy: 21% Conflict; 58% Independent; 15% Collaborative; 5% Don't Know. Taiwan: 10% Conflict; 62% Independent; 21% Collaborative; 7% Don't Know. Turkey: 26% Conflict; 35% Independent; 33% Collaborative; 7% Don't Know. UK: 29% Conflict; 51% Independent; 12% Collaborative; 7% Don't Know. US: 35% Conflict; 47% Independent; 12% Collaborative; 7% Don't Know. But, as we have just seen, the proper response to questions about 'the relationship between science and religion' is that it all depends upon which denomination or sect is being considered: some denominations and sects conflict with science; other denominations and sects are independent of science.

5. What do religions say about science?

Religious teachings about science vary widely. Some branches of some religions claim to reject science; often, the relevant branches of these religions avow scepticism towards almost all claims beyond the teachings of the branches of the religion in question. Some branches of some religions profess to accept much, but not all, of the teachings of science, drawing the line at scientific teachings that they take to be inconsistent with the teachings of the relevant branches of these religions. Some branches of some religions say that there is no conflict between 'true science' and the teachings of the relevant branches of those religions, but reject some teachings that have universal – or near-universal – expert scientific consensus on the grounds that those teachings are not 'true science'. Some branches of some religions say that there is no conflict between science and the teachings of the relevant branches of those religions, but also insist that the teachings of science have a lower standing than the teachings of the relevant branches of those religions. Some branches of some religions insist that the teachings of science are on all fours with the teachings of the relevant branches of those religions, while nonetheless having a history of rejecting universal – or near-universal – expert scientific consensus on the grounds of (perceived) conflict with the teachings of the relevant branches of those religions. And some branches of some religions insist that the teachings of science are on all fours with the teachings of the relevant branches of those religions without having any history of rejecting universal – or near-universal – scientific consensus.

Attributions of rejection of science are controversial. I shall give just one tendentious example; there are many other cases from different times and places that would serve as well as the example I give. Bodde (1991) includes religious attitudes among a wide range of intellectual and social forces that may have militated against the development of science and technology in pre-modern China. In some parts of China, at some times, these religious attitudes supported antipathy towards science and scientific advancement. While the full history of the connection between the various Chinese religions – Confucianism, Daoism, Buddhism, and Chinese folk religions – remains to be written, it seems plausible to claim that we do here find examples of branches of religions that explicitly reject large parts of science. Of course, this is not to say that Confucianism, Daoism, Buddhism, and/or Chinese folk religions now reject large parts of science; and nor is it to say that, at some point in history Confucianism, Daoism, Buddhism, and/or Chinese folk religions rejected large parts of science. Rather, it is to say that there have been – and perhaps still are – sects or groups of Chinese people belonging to these religions who have, on the basis of their religion, rejected large parts of science.

There are various cases in which religious adherents have rejected well-established science on the basis of their religious convictions; and there are also various cases in which religious adherents have adopted views that are clearly not well-established science on the basis of their religious convictions. Perhaps the most notorious case of the *former* kind is the rejection, by fundamentalist adherents of Christianity and Islam, of claims in evolutionary science – e.g., that human beings and chimpanzees have relatively recent common ancestry – that have universal expert consensus. While, by and large, within a few decades of the publication of *The Origin of Species*, religious adherents in the UK came to accept the claim about common descent, history ran very differently in the US. A significant proportion of Christians in the US based their rejection of common descent on a literal reading of scripture, and, over time, successfully exported this rejection to other countries and other religions. Today, there are large numbers of Christians, Muslims, and Jews – and not insignificant numbers of proponents of some other major religions – who, on the basis of their religion, reject common descent despite universal expert scientific consensus that human beings and chimpanzees do have relatively recent common ancestry. Perhaps the clearest case of the *latter* kind is the acceptance, by fundamentalist adherents of Christianity and Islam, of the claim that natural reality has a finite history, despite the lack of universal expert scientific consensus on this claim. While, since the mid-1960s, there has been near-universal expert scientific consensus that our universe arose from something like an initial singularity about 13.8 billion years ago, there is currently no universal – or near-universal – expert scientific consensus on the question of whether our universe is part of a multiverse, and nor is there any universal – or near-universal – expert scientific consensus on the question of whether, if there is a multiverse, that multiverse has an infinite past. In this case, there are large numbers of Christians, Muslims, and Jews who, on the basis of their religion, accept that natural reality has a finite past even though there is no universal – or near-universal – expert scientific consensus on this matter.

Bahá'i provides one example – among many – of a religion that says that there is no conflict between 'true science' and 'true religion', but which rejects some teachings that have universal or near-universal expert scientific consensus on the grounds that those teachings are not 'true science'. In particular – as is made clear by Bahá'-ulláh (1990: 162–163) – Bahá'i teaches that every star is orbited by inhabited planets. But the universal or near-universal expert scientific consensus is that only a small fraction of stars are orbited by inhabited planets. Those who accept this teaching of the Bahá'i faith believe against universal or near-universal expert scientific consensus. ('Abdul'-Bahá (2014: 183–184) also makes it clear that Bahá'i teaches that humans do not share common ancestry with other animals, but rather evolved along a separate evolutionary path. While the positive view that is adopted here is different from the positive views standardly adopted by fundamentalist Christians, Muslims and Jews, it is still a view that goes against universal or near-universal expert scientific consensus.)

Buddhism comes in many varieties. Among the Buddhist traditions, there are some that claim to privilege proper assessment of evidence above reliance on faith, hearsay, and speculation. However, these Buddhist traditions typically assimilate science to 'conventional' truth, except, perhaps, where the teachings of science – e.g., in quantum mechanics and relativistic physics – can be 'interpreted' to fit with Buddhist teachings about 'ultimate' truth. Given the length of the bow that must be drawn to find even the remotest connection between contemporary physics and Buddhist teachings on dependence and emptiness, the upshot here is that, in fact, Buddhist teachings assimilate science to 'conventional' truth. In this case, it seems that, while there is no conflict between science and the religious teachings of those Buddhist traditions, the teachings of science clearly have a lower standing than the religious teachings of those Buddhist traditions.

The official position of the (Roman) Catholic Church is that there is no conflict between science and religion. Moreover, the Church promotes itself as a patron of science and the sciences. Historically, the Church played an important role in the foundation of universities, and in the sponsorship of research in the formal, natural and applied sciences, including mathematics, astronomy, physics, chemistry, geology, biology, architecture, engineering, and medicine. Many famous scientists were Catholic, particularly during the earlier stages of the scientific revolution: for example, Agricola, Boscovich, Copernicus, Descartes, Galileo, Grimaldi, Kircher, Lamarck, Lavoisier, Lemaitre, Mendel, Mersenne, Pascal, Pasteur, Scheiner, Steno, and Vesalius. The Vatican Observatory (established in 1789) and the Pontifical Academy of Sciences (established in 1936) continue to make a contribution to ongoing scientific research. Nonetheless, there is on-going scholarly controversy about the Church's historical engagement with science, and, in particular, about whether it has persisted in its religious opposition to certain teachings long after the establishment of universal – or near-universal – expert scientific consensus on their truth. For example, the Church's repudiation of geocentrism was not official until 1835, when Galileo's *Dialogues Concerning the Two Chief World Systems* and Copernicus' *De Revolutionibus Orbium Coelestium* were finally removed from the Church's Index of Prohibited Books. While there is certainly justice in the suggestion that some claims of critics of the Church's treatment of scientific innovations are overblown, there are reasonably good grounds for claiming that there have been cases in which the Church has rejected universal – or near-universal – expert scientific consensus because of (perceived) conflict between that consensus and its teachings.

The claim, that there is nothing in the history of some branches of some religions that is in tension with their insistence that the teachings of science are on all fours with their religious teachings, is widely contested. However, it is not hard to see that the definition of religion that I have adopted certainly *permits* the existence of religions that are in no conflict with science. Imagine, for example, deists whose doctrinal commitments do not extend beyond belief in a creator God and a life to come, whose practical commitments do not extend beyond sacrifices of goods, property, and time in the service of the happiness and welfare of others; who engage in communion, congregation, and intimate fellowship following long-established historical tradition in their communities; and who, as a result of all of the above, achieve some mastery of their existential anxieties. I see no reason why such deists could not be fully committed to all of the established teachings of all of the sciences: formal, natural, social, and applied. Moreover, I think that there is good reason to suppose that there have been – and are – people like this: people whose religious doctrinal commitments are so 'minimal' that they cannot get into conflict with established science. Of course, the religious doctrinal commitments of these people, however 'minimal' they may be, will be in conflict with naturalism. But naturalism is not, itself, a doctrine on which there is universal – or near-universal – expert scientific consensus.

In the late nineteenth century, Draper (1874) and White (1896) argued that there is an inevitable state of 'warfare' between religion and science. More recent scholarship – see, for example, Numbers (2009) – has established a broad consensus that the works of Draper and White are riddled with factual errors. Nonetheless, there is no shortage of contemporary support for the claim that there is inevitable and irreconcilable conflict between science and religion. Consider, for example:

> There is no common ground between science and religion. ... The claims of science rely on experimental verification, while the claims of religions rely on faith. These are irreconcilable approaches to knowing.
>
> (Tyson 1999)

> Religious moderates are themselves the bearers of a terrible dogma: they imagine that the path to peace will be paved once each of us has learned to respect the unjustified beliefs of others. What is the alternative to religion as we know it? As it turns out, this is the wrong question to ask. Chemistry was not an "alternative" to alchemy; it was a wholesale exchange of ignorance at its most rococo for genuine knowledge. We will find that, as with alchemy, to speak of "alternatives" to religious faith is to miss the point.
>
> (Harris 2004: 24)

> Fundamentalist religion debauches the scientific enterprise. ... The teachings of 'moderate' religion, though not extremist in themselves, are an open invitation to extremism. ... We should blame religion itself, not religious extremism.
>
> (Dawkins 2006: 284, 306)

> Religion has run out of justifications. Thanks to the telescope and the microscope, it no longer offers an explanation of anything important. Where once it used to be able, by its total control of a worldview, to prevent the emergence of rivals, it can now only impede and retard – or try to turn back – the measureable advances we have made.
>
> (Hitchens 2007: 282)

> Irreconcilable differences arising from the differing viewpoints and methodology of science and religion include the origin of the universe and its physical parameters, the origin of complexity, the concepts of holism versus reductionism, the nature of mind and consciousness, and the sources of morality.
>
> (Stenger 2012: 29)

> It's ironic, really, that so many people are fixated on the relationship between science and religion: basically, there isn't one. ... It's inevitable that science draws people away from religion.
>
> (Krauss 2015)

These views, and numerous others like them, allege a wide range of different – and conflicting – negative assessments of the claim that it is possible for there to be religion that is in no conflict with science. Tyson claims that science and religion support irreconcilable methods of forming beliefs. Dawkins implies that religion – not merely 'extreme' or 'fundamentalist' religion – debauches science. Hitchens suggests that, after the development of science, there is nothing important that is successfully explained by religion, even though religion aspires to explain things that are not explained by science. Harris suggests, I think, that it is something akin to a category mistake to suppose that religion is in competition with science. Stenger identifies a range of topics on which, he says, there are irreconcilable differences between science and religion. Krauss says both that there is no relationship between science and religion, and that there is an adversarial relationship in which science inevitably has the upper hand.

I do not think that any of these authors makes a convincing case for the claim that there cannot be religion that is not in conflict with well-established science; and nor do I think that any of these authors makes a convincing case for the claim that are no religious believers whose religious beliefs are not in conflict with well-established science. As I have already noted, I agree with these authors that there certainly has been – and that there certainly still is – conflict between some of the teachings of some branches of some religions and some of the teachings of established science. But none of these authors provides us with good reason to suppose that it is necessary that there be 'warfare' between science and religion.

6. What does science say about religion?

There are many sciences that include branches that study religion. Moreover, there are interdisciplinary ventures that seek to draw on a broad cross-section of sciences in studying religion. We can provide no more than the briefest overview here.

Anthropology of religion provides comparative studies of religious beliefs and practices across different cultures, often with a focus on relationships between religions and other social institutions. Landmark fieldwork studies that made significant contributions to the anthropology of religion include Maurice Bloch's work in Madagascar, Edward Evans-Pritchard's study of the Azande, Arthur Hocart's work in the South Seas, Alfred Radcliffe-Brown's study of the Andaman Islanders, Mary Steedly's work with the Sumatran Karobatak, Paul Stoller's study of the Nigerian Songhay, and Edith Turner's work on the Zambian Ndembu. Historically influential theorists in the field – in addition to those already mentioned – include Edward Tylor, James Frazer, Franz Boas, Claude Lévi-Strauss, Lucien Lévy-Bruhl, Byron Good, and Mary Douglas.

Sociology of religion uses quantitative methods – census analysis, demographic analysis, polls, and surveys – and qualitative methods – archival analysis, documentary analysis, historical analysis, interviews, and participant observation – to study religious beliefs, religious practices, and forms of religious organisation in particular societies. Historically significant figures in the field include Karl Marx, Emile Durkheim, Max Weber, Ernest Gellner, and Michel Foucault. Secularisation theses – i.e., claims about the (alleged) loss of authority of religion in political and social life, at least in Western Europe and North America – have been a major topic in sociology of religion.

Economics of religion uses economic theories and methods to explain the religious behaviour of individuals, groups, and cultures. Two often-cited examples are: (a) Adam Smith's analysis of variation in the quantity and quality of provision of religious services with competition among religious providers, government regulation of religious providers, and differential government support for religious providers; and (b) Max Weber's account of the role that 'the Protestant work ethic' played in the rise and entrenchment of capitalist modes of production. The economics of religion is not to be confused with 'religious economy' theories – developed by Rodney Stark and others – which model religions as products and religious adherents as consumers.

Political science of religion studies the mutual influence that politics and religion have upon one another, with a focus on relationships between political actors – government, judiciary, political parties, political lobbies, etc. – and religious communities at local, national, and international levels. A significant issue for political science of religion is whether it is anything more than a nascent discipline. Kettell (2012) notes that, in the preceding decade, religion received far less attention than other themes in political science, and far less attention in political science than in sociology. Central topics for political science of religion include separation of church and state, religious toleration, and the role of religion in public deliberation.

Psychology of religion applies psychological methods and interpretative frameworks to religious traditions and religious/non-religious individuals in search of detailed accounts of the origin and function of religious beliefs and religious behaviours. Early influential figures in the field include William James, the psychoanalysts Sigmund Freud, Alfred Adler and Erich Fromm, and the 'trait' theorist Gordon Allport. Psychologists of religion have conducted empirical studies of correlations between religiosity and physical health, religiosity and mental health, religiosity and prejudice, based on psychometric assessments of religiosity and psychological typologies of religions and religious development. Psychologists of religion have also conducted empirical studies on the effect of petitionary prayer on the health outcomes of objects of those prayers.

Cognitive science of religion – which might be viewed as a sub-field of psychology of religion – studies religions, religious thought, and religious behaviour, from the perspective of cognitive and evolutionary sciences. Major figures in this new field include Scott Atran, Patrick Boyer, Stewart Guthrie, Thomas Lawson, Robert McCauley, Ara Norenzayan, Jason Slone, Richard Sosis, Dan Sperber, Harvey Whitehouse and David Sloan Wilson, among many others.

There is much that remains contested in the scientific study of religion. While a significant amount of data has been collected – including, in particular, a significant amount of demographic data – the data that we have is not globally representative. Moreover, for controversial questions – e.g., concerning correlations between religiosity and other valued or disvalued attributes – there are questions about the interpretation of the data that we do have even in the case of well-studied populations, e.g., in the United States. The studies in this area that most bear reporting are carefully conducted meta-analyses that analyse a significant range of prior studies. I shall here just mention a few meta-analyses from the psychology of religion.

Hall *et al.* (2010) found that greater religious identification, greater extrinsic religiosity, and greater religious fundamentalism are all positively correlated with racism; only those religious individuals with a questioning orientation towards religion proved racially tolerant. Whitely (2009) found that all forms of religiosity except quest and extrinsic orientation had at least small negative correlations with attitudes towards lesbians and gay men. Masters and Spielmans (2007) found that distant intercessory prayer has no discernible effect on the health outcomes of the objects of those prayers. Jim *et al.* (2015) found that religion or spirituality is positively correlated with better physical health outcomes in cancer patients. Ano and Vasconcelles (2016) found that there is a positive correlation between religious coping strategies and psychological adjustments to stress. Lodi-Smith and Roberts (2007) found that the extent of investment in religion is positively correlated with agreeableness, conscientiousness, emotional stability, and low psychotism (and that there are similar correlations for investment in family, work, and volunteerism). Wu *et al.* (2015) found that religion plays a protective role against suicide in a majority of settings where suicide research is conducted, but the effect varies based on cultural and religious context.

Results in psychology of religion are correlational; they do not establish loci of causation. Moreover, as suggested in the parenthetical observation in connection with Lodi-Smith and Roberts (2007), results in the psychology of religion do not show that religiosity – or irreligiosity – is a *unique* source of benefits or harms with which it correlates. When we dig into the details provided by sciences that are actually engaged in the study of religion, we see that these sciences do not now – and are not ever likely to – provide decisive reasons for humanity to abandon religion.

7. Concluding remarks

The question posed at the beginning of this chapter is whether science defeats religion.

Science is a collective enterprise of data-driven description, prediction, and understanding in which universal expert agreement functions as regulative ideal, and hence in which (a) reproducibility, parsimony, and consilience are fundamental values; (b) there are strict protocols governing the conduct of experiments and the collection and analysis of data; and (c) there are significant institutions devoted to protecting the integrity of scientific investigation, publication, accreditation, recognition, and reward.

Given what science is, it is clear that science is not a religion, even though the institutions of science are grounded in commitments to the values and imperatives (a)–(c). So the claim that science defeats religion does not fall at the very first hurdle.

While there is clear evidence that collectively pre-eminent scientists are less religious than the population at large, scientists are distributed across the full spectrum of religiosity; there is no good argument from the collective diminished religiosity of pre-eminent scientists to the claim that science defeats religion.

There is nothing in the detailed findings of the sciences that study religion that suggests that there is reason for humanity to abandon religion; on the contrary, research in, for example, psychology of religion, paints a mixed picture of the costs and benefits of religious adherence.

Many religious denominations and sects make false claims about the global compatibility of their religious teachings with science. However, that many religious denominations and sects make these false claims does not justify the claim that there is, and must be, 'war' between science and religion; it is consistent with there being many religious denominations and sects that make false claims about the global compatibility of their religious teachings with science that the teachings of some religious denominations and sects are globally compatible with the teachings of science.

Standard 'models' of 'the relationship between science and religion' should all be rejected. There is no room for 'dialogue' between religion and science, and no possibility of 'integration'. Since the views of some religious denominations and sects conflict with science, it is not true that religion and science are 'independent'. And, as already noted, whether religion and science are in 'conflict' depends upon whether there are religious denominations and sects whose teachings are globally compatible with the teachings of science.

Finally – the key observation – there is good reason to think that there can be – and that there are – religious denominations and sects whose religious beliefs are not in conflict with science. In particular, religious adherents who accept that natural reality does not have any on-going causal interaction with non-natural causal reality need not find themselves in conflict with any established science.

8 Does naturalism defeat religion?

The claim that naturalism defeats religion is not plausible on its face. Naturalism has been widely discussed in academic philosophy for at least the past sixty years. If it is true that naturalism defeats religion, then it is hard to understand why a substantial proportion of academic philosophers are religious. In this chapter, I shall make the strongest case for naturalism that I am able to construct, and then I shall examine the shortcomings of that case.

1. Outline

The best case for naturalism that I have been able to construct depends upon three principal claims.

The first claim is that there is a sense in which best naturalistic big pictures are *minimal*: the only theoretical commitments that best naturalistic big pictures have are theoretical commitments that they share with all other best big pictures; all other best big pictures have additional theoretical commitments beyond the theoretical commitments of best naturalistic big pictures.

The second claim is that there is a sense in which best naturalistic big pictures are *maximal*: with respect to breadth, depth, and adequacy of explanation, best naturalistic big pictures do at least as well as any other best big pictures.

The third claim is that, if, among best big pictures, there is a type of big picture that is minimal with respect to theoretical commitments and maximal with respect to breadth, depth, and adequacy of explanation, then those best big picture are *the very best* big pictures.

These three principal claims jointly entail that the very best big pictures are best naturalistic big pictures. Hence, given that no consistent religious big pictures are naturalistic – which entails, in particular, that no best religious big pictures are naturalistic – it follows that naturalism defeats religion: best naturalistic big pictures are better than best religious big pictures.

Before I turn to the task of assessing the truth of these claims, I need to give some further explanation of their content.

2. Background: big pictures

In Chapter 2, Section 4, I said that big pictures are the best approximations that we can have to worldviews, i.e., to comprehensive descriptive, evaluative, and normative theories of everything.

I take it that, roughly, the true comprehensive theory of everything is a non-trivial theory that contains every truth. I say 'roughly' because this account may require some finessing in order to handle truth-theoretic paradoxes such as the liar paradox. Note that this formulation leaves it open that the comprehensive theory of everything contains true contradictions.

For convenience, I shall say that the true comprehensive theory of everything is a set of *propositions*; others might prefer to couch this part of the discussion in terms of sentences. Moreover, I shall suppose – for convenience, for this part of the discussion – that the true comprehensive theory of everything is the logical closure of a finite set of logically independent, non-negated, propositions $p_1, \ldots, p_n$. Given these simplifying assumptions, *non-trivial worldviews* are all of the finite sets of logically independent propositions $q_1, \ldots, q_n$, where each of the q_i is either p_i or $\sim p_i$.

It seems reasonable to say that the true theory of everything is not something that we will ever be able to formulate. It may require for its formulation concepts that we shall never grasp, perhaps because those concepts lie forever beyond our grasp. Even if it doesn't require for its formulation concepts that we shall never grasp, it does require for its formulation information that we shall never possess, perhaps because that information is such that it is impossible for us to acquire it. (Consider, for example, detailed information that is never accessible within our light-cone.)

It also seems reasonable to say that, if we could formulate non-trivial worldviews, it might turn out that we were undecided between some of them. Suppose, for example, that I am undecided whether q_j, and that W_1 and W_2 are the two worldviews that differ only on qj. In that case, by a natural extension of terminology, we might say that my worldview is $W_1 v W_2$.

Suppose that one person has the worldview W_1 and another person has the worldview W_2. If they were somehow able to discuss their worldview disagreement, these people could take for granted all of the propositions on which they agree: all of the q_i except for q_j. I shall say that, in a worldview disagreement of this kind, the logical closure of the propositions on which the parties agree is what they are entitled to take to be *data* to their disagreement. (True enough, in this case, the data is irrelevant to the disagreement, since the p_i are logically independent. But there is nothing else that is a candidate to be data to their disagreement.)

Given that big pictures are our best approximations to worldviews, what can we say about them?

One thought is that a big picture is a worldview in which no judgment is made about most propositions: while big pictures aspire to be complete worldviews, they simply fall short in this aspiration. On this proposal, perhaps, at any given time a person's big picture is just the set of that person's beliefs at that time. (Or perhaps it is the set of that person's commitments at that time, where a person's commitments are whatever falls in the logical closure of their beliefs, or, perhaps, whatever falls in some suitably restricted part of the logical closure of their beliefs.) It is not clear that this is the most fruitful way of thinking about big pictures.

A better thought is that a big picture is something like the logical closure of a set of *big picture propositions*, where big picture propositions are the contents of answers to *big picture questions*: Do we have *a priori* knowledge? Are there abstract objects? Are there objective aesthetic values? Are there analytic propositions? Is epistemic justification internalist? Is there an external world? Do we have libertarian free will? Does God exist? Are there laws of nature? Is logic classical? Is mental content internalist? Is the mind purely physical? Is moral motivation internalist? Should normative ethics be consequentialist? Is perceptual experience representational? Is personal identity biological? Should politics be egalitarian? Are proper names Fregean? Is time B-theoretic? Is truth epistemic? And so on. Given that we think about big pictures in this way, we can take those who are undecided on some questions to have disjunctive big pictures. However, we cannot merely stipulate or assume that big picture propositions are – or are not – logically independent from one another. And we need an alternative account of data that we can use when considering big picture disagreement: in my view, the best path is to include everything that is commonly established, including everything that is established science, to be data to any such disagreement.

The view of participants in big picture disagreements that emerges is something like this: they believe a set of big picture propositions, which gives them a commitment to the logical closure of that set of big picture propositions; and they believe a whole bunch of other stuff, much of which can serve as data in big picture disagreements if it is accepted by other parties to the disagreement.

3. Background: idealisation

Given what I have just said about big pictures and data, it is clear that no two people will have the same big picture and data. Among people who share particular big picture propositions – e.g., among those who believe that natural reality exhausts causal reality and that scientific method is our touchstone for identifying denizens of causal reality – there will be significant variation in the epistemic merits of their big pictures, and there will be significant variation in the epistemic merits of their data. Moreover, among those people, there will also be significant variation in, for example, intelligence, analytical skills, debating skills, and so forth.

When we think about big picture disagreement – or, equivalently, when we think about the philosophical assessment of the merits of big pictures – we are not interested in idiosyncratic disputes that arise due to variation in intelligence, analytical skills, debating skills, and so forth. Rather, we are interested in the merits of the big pictures themselves. But what exactly does that mean? Not that we are interested in the merits of big pictures that people actually have: as we have already noted, the big pictures that people actually have are idiosyncratic in all kinds of respects. What we are interested in is *idealised* big pictures: *the best big pictures* that we can formulate that are committed to particular big picture propositions.

At least roughly, then, the framework for subsequent discussion is this. We are interested in assessing best big pictures: the best theories incorporating answers to the big questions. In assessing best big pictures, we need to consider them in conjunction with data, i.e., in conjunction with everything that is commonly established, including everything that is established science. We can think of axiomatisations of best big pictures and data as idealisations of complete networks of individuals' beliefs; and we can think of the logical closure of those axiomatisations as idealisations of the commitments of complete networks of individuals' beliefs.

4. Background: method

In principle, there are three steps to be taken in the resolution of big picture disagreement, i.e., in the ranking of the merits of competing big pictures.

The first step is *articulation*. Ideally, we should give a complete statement of the big pictures that are up for assessment, and a complete statement of the data that is, or may be, relevant to that assessment. In practice, the best that we can do is to provide articulations of the competing big pictures with the same degree of care, and to the same level of detail, and to say enough about the relevant data to allow assessment to proceed. Where there is dispute about whether something is data – i.e., where there is dispute about whether something is commonly established – we might consider counting the relevant claims as part of the big pictures rather than as part of the data. Whether we should do this depends upon the goals of the particular analysis of competing big pictures.

The second step is *internal review*. Ideally, we should determine (a) whether the big pictures are consistent, and (b) whether the conjunctions of big pictures and data are consistent, for a range of relevant kinds of consistency: logical, probabilistic, explanatory, and so forth. In practice, the best we can do is to search for inconsistencies in the competing big pictures and the competing conjunctions of big pictures with data, with the same degree of care and effort. Where inconsistency is discovered, we have sufficient reason to claim that the particular big picture under assessment is not one of the very best big pictures. (Those who think that some kinds of inconsistency are tolerable should suppose that I am here just talking about intolerable inconsistencies.)

The third step is *comparison*. Ideally, we compare all of the theoretical virtues of all of the big pictures that are up for assessment, and make a ranking of these big pictures in terms of their overall theoretical virtue relative to the data that is being used for the purposes of the evaluation. In practice, we make the best assessment that we can of the overall theoretical virtue of the big pictures that are up for assessment, relative to the data that is being used for the assessment, giving the same level of care and effort to our assessment of each of the competing big pictures. At the end of this third stage of our procedure, we have identified the big picture that is the very best big picture, or the big pictures that are the very best big pictures.

In Oppy (2013a), I exhibit the use of this method in the assessment of the relative merits of best naturalistic and best theistic big pictures.

5. Background: theoretical virtues

There are many things that are said to be theoretical virtues. Ultimately, for our purposes, the assessment of overall theoretical virtue is a trade-off between two overarching virtues: minimisation of theoretical commitments and maximisation of explanatory breadth and depth.

One family of theoretical virtues concerns the 'internal' merits of theories: consistency of the theory, coherence of the theory, consistency of the theory with the data, and so forth. This family of theoretical virtues is assessed in the second stage of our assessment process. Theories that lack these virtues are not worth assessing for other theoretical virtues.

Another family of theoretical virtues concerns the utility of theories: fruitfulness, applicability, predictive power, and so on. While these virtues are important for scientific theories, they have no role to play in the comparative assessment of big pictures.

The final two families of theoretical virtues are, in some sense, in competition with one another. On the one hand, there are the virtues associated with the minimisation of theoretical commitment: simplicity, unification, beauty, and the like; and on the other hand, there are the virtues associated with maximisation of explanatory breadth and depth: explanatory breadth, explanatory depth, explanatory fit with established science, and so forth. Almost all accounts of theoretical virtues recognise that best theories make the best trade-off between minimisation of theoretical commitment and maximisation of explanatory breadth and depth.

When we compare big pictures on given data, we are looking to see which of those big pictures makes the best trade-off between minimisation of theoretical commitment and maximisation of explanatory breadth and depth. While it is controversial whether there is a general algorithm for making these evaluations – and while it is also controversial, given that there is a general algorithm for making these evaluations, which algorithm that is – it is not controversial that there are some decidable cases. In particular, if some theories have fewer commitments than all other theories, and yet do not worse on the count of explanatory breadth and depth than all other theories, then those theories are the very best theories.

6. Background: shortcut

Given what I have said to this point, it is clear that a full, detailed argument for the superiority of the best naturalistic big pictures to other best big pictures would be a Herculean task. I am not proposing to try to carry out this task, here or elsewhere. Rather, I aim to develop an argument about what the outcome of carrying out that task of comparing best big pictures would be. That argument has two major premises.

The first major premise is that the best naturalistic big pictures are *minimal*: the best naturalistic big pictures have fewer commitments than any of the best big pictures that are in serious competition with it.

The second major premise is that the best naturalistic big pictures are *maximal*: the best naturalistic big pictures have no less explanatory breadth and depth than competing best big pictures.

Given these two premises, and given the conclusion of the preceding description of theoretical virtues, we arrive at the view that the best naturalistic big pictures are the best big pictures. So, in particular, best naturalistic big pictures are better than religious big pictures. In this sense, naturalism defeats religion.

7. Premise 1

Naturalistic big pictures are characterised by their commitment to the following two claims: (1) causal reality is natural reality; and (2) scientific method is our touchstone for identifying denizens of causal reality. Why should we suppose that it follows that best naturalistic big pictures are *minimal*?

The first point to note is that every best big picture that is in serious competition with best naturalistic big pictures is committed to natural causal reality. Moreover, any best big picture that is in serious competition with best naturalistic big pictures is committed to the claim that scientific method correctly identifies denizens of natural causal reality. Thus, every best big picture that is in serious competition with best naturalistic big pictures is committed to the full inventory of denizens of natural causal reality – objects, powers – that is vouchsafed by science. But that's just to say that any best big picture that is in serious competition with best naturalistic big pictures is committed to everything to which naturalistic big pictures are committed. Moreover, given that any best big picture that is in serious competition with best naturalistic big pictures is not naturalistic, any best big picture that is in serious competition with best naturalistic big pictures has commitments to causal entities – objects, powers – beyond the denizens of natural reality. So, insofar as we limit our attention to the causal domain, best naturalistic big pictures have fewer commitments than any of the best big pictures with which they are in competition.

The next point to note is that other potential sources of theoretical commitments – e.g., the evaluative, the normative, the abstract, and so forth – are, from the standpoint of the development of further types of theoretical commitments, entirely independent of the causal domain: there is no reduction of the types of commitments engendered by the evaluative, or the normative, or the abstract, to the types of commitments engendered by the causal. But, if the types of commitments engendered by the evaluative, the normative, the abstract, and so forth are independent of the types of commitments engendered by the causal, then the best big pictures are simply best big picture treatments of the causal conjoined with best big picture treatments of the evaluative, the normative, the abstract, and so forth. And, if the best pictures are simply best big picture treatments of the causal conjoined with best big picture treatments of the evaluative, the normative, the abstract, and so forth, then, given that best naturalistic big pictures have fewer commitments than other best big pictures with respect to the causal domain, best naturalistic big pictures have fewer commitments than other best big pictures *tout court*.

The claim that the types of commitments engendered by the evaluative, the normative, the abstract, and so forth are independent of the types of commitments engendered by the causal is controversial, at least in some quarters. For example, some *theists* have claimed that the evaluative and the normative can be reduced to divine commands, and that the abstract can be reduced to divine mental activities. However, the putative reduction of the evaluative, the normative, the abstract, and so forth, to the causal activities of a causal agent makes it impossible for the evaluative, the normative, the abstract, and so on, to apply to that agent prior to those causal activities. Theists who suppose that God is good, and right, and one, independently of God's issuing commands and having thoughts, cannot consistently suppose that the evaluative and the normative reduce to divine commands and that the abstract reduces to divine mental activities. And theists who deny that God is good, and right, and one, independently of God's issuing commands and having thoughts, can give no adequate account of the necessity of the evaluative, the normative and the abstract. (See Oppy [forthcoming a][forthcoming b] for much more elaborate development of this argument.)

The claim that every best big picture has all of the causal commitments of best naturalistic big pictures, and more besides, is also controversial, at least in some quarters. For example, some *idealists* have claimed that they do not have any commitment to natural causal reality: they deny that there is anything other than minds and their contents. However, it seems to me that best idealist big pictures are bound to have commitments that exactly mirror – and so carry the same theoretical cost as – the commitments of best naturalistic big pictures, and more besides. After all, plausible idealist big pictures do not treat experience as surd; rather, they offer causal explanations for our having the experiences that we do. Typically, these explanations advert to models of natural reality – in a divine mind – the description of which is the task of the natural sciences: for each causal item or relation that is reckoned by naturalists – on the basis of some range of experience – to occur in natural reality, there is a causal item or relation in the divine model that the idealist reckons on the basis of that same range of experiences. Since the match between the naturalist's natural reality and the idealist's model in the divine mind is perfect – at least in principle – and since idealists are committed to causal entities – e.g., God – to which naturalists are not committed, it is clear that best naturalistic big pictures are less committing than best idealist big pictures. (See Oppy [forthcoming a] for a much more elaborate rendition of this argument.)

Despite the demurral of some, the claim that best naturalistic big pictures are *minimal* is widely accepted, even by those who suppose that there are better big pictures than best naturalistic big pictures. Particularly given my account of science, naturalism, and religion, it really is very plausible to suppose that best naturalistic big pictures are less committing than best religious big pictures.

8. Premise 2 (overview)

The claim that best naturalistic big pictures have no less explanatory breadth and depth than competing best big pictures is evidently controversial. There are many areas where proponents of competing best big pictures suppose their views have greater explanatory breadth and depth than the best naturalistic big pictures.

Some suppose there are competing best big pictures that give better explanations than those given by best naturalistic big pictures for what I shall call *general causal features* of natural causal reality: (1) the *existence* of natural causal reality; (2) the *continuing existence* of natural causal reality; (3) the *occurrence* of causal processes in natural causal reality; and (4) the *continuing occurrence* of causal processes in natural causal reality. According to some, one or more of these general causal features of natural causal reality is better explained by best big pictures that are not best naturalistic big pictures than by best naturalistic big pictures.

Some suppose that there are competing best big pictures that give better explanations than those given by best naturalistic big pictures for what I shall call *general design features* of natural causal reality: (1) the alleged fine-tuning of fundamental cosmic parameters in natural causal reality; (2) the emergence of life in natural causal reality; and (3) the continuing existence of life in natural causal reality. According to some, one or more of these general design features of natural causal reality is better explained by best big pictures that are not best naturalistic big pictures than by best naturalistic big pictures.

Some suppose that there are competing best big pictures that give better explanations than those given by best naturalistic big pictures for the existence of *mental capacities and phenomena* in natural causal reality: (1) consciousness; (2) reason; and (3) *a priori* knowledge. According to some, the instantiation of one or more of these mental capacities and phenomena in natural causal reality is better explained by best big pictures that are not best naturalistic big pictures than by best naturalistic big pictures.

Some suppose that there are competing best big pictures that give better explanations than those given by best naturalistic big pictures for what I shall call *reports of the naturalistically anomalous* in natural reality: (1) reports of miraculous interventions, episodes, activities, and phenomena; (2) reports of other non-natural interventions, episodes, activities, entities, and phenomena. According to some, one or more of these reports of the naturalistically anomalous is better explained by best big pictures that are not best naturalistic big pictures than by best naturalistic big pictures.

Some suppose that there are competing best big pictures that give better explanations than those given by best naturalistic big pictures for the existence and nature of *religious experience* in natural causal reality: (1) mystical experience; (2) religious dreams; (3) religious visions; (4) religious perception of the mundane; and (5) religious perception of the religious. According to some, the occurrence of instances of one or more of these kinds of religious experiences in natural causal reality is better explained by best big pictures that are not best naturalistic big pictures than by best naturalistic big pictures.

Some suppose that there are competing best big pictures that give better explanations than those given by best naturalistic big pictures for the initial and/or continuing existence of *religiously significant artifacts*: (1) religious texts; and (2) religious relics. According to some, the occurrence of instances of one or more of these kinds of religiously significant artifacts in natural causal reality is better explained by best big pictures that are not best naturalistic big pictures than by best naturalistic big pictures.

Some suppose that there are competing best big pictures that give better explanations than those given by best naturalistic big pictures for what I shall call *religious communication*: (1) divination; (2) omens; (3) linguistic communication with non-natural agents; and (4) non-linguistic communication with non-natural agents. According to some, the reported efficacy of one or more of these methods is better explained by best big pictures that are not best naturalistic big pictures than by best naturalistic big pictures.

In the following sections of this chapter, we shall consider whether any of these cases gives us reason to suppose that there are some areas in which best big pictures that are not best naturalistic best pictures have greater explanatory breadth and depth than best naturalistic big pictures.

9. Premise 2 (general causal features)

Either causal reality involves an infinite regress or causal reality has an initial part: 'the initial singularity'. Whether or not there is an 'initial singularity', causal reality continues to exist, and the state of causal reality evolves, without any external input. If there is an initial singularity, then either it exists of necessity, or its existence is brutely contingent; if there is an initial singularity, then either it possesses some of its properties as a matter of brute contingency or it possesses all of its properties as a matter of necessity. Whether or not there is an initial singularity, the continuing existence of causal reality is either a matter of necessity or it is a matter of brute contingency.

It is currently a matter of dispute whether causal reality involves an infinite regress; it is currently a matter of dispute whether the existence of an initial singularity is necessary or brutely contingent; it is currently a matter of dispute whether the properties of an initial singularity are all necessary or include some that are brutely contingent; it is currently a matter of dispute whether the continuing existence of causal reality is necessary or a matter of contingency.

Suppose that best big pictures say that causal reality involves an infinite regress. Then best naturalistic big pictures say that there is just an infinitely regressing natural reality whose state evolves without any external input. Competing best big pictures postulate either another kind of infinitely regressing entity that evolves the state of an infinitely regressing natural reality without any kind of external input, or else another kind of infinitely regressing entity that evolves the state of a finite natural reality without any external input. Either way, competing best big pictures clearly score no better than best naturalistic big pictures in point of their explanatory adequacy; either way, the [continuing] existence of causal reality and the [continuing] occurrence of causal processes in causal reality are explained by appeal to infinite regress on state evolution in the absence of external input.

Suppose that best big pictures say that there is an initial singularity that exists of necessity and that has all of its properties of necessity. Then, best naturalistic big pictures say that there is just a causal-past-finite, necessarily existing natural reality whose state evolves without any external input. Competing best big pictures say that there is a causal-past-finite, necessarily existing causal reality whose state evolves without any external input in which natural reality is a merely contingently existing sub-part whose evolution of state is, at least in part, due to causes external to it. Competing best big pictures clearly score no better than best naturalistic big pictures in point of their explanatory adequacy: either way, the [continuing] existence of causal reality and the [continuing] occurrence of causal processes in causal reality are explained by appeal to [brute] necessity.

Suppose that best big pictures say that there is an initial singularity that exists contingently and that has some of its properties contingently. Then, best naturalistic big pictures say that there is just a causal-past-finite, brutely contingently existing natural reality whose state brutely contingently evolves without any external input. Competing best big pictures say that there is a causal-past-finite, brutely contingently existing causal reality whose state brutely contingently evolves without any external input, in which natural reality is a contingently existing sub-part whose evolution of state is, at least in part, due to contingent causes external to it. Competing best big pictures clearly score no better than best naturalistic big pictures in point of their explanatory adequacy: either way, the [continuing] existence of causal reality and the [continuing] occurrence of causal processes in causal reality are explained by appeal to [brute] contingency.

Suppose, finally, that best big pictures say that there is an initial singularity that exists of necessity, but that has some of its properties contingently. Then, best naturalistic big pictures say that there is just a causal-past-finite, necessarily existing natural reality whose state brutely contingently evolves without any external input. Competing best big pictures say that there is a causal-past-finite, necessarily existing causal reality whose state brutely contingently evolves without any external input, in which natural reality is a contingently existing sub-part whose evolution of state is, at least in part, due to contingent causes external to it. Competing best big pictures clearly score no better than naturalistic best big pictures in point of their explanatory adequacy: either way, the [continuing] existence of causal reality and the [continuing] occurrence of causal processes in causal reality are explained by an appeal to exactly the same kind of mix of [brute] necessity and [brute] contingency.

No matter what turns out to be the best view to take on the currently disputed questions about the explanation of the [continuing] existence of causal reality and the [continuing] occurrence of causal processes, best big pictures – whether naturalistic or non-naturalistic – will incorporate that view. Consequently, consideration about these general causal features cannot possibly give any explanatory advantage to non-naturalistic big pictures.

I anticipate that some may object that there is explanatory advantage to be gained by judicious postulation of the properties of the cause of the [continuing] existence of natural reality and the [continuing] occurrence of causal processes in natural reality. Suppose, for example, that you insist that the cause, of the [continuing] existence of natural reality and the [continuing] occurrence of causal processes in natural reality, is existence itself, pure act, a simple, eternal, infinite, and largely incomprehensible we know not quite what. Aren't you better placed than naturalists because you – but not they – have no causal explanation of the [continuing] existence of natural reality and the [continuing] occurrence of causal processes in natural reality?

Not at all! True enough, you do have a causal explanation of the [continuing] existence of natural reality and the [continuing] occurrence of causal processes in natural reality. But, on your view, causal reality also includes existence itself, pure act, a simple, eternal, infinite, and largely incomprehensible we know not quite what. What explains the [continuing] existence of existence itself, pure act, a simple, eternal, infinite, and largely incomprehensible we know not quite what, and what explains its [continuing] participation in causal processes? Don't say that these things explain themselves! That's absurd: 'A because A' is *always* an explanatory solecism. There are no options beyond those that we have already canvassed: either brute necessity or brute contingency. But if, for example, you suppose that it is brutely necessary that existence itself – pure act, a simple, eternal, infinite, and largely incomprehensible we know not quite what – exists, then your view has no explanatory advantage, over the view of the naturalist who supposes that it is brutely necessary that there is an initial singularity, when it comes to explanation of the [continuing] existence of natural reality and the [continuing] occurrence of causal processes in natural reality.

10. Premise 2 (general design features)

In the current standard model of particle physics, there are twenty-five 'freely adjustable' parameters (plus the cosmological constant). The current standard model is not final physical theory: it includes both quantum mechanics and general relativity, even though these theories are known to be inconsistent at sufficiently high energy levels. While it is uncertain whether any of the current contenders for final physical theory – string theory, loop quantum gravity – are final physical theory, it is clear that we should not just assume that there are so many – or, indeed, any – 'freely adjustable' parameters in final physics.

But let's pretend. Suppose it is true that there are dozens of 'freely adjustable' parameters in final physical theory. Suppose, too, that – as is currently the case for the twenty-five independent universal dimensionless physical constants in the standard model of particle physics – if any one of these 'freely adjustable' parameters took a value only very slightly different from its actual value, then either our universe would have been very short-lived – on the order of a second or less – or else our universe would have expanded so rapidly that it would always have consisted of more or less nothing but empty space. Is this 'fine-tuning' of the 'freely adjustable' parameters in the standard model of particle physics something that is less well-explained in best naturalistic big pictures than in other best big pictures?

We are supposing that, somewhere in actual causal history – i.e., somewhere in actual causal reality – the values of the 'freely adjustable' parameters are set. While, in principle, given the independence of these parameters, it may be that the actual current values of different parameters are set at different points in actual causal history, it is a harmless simplification in the ensuing discussion to suppose that there is no more than one point at which all of the actual current values of the various parameters are set.

What does it mean to say that, at some point in the actual causal order, the values of the parameters are 'set' to be their current actual values? At least this: that, at all subsequent points in the actual causal order at which the parameters take values, absent causal intervention, the values of the parameters are their current actual values. (In order to simplify the subsequent discussion, I shall assume that there is no subsequent causal intervention: if, at some point in the causal order, the values of the parameters are set to their current actual values, then the parameters do not take anything other than those current actual values in subsequent actual causal history.)

Given the simplifying assumption that there is no more than one point in causal reality at which the actual current values of the parameters are set, there are two significant hypotheses about where in the actual causal order the values of the parameters are set. It could be that, at every point in the actual causal order, the values of the parameters are set; or it could be that there is some initial part of the actual causal order in which the values of the parameters are not set, leading up to a point at which the parameters are set to their current actual values.

Suppose that it is true at all points in the actual causal order that the values of the parameters are set to their current actual values. Given that the parameters are 'freely adjustable', we assume that it is possible for the parameters to take values other than the values that they currently actually take: it could have been that the values of the parameters are other than the current actual values. But, necessarily, given that it is possible for the parameters to take values other than the values that they currently actually take, and given that, at *all* points in the actual causal order, the values of the parameters are set to their current actual values, there is nothing that *initially assigns* the current actual values to the parameters. (If there is an initial assigning of the current actual values of the parameters, then (a) that initial assigning is part of the causal order, and (b) that initial assigning brings about a transition from a state in which the values of the parameters are not yet set to a state in which the values of the parameters are set. Yet, *ex hypothesi*, there can be no such transition.) So, on the hypotheses in play, it is a matter of *brute contingency* that the parameters initially take the values that they do. That is: given that it is true, at all points in the causal order, that the values of the parameters are set to their current actual values, any best big picture will be committed to the claim that it is simply a matter of brute contingency that the values of the parameters are initially set to their current actual values.

Suppose, instead, that there is some initial part of the actual causal order in which the values of the parameters are not already set, leading up to a 'choice point' at which the parameters are set to their current actual values. Given that the parameters are 'freely adjustable', it is possible, at the 'choice point', for the parameters to be set to values other than the values that the parameters currently actually have. But, given that (a) the values of the parameters are not set prior to the 'choice point', and (b) that it is possible at the 'choice point' for the parameters to be set to values other than the values that the parameters currently actually have, the setting of the values at the 'choice point' is a matter of *brute contingency*. (We are supposing that it is possible that, at the 'choice point', the values of the parameters are set so that the universe is very short-lived; and we are supposing that it is possible at the 'choice point', that the values of the parameters are set so that the universe is almost always and everywhere empty space. It must be that, if we suppose that it is not a matter of brute contingency that the values of the parameters are set to the current actual values rather than to some other possible values, then we suppose that there is an explanation why, at the 'choice point', the values of the parameters were set to the current actual values rather than to some other possible values. But it also must be that any explanation why, at the 'choice point', the values of the parameters were set to the current actual values rather than to some other possible values appeals to features of some prior point of causal reality that themselves set the values of the parameters at that earlier point in causal reality.) So, on the hypotheses in play, it is a matter of brute contingency that the parameters take on the values that they do. That is: given that there is some initial part of the actual causal order in which the values of the parameters are not already set, leading up to a 'choice point' at which the parameters are set to their current actual values, any best big picture will be committed to the claim that it is simply a matter of brute contingency that the values of the parameters are set to the current actual values.

Drawing the threads together, I conclude that, *given* that it is true that the 'freely adjustable' parameters in final physical theory are set to certain values, and *given* that it is possible for those parameters to be set to very different values, all best big pictures say that it is ultimately a matter of brute contingency that the 'freely adjustable' parameters are set to the values to which they are actually set. While this conclusion holds whether there is just one setting of 'adjustable parameters' that holds for all of natural causal reality, or whether there are different settings of 'adjustable parameters' for different parts of natural causal reality, it is worth noting that, in the latter case, there must be 'choice points': it cannot be that there is an 'initial setting' for all of natural causal reality if there are different settings for different parts of natural causal reality. It will simplify the rest of our discussion if we suppose that our universe exhausts natural causal reality.

Given the abstract level at which the argument has preceded, it may help to fill in some details for competing best big pictures (under the simplifying assumptions that we have made).

According to best naturalistic big pictures, our universe is characterised by a set of brutely contingent 'adjustable parameters' that either have always characterised it, or else that have characterised it since the universe reached a 'choice point' at which the values were fixed. (If our universe is characterised by a set of 'adjustable parameters' that have always characterised it, then it is possible – for all that has been argued to this point – that best naturalistic big pictures say that it is *necessary* that the 'adjustable parameters' take the values that they do. That the 'parameters' are 'adjustable' entails only that they must be 'put in by hand': they are not fixed by any more fundamental theory; it is consistent with the 'adjustable' nature of the 'parameters' that their values are nonetheless necessary: the values simply could not be other than what they actually are. While I think that this is an attractive theoretical option, I do not propose to spruik for it here.)

According to competing best big pictures on which there is some non-natural agency that *assigns* the values of the 'adjustable parameters' in our universe, there is some feature of that non-natural agency that is keyed to the setting of the values of the 'adjustable parameters' and that explains why the 'parameters' take the values that they do. To the extent that this explanation is not itself an appeal to brute contingency – the non-natural agency rolls the cosmic dice – the relevant features of the agency that ultimately explains the assignment of values to the 'parameters' are brutely contingent features of that agency. Given the assumption that it is possible for the 'parameters' to take on values other than the values that they actually take on, there is no alternative theoretical option. Thus, according to other best big pictures, our universe is characterised by a set of 'adjustable parameters' that either have always characterised it, or else that have characterised it since the universe reached a 'choice point' at which the values were fixed, where the features of the non-natural agency that explain the assignment of values to the 'adjustable parameters' are brutely contingent in just the same way that the 'parameters' themselves are brutely contingent in best naturalistic big pictures. (As we noted in connection with best naturalistic big pictures, it is possible – for all that has been argued to this point – that best competing big pictures on which there is some non-natural agency that assigns the values of the 'adjustable parameters' in our universe hold that it is necessary that those agents have features that determine that they assign the values that they do to the 'adjustable parameters'. This is an equally attractive theoretical option for those competing best big pictures.)

The upshot is clear: there is no explanatory advantage that accrues to either best naturalistic big pictures or to competing best big pictures that hold that there is some non-natural agency that *assigns* the values of the 'adjustable parameters' in our universe. Exactly the same mix of brute contingency and brute necessity figures in the ultimate explanations in both kinds of best big pictures.

I anticipate that some will object that the costs of the postulation of non-natural agency are met – at least in part – by the explanation of the setting of the values of the 'adjustable parameters' as the result of assignment by that non-natural agency. But this assessment just gets the accounting wrong. There is exactly as much that has no explanation on views that postulate non-natural agency as there is on naturalistic views: insofar as we restrict our attention to the 'freely adjustable parameters' in the current standard model of particle physics, the postulation of that non-natural agency is pure cost.

I anticipate that some will say that there are 'general design features' other than the 'freely adjustable parameters' of the current standard model of particle physics that are given better explanations in competing best big pictures than in best naturalistic big pictures. In particular, I anticipate that some will say that this is true for (a) the emergence of life in natural reality, and (b) the continuing existence of life in natural reality. However, I think that it is obvious, given the case that I have made that best naturalistic big pictures do no worse than competing best big pictures in explaining general causal features of causal reality *and* the values taken by the 'freely adjustable parameters' of the current standard model of particle physics, that best naturalistic big pictures do no worse than competing big pictures in explaining (a) the emergence of life in natural reality, and (b) the continuing existence of life in natural reality.

11. Premise 2 (mind)

Well-established science gives us no reason to suppose that minded entities are anything other than *late* and *local*. The only minded entities currently recognised by established science are relatively recently evolved biological organisms on our planet. It is an open question whether science will one day identify minded entities on other planets; but, if it does, there is nothing in established science to suggest that those entities will be anything other than either (1) relatively recently evolved biological organisms or (2) downstream causal products of the activities of relatively recently evolved biological organisms.

According to well-established science, human beings are relatively recently evolved biological organisms. Each human organism has its origins in the fusion of a human sperm and a human ovum. In each human organism, there is ante-natal development of various biological systems, including neural systems, whose operations are necessary for the continuing post-natal existence of that human organism. For each human organism, those various biological systems eventually cease working, never to resume. The death of each organism is followed by decay: eventually, there are no 'mortal remains' for any human organism.

Much well-established science allows that minded organisms are properly described using a range of *mental* vocabulary: minded organisms are *conscious* organisms; minded organisms have *agency*; minded organisms *perceive* their immediate surroundings; some – perhaps all – minded organisms *believe, desire,* and *intend*; some – perhaps all – minded organisms *remember, learn,* and *predict*; some – perhaps all – minded organisms *feel, empathise,* and *suffer*; some – perhaps all – minded organisms *reason, calculate,* and *communicate*; and so on. There are controversial borderline cases – contemporary and historical – where it is unclear whether organisms are minded, but there are clear cases of non-minded entities: organisms that do not have nervous systems – bacteria, amoeba, and paramecia – and non-organisms, such as cups, tables, trains, towns, continents, gas giants, solar systems, and galaxies. It is currently controversial whether there can be artificial minded entities; many think that it is just a matter of time before there are minded non-organisms, e.g., androids.

Well-established science gives us no reason to suppose that we need to appeal to anything beyond biological processes in organisms, the local environments of those organisms, and the local, social, and evolutionary histories of those organisms, in order to explain the proper application of mental vocabulary to those organisms. That minded organisms are *conscious* – when, indeed, they are conscious – is just for those organisms to be engaged in certain kinds of neural processing. That minded organisms are *perceiving* their immediate environments just is for them, in those environments, to be engaged in certain kinds of neural processing that have been appropriately shaped by local, social, and evolutionary history, and that are appropriately causally related to those environments, etc.

I say that naturalists suppose that the story that is licensed by well-established science is the *full* story about all of the minded entities that there have been and that there ever will be. Not all who call themselves 'naturalists' agree. We saw in Chapter 4 that some who call themselves 'naturalists' believe in minded entities that do not figure in the above inventory. Moreover, some who call themselves 'naturalists' suppose that minded entities have minds, where this claim is understood to commit us to more than the claim that there are minded entities. However, at least as far as well-established science is concerned, talk of 'minds' is no more than mere idiomatic convenience. I say – and will assume, at least for now – that naturalists maintain that there is no *non-pleonastic* sense in which minded entities have minds.

Some non-naturalists suppose that there are non-natural minded entities: gods, angels, demons, and the like. Some non-naturalists suppose that universes are created by non-natural minded entities. Some non-naturalists suppose that mindedness is ubiquitous: each and every thing that exists is minded. Some non-naturalists suppose that entire universes are minded entities. Some non-naturalists suppose that mindedness extends beyond minded organisms to particular, special, natural non-organisms: particular mountains, particular trees, particular rocks, and so forth. Some non-naturalists suppose that mindedness extends beyond minded organisms to particular, special artifacts: particular weapons, particular relics, and so on. Some non-naturalists suppose that the very same human being – or, more generally, the very same sentient being – can be identical with a succession of human organisms – or, more generally, with a succession of sentient organisms. Some non-naturalists suppose that minds can exist independently of minded organisms. Some non-naturalists suppose that the minds of minded organisms in our universe are not located in our universe. Some non-naturalists suppose that the elsewhere-located minds of minded things in our universe causally interact with things in our universe. Some non-naturalists suppose that it *can be* that the only things that exist are minds and their 'contents'. Some non-naturalists suppose that it *is* the case that the only things that exists are minds and their 'contents'. Some non-naturalists suppose that human beings are non-natural 'spiritual' beings that are merely contingently tied to human organisms, and that have non-terminating existence – either separately, or as a merged part of some greater entity – in a separate, non-natural, 'spiritual' realm.

The question before us is whether any of the non-naturalist alternatives carry some explanatory advantage over naturalism. This question breaks down into a large number of sub-questions: (a) Is there anything that is better explained by the addition of gods, angels, demons, and so forth, to the entities postulated by naturalism? (b) Is there anything that is better explained by the addition, to the postulates of naturalism, of the further claim that mindedness is ubiquitous? (c) Is there anything that is better explained by the addition, to the postulates of naturalism, of the further claim that entire universes are minded entities? (d) Is there anything that is better explained by the addition, to the postulates of naturalism, of the further claim that mindedness extends beyond minded organisms to particular, special, natural non-organisms: particular mountains, particular trees, particular rocks, and so forth? (e) Is there anything that is better explained by the addition, to the postulates of naturalism, of the further claim that mindedness extends beyond minded organisms to particular, special artifacts: particular weapons, particular relics, and so on? (f) Is there anything that is better explained by the addition, to the postulates of naturalism, of the further claim that the very same human being – or, more generally, the very same sentient being – can be identical with a succession of human organisms – or, more generally, with a succession of sentient organisms? (g) Is there anything that is better explained by the addition, to the postulates of naturalism, of the further claim that minds can exist independently of minded organisms? (h) Is there anything that is better explained by the addition, to the postulates of naturalism, of the further claim that the minds of minded organisms in our universe are not located in our universe? (i) Is there anything that is better explained by the addition, to the postulates of naturalism, of the further claim that the elsewhere-located minds of minded things in our universe causally interact with things in our universe? (j) Is there anything that is better explained by the addition, to the postulates of naturalism, of the further claim that the only things that fundamentally exist are minds and their 'contents'? (k) Is there anything that is better explained by the addition, to the postulates of naturalism, of the further claim that human beings are non-natural 'spiritual' beings that are merely contingently tied to human organisms, and that have non-terminating existence – either separately, or as a merged part of some greater entity – in a separate, non-natural, 'spiritual' realm?

Discussion of (a) commenced in Chapter 6, Sections 1.9 and 1.10, and continues in Chapter 6, Sections 1.12 through 1.15. So it would be premature to say anything about it here.

I say that a negative answer is immediately appropriate for (b), (c), (d), (e), (h), (i), and (j). I suppose that it might be suggested that the mindedness of minded organisms is, itself, evidence for the mindedness of everything, or the mindedness of the universe, or the mindedness of particular entities that lack nervous systems. In particular, I suppose that it might be suggested that the consciousness of minded organisms is, itself, evidence for the consciousness – or, perhaps, proto-consciousness – of other things. But, as I have already noted, for minded organisms to be conscious – when they are conscious – is just for them to be engaged in certain kinds of neural processing: the consciousness of minded organisms *isn't* evidence for the consciousness – or proto-consciousness – of other things.

There is more to say about (f), (g), and (k). In each of these cases, there are two types of explanatory advantage that might be claimed. On the one hand, it might be said that these hypotheses can explain how it is possible for there to be cosmic justice and/or how it is possible for there to be some kind of survival of death. On the other hand, it might be said that there is scientific data that justifies these explanatory hypotheses. I do not think that either of these proposals survives scrutiny. On the one hand, we need some independent evidence that cosmic justice is realised and/or that there is some kind of survival of death before we have the least reason to think that the ability to explain the possibility of the realisation of cosmic justice and/or the possibility of survival of death is some kind of explanatory advantage. On the other hand, the plain truth is that there is no well-established science that supports any of these claims. True enough, there are individual scientific studies that purport to provide evidence that there is survival of death – e.g., scientific studies of near-death and out-of-body experiences – but all reputable meta-analyses have concluded that the scientific literature does not support (f), (g), and (k).

On my assessment – pending the completion of the discussion of (a) – there is nothing in considerations about mindedness that is better explained by non-naturalistic big pictures than by naturalistic big pictures. Moreover, on my assessment – again pending the completion of the discussion of (a) – there is no reason to be shy about suggesting that there are no considerations about mindedness that are better explained on best non-naturalistic big pictures than on best naturalistic big pictures.

My assessment of (a)–(k) skips past a large amount of philosophical literature in which many take up contrary views. Some – e.g. Chalmers (1996) – think that it is possible that there be creatures that have the same kinds of neural states and processes as actual human beings but that lack the subjective conscious experiences had by actual human beings. (I say this is impossible: you may be able to describe, or imagine, such creatures, but they could not be anything other than creatures of description or imagination.) Some – e.g., Moreland (2003)(2007)(2009) – think that there are 'arguments from consciousness' that establish that theistic big pictures are better than naturalistic big pictures. (I say that, since these arguments take it as a premise that there are non-natural mental entities, they certainly do not show that theistic big pictures are better than naturalistic big pictures.) Some – e.g., Reppert (2009) – think that there are 'arguments from reason' that establish that theistic big pictures are better than naturalistic big pictures. (I say that, since these arguments rely on the assumption that our reasoning capacities could not be a socially filtered mix of evolutionary adaptations and exaptations, they fail for much the same reasons that Plantinga's EAAN fails.) I have discussed some of this literature in more detail elsewhere: see Oppy (2013a)(2013b)(2014a).

12. Premise 2 (anomalies)

All religions include reports of *miracles*: events that involve non-natural agents and/or the exercise of non-natural powers.

Some reports of miracles concern the lives and deeds of central figures in particular religions, e.g., Buddha, Jesus, and Mohammad. According to the works in the Pali Canon, Buddha's birth was painless and everywhere that the infant Buddha placed his foot, a lotus flower bloomed; Buddha was able to walk on water and through walls. He was clairaudient, telepathic, able to recall his own past lives, privy to the karmic destiny of others, and free from greed, hatred, delusion, ignorance, and craving; and, on particular occasions, Buddha commanded flood waters to recede and walked between the parted waters on dry land, levitated while fire and water streamed from different parts of his body, and divided his body into pieces before reuniting the separated pieces. According to one or more of the Christian gospels, Jesus was born of a virgin, raised from the dead, walked on water, calmed a storm, raised other people from the dead, turned water into wine, caught fish in apparently empty waters, fed multitudes with next to nothing, cast demons into pigs, withered fig trees, and healed a vast range of conditions, including leprosy, paralysis, blindness, deafness, dumbness, withered limbs, lameness, severed ears, and dropsy. According to one or more of the Hadith, Muhammad revealed the *Qu'ran*, split the moon in order to convince unbelievers, blinded enemies with handfuls of dust, made numerous accurate prophecies, caused rain during drought, fed multitudes with next to nothing, caused trees to move at his command, made barren ewes produce milk, healed injured eyes with spittle, understood the languages of animals, was greeted by stones and trees, made prayers that were instantly answered, and ascended into heaven from Jerusalem.

Many reports of miracles are woven into central religious texts. For example, according to the Hebrew scriptures, God was responsible for the Noahide flood, the confusion of tongues at Babel, the destruction of Sodom and Gomorrah, the turning of Lot's wife into a pillar of salt, the changing of Aaron's rod into a serpent, the plagues of Egypt, the parting of the Red Sea, the sweetening of the waters at Marah, the raining of manna from heaven, the talking by Balaam's donkey, the destruction of the walls of Jericho, the stilling of the sun and moon to allow the Israelites to destroy their enemies, the raising of Shunammite's son from the dead, and much, much more.

Many reports of miracles belong to historical religious traditions. For example, according to Hindu tradition, Ahalya was turned to stone but later brought back to life by Rama's touch, Draupadi's sari became never-ending so that she could not be disrobed and shamed by Duryodhana, Jnandeva instructed a water buffalo to give a sixty minute recital of the Vedas in order to show up Brahmin ridicule, Chaitanya caused Lord Jagannath's chariot to move – when even teams of elephants could not budge it – simply by resting his head against it, Manikkavasagar restored speech to the dumb daughter of the Sri Lankan Buddhist king, and so on.

Reports of religious miracles continue to appear. Here are a few recent examples. In October, 1917, 100,000 people witnessed the sun plummeting towards the earth in a zigzag pattern at Fatima in Portugal. Between 1987 and 2007, Audrey Marie Santo was a conduit for miracles, ranging from healing of diseases and injuries to blood-weeping icons, bleeding statues, stigmata, and appearances of the Virgin Mary in cloud formations. Before dawn, on September 21, 1995, a statue of Ganesha in New Delhi drank milk offerings; within hours, statues from the entire Hindu pantheon all over India were drinking milk. (This episode was repeated on August 20, 2006, though this time only statues of Ganesha, Shiva, and Durga were involved.) In May 2008, Assad Busool discovered a piece of tree bark in front of his house with

Does naturalism defeat religion? 171

the Arabic word for 'Muhammad' carved into it by insects. In July 2008, a marble statue of Shirdi, Sai Baba opened one of its eyes. In November 2012, an image of the Madonna appeared on a hospital window near Kuala Lumpur.

Not all reports of events that involve non-natural agents and/or the exercise of non-natural powers are reports associated with religions. There is a vast range of reports of events and entities that are *anomalous*, i.e., that have no support from well-established science.

There are many reports of sightings of cryptids, i.e., of animals whose existence is entirely unsubstantiated: aswangs, barmanous, bunyips, chupacabras, gunnis, hoop snakes, Loch Ness monsters, mahambas, man-eating trees, mermaids, owlmen, popobawas, werewolves, will-o'-the-wisps, and yeti.

There are many reports of a vast range of other anomalous events and entities: astrological influences, alien abductions, alien visitations, channelling, clairvoyance, demons, dowsing, ESP, fairies, fortune-telling, ghosts, goblins, haunting, levitation, out-of-body travels, reincarnation, telekinesis, telepathy, and witchcraft.

There are many conspiracy theories that contradict well-established science while receiving no support from established scientific methods. Some conspiracy theories have ethnic, racial, and/or religious origins: e.g. Holocaust denial is rooted in anti-Semitism. Some conspiracy theories emerge after the deaths or disappearances of well-known people: e.g, theories about the assassination of JFK. Some conspiracy theories allege cover-ups of extra-terrestrial visitation or control: e.g, theories about world control by shape-shifting alien reptiles. Many conspiracy theories challenge well-established science: e.g., flat earth theories, allegations that the science of global warming is a fiction, and claims that the moon-landings were faked. Some conspiracy theories challenge well-established medical science: e.g., scares about artificial diseases, fluoridation, and vaccination. Some conspiracy theories focus on economics and politics at either local or global levels: e.g., theories about the 9/11 attacks, the Sandy Hook shootings, and a child-sex ring run by Democrats from a pizza restaurant in Washington. There are conspiracy theories about business, sport, espionage, aviation, and almost any other domain of human activity.

There are many reports affirming the virtues of alternative medicine and 'spiritual healing': acupuncture, apitherapy, Bach flower remedies, Bates method, chiropractic, chromotherapy, crystal healing, cupping, ear candling, energy therapies, havening, homeopathy, hypnotherapy, iridology, magnotherapy, naturopathy, numerology, orgonomy, osteopathy, pilates, rebirthing, reflexology, reiki, rolfing, thalassotherapy, and urine therapy.

When we consider the full range of reports of anomalous events and entities, it is impossible to resist the conclusion that almost all of them are cut from the same cloth. We all know that almost all reports of sightings of cryptids, and almost all reports of other anomalous events and entities, and almost all conspiracy theories, and almost all reports of the virtues of alternative medicine and 'spiritual healing' are false. We all know that the entire field of reports of anomalous events and entities is rife with knavery and folly:

we all know that almost everything in this field pivots on exploitation of human frailties. Moreover, we all know that the reports of miracles from across the religions of the world are also cut from that same cloth: we all know that almost all of the reports of miracles from across the religions of the world are false.

The main contours of the general explanation of the production and reproduction of all of these various kinds of reports are widely understood. We are all disposed to make false attributions of agency. We are all disposed to believe what we are told by those we take to be authoritative. We all aspire to be taken to be authoritative with respect to some domains. It is inevitable that falsehoods about what matters to us are uttered and have local uptake. Mostly, these falsehoods don't get far: for one reason or another, they are not sufficiently exciting or sufficiently memorable. But we are all disposed to remember 'minimally counter-intuitive' falsehoods, i.e., falsehoods invoking entities that differ strikingly from familiar entities along just one or two dimensions. Often enough, minimally counter-intuitive falsehoods receive wide uptake and become entrenched in particular sub-communities. Sometimes, these minimally counter-intuitive falsehoods are attractors for further theorisation; sometimes, they even receive various kinds of institutional support. Of course, except perhaps in cases where oppressive regimes are promulgators of their truth, there are many who do not accept these beliefs. So, these kinds of beliefs do not achieve the standing of well-established science; these kinds of beliefs are never the focus of expert consensus. But these kinds of beliefs can have very high levels of acceptance; and these kinds of beliefs can persist for millennia.

Claims about the distribution of 'anomalous' beliefs has mostly not been subject to meta-analytic review. Thus, while the following figures are drawn from reliable sources, they should be treated with some degree of caution: 40% of adult Americans self-identify as superstitious; 32% knock on wood to avoid bad luck; 38% of adult Americans use alternative medicine; 54% of adult Americans believe that the US Government is concealing what it knows about the 9/11 attacks; 50% of adult Americans believe that the US Government is concealing what it knows about the JFK assassination; 50% of adult Americans believe in astrology; 17% of adult Americans believe that cryptids – such as Bigfoot and the Loch Ness monster – will eventually be discovered by science.

Naturalists suppose that no current reports of anomalous events and entities should be accepted; moreover, naturalists suppose that almost no current reports of anomalous events and entities will end up being accepted. Naturalists suppose that something like the above sketch of the contours of the general explanation for the production and reproduction of reports of anomalous events and entities applies across the board: there is a *uniform* general account that holds for all reports of anomalous events and entities. Of course, for each report of anomalous events and entities, there is a detailed history of exactly how it arose and spread; but there is no reason to think that naturalists need to be interested in the details of histories in particular cases, or that they need to know the details of the histories in particular cases before they are entitled to maintain that a given case is properly to be treated like all of the rest of the reports of anomalous entities and events.

Non-naturalists who suppose that there is a small range of true reports of anomalous events and entities are not able to adopt a uniform account of anomalous events and entities. True enough, they can hold that, for a large range of cases, the account that the naturalist applies across the board does hold. But, for the narrow range of cases of reports of anomalous events and entities that they take to be true, non-naturalists adopt a stance that requires a different kind of explanation. Unless there is some significant gain in explanatory breadth and depth that goes along with the adoption of that stance, the result is simply pure loss for non-naturalists.

Of course, it is the case that scholars in all of the world's religions have expended enormous effort seeking to establish that the reports of anomalous events and entities that they accept really are true. But, as Hume observed long ago, success for any one party in this enterprise is defeat for all of the other parties to the enterprise. If, for example, the Christian miracles happened, then the Islamic, Buddhist, and Hindu miracles did not happen (and the Jewish miracles did not have the significance that Jews might take them to have). In order to effectively defend the reports of anomalous events and entities that belong to a given religion, it needs to be argued that those reports are much better – much more credible – than the reports of anomalous events and entities that belong to other religions *and* much better – much more credible – than all of the reports of anomalous events and entities that do not belong to any religions. If, for example, there is no better support in the historical record for the miracles attributed to Buddha than for the miracles attributed to Jesus, then there is no good reason to accept either set of miracle attributions.

I take it that the clear verdict of consideration of reports of anomalous events and entities is that naturalistic big pictures do no worse than competing big pictures on the count of explanatory breadth and depth, and that, in consequence, it is reasonable to infer that best naturalistic big pictures do no worse than competing best big pictures. Naturalistic big pictures are the only big pictures that give a uniform treatment of all reports of anomalous events and entities. By comparison, non-naturalistic big pictures are locked into competitive special pleading, each trying to claim greater explanatory breadth and depth on the basis of different applications of similarly questionable explanatory techniques to very similar sets of claims.

13. Premise 2 (experience)

Reported religious experience is multifarious.

Some religious experience is directly generated by religious practice. Consider, for example, the natural – mundane – experiences of religious adherents during their participation in religious dances, feasts, festivals, initiations, marriages, musical performances, prayers, sacrifices, sermons, worship, and so forth. This kind of religious experience is explained by the existence of religious organisations, practices, traditions, and the like. While it may not be *exactly* right to say that these kinds of religious experiences are open to non-religious participants in religious events – because, say, experience of these events is sensitive to differences in beliefs between religious adherents and 'outsiders' – it is nonetheless the case that there is no reason to suppose that naturalistic big pictures and non-naturalistic big pictures differ in their capacity to explain this category of religious experience. There are experiences *of* religion because there *is* religion.

Some religious experience involves particular kinds of responses to what is acknowledged to be the natural world. For example, some religious adherents report 'seeing the divine' in certain aspects of the natural world: the starry sky, sunflowers, cherry blossom, totemic animals, virtuous actions, sublime music, feelings of remorse and shame, and so forth. This kind of religious experience is readily explained in terms of prior religious beliefs. Those – and only those – who have already adopted a certain kind of religious explanatory framework make use of that kind of religious explanatory framework to add interpretative overlay to their experiences of the natural world. Of course, these patterns of interpretative overlay vary from one religious adherent to the next, depending upon the precise content of their religious beliefs. For example, indigenous Australians did not interpret any of their experiences of the natural world in monotheistic terms prior to their contact with monotheistic religious believers. Given the characteristic patterning of this kind of religious experience across time and place, it is obvious that there is no explanatory disadvantage that accrues to naturalists in connection with this kind of religious experience: naturalists can fully endorse an entirely uniform account of the kind that has just been outlined.

Some religious experience involves the (alleged) witnessing of miracles. In the preceding section of this chapter, we discussed the evidential force of reports of this kind of religious experience. Is there any residual question to be addressed about the religious experiences themselves? I don't think so. The reports that we make to ourselves based on the experiences that we have are just some among the many reports that we may be obliged to weigh in order to arrive at suitably considered judgments. In cases where we are disposed to judge that we have witnessed a miracle – i.e., that we have witnessed the exercise of non-natural causal powers by non-natural causal agents – we *ought* to reflect upon the considerations that were aired in the preceding discussion. Given that naturalists do not take themselves to witness miracles, there is nothing in religious experience of (alleged) miracles that creates any kind of explanatory disadvantage for naturalists.

Some religious experience involves *dreams* and *visions*.

Dreams are successions of images, emotions, sensations, and thoughts that occur involuntarily during sleep. In some cultures, dreams have been taken to be messages from gods and/or ancestors; in many cultures, dreams have been taken to have utility in predicting the future. Expert oneirologists have not reached consensus on either the purpose of dreaming or the interpretability of dreams. Some follow Freud in thinking that dreams disclose desires and emotions that would otherwise not be brought to consciousness. Some suspect that dreams have a role in formation of memories and/or problem-solving. Some think that dreams are merely products of random brain activation. Given the lack of consensus among expert oneirologists, there are no good grounds for making positive assertions about the purpose of dreaming or the interpretability of dreams. However, there is consensus among expert oneirologists that we should not take dreams to be messages from gods and/or ancestors. Naturalists are fully justified in supposing that dreams are not messages from gods and/or ancestors; and they are also fully justified in supposing that best naturalistic big pictures will say that dreams are not messages from gods and/or ancestors.

Visions are successions of images, emotions, sensations, and thoughts that occur in states other than regular wakefulness and sleep, i.e., in 'altered states of consciousness'. These states are very diverse. They include: day-dreaming, near death experiences, and states that may be induced by, for example, drugs (such as alcohol, cocaine, ecstasy, heroin, LSD, marijuana, and morphine), exercise, fasting, hypnosis, meditation, mental illness, music, and sex. It is obvious to everyone that many visions provide neither information nor insight to those who have them: the visions of those with crippling drug addictions and/or debilitating mental illnesses are typically nothing more than symptoms of their conditions. Moreover, it is obvious to everyone that most of the states in which visions are produced are not cognitively reliable: I am likely to impair my performance on even quite cognitively undemanding tasks by preceding my undertaking of those tasks with prolonged strenuous exercise, extensive fasting, ingestion of mind-altering drugs, long periods of sleeplessness, and/or marathon sessions of sex. Those who hold that religious visions provide information and insight for those who have them face a difficult task. If religious visions occur in states that typically impair performance even on cognitively undemanding tasks, then there is clearly good reason not to take them to be reliable sources of information and insight. But, even if religious visions are in altered states of consciousness that are not yet known to typically impair performance even on cognitively undemanding tasks, our knowledge about other altered states of consciousness provides us with good reason to suppose these religious visions are not reliable sources of information and insight. Naturalists are fully justified in supposing that religious visions are not messages from gods and/or ancestors; and they are also fully justified in supposing that best naturalistic big pictures will say that religious visions are not messages from gods and/or ancestors.

The most interesting kind of religious experience is what I shall call 'mystical experience'; others sometimes call it 'sacred experience' or 'spiritual experience'. I divide mystical experiences into five kinds: ecstatic, numinous, unitive, salvific, and natural. *Ecstatic* mystical experiences are the experiences of shaman and mediums; they are often interpreted as possession by the divine. *Numinous* mystical experiences – described by Otto (1917/1923) – are characterised by fear, compulsion, and sense of personality; they are often interpreted as theistic encounters. *Unitive* mystical experiences – described by James (1902/2012) – are characterised by evanescence, ineffability, passivity, pedagogical value, and tranquillity; they are often said to invoke a sense of oneness with the divine. *Salvific* mystical experiences are hypothesised to accompany salvation in given religions; these experiences are said to accompany liberation, or enlightenment, or rebirth, or the like. *Natural* mystical experiences are characterised by the same kinds of properties that characterise unitive mystical experiences, except that the invoked sense of oneness is with nature, rather than with the divine.

Insofar as ecstatic mystical experience involves visions, it falls under matters that we have already discussed. Insofar as ecstatic mystical experience does not involve visions, we can group it with numinous mystical experiences and unitive mystical experiences. What I then take to be common to these three kinds of mystical experiences is that they have negligible communicable content. On the side of the experiencing, there is tranquillity, or fear and compulsion, or ecstasy and enthusiasm; but, on the side of that which is experienced, we are given no more than a sense of oneness with the divine, or a sense of personality, or the like.

This lack of content – which has been seized upon by perennialists, transcendentalists, universalists, theosophists, 'pizza effected' syncretists, and the like – means that mystical experience could not play a significant role in promoting some religious big pictures above others. True enough, Otto's 'sense of personality' might be taken to be weak evidence in favour of theistic big pictures; but James' 'sense of oneness with the divine' is neutral between almost all religious big pictures. At best, mystical experience might have some role to play in deciding between religious big pictures and their competitors. However, there are good reasons for thinking that, in fact, mystical experience does not generate reasons for favouring religious big pictures.

First, much mystical experience is generated by conditions that are negatively correlated with performance on even quite simple cognitive tasks. As we noted above, mental illness – depression, epilepsy, schizophrenia, stroke – bodily insult – extreme exercise, extreme sexual activity, mortification, near-death experience, sensory deprivation, starvation – and ingestion of mind-altering drugs – ayahuasca, mescaline, muscimol, psilocybin, salvinorin A – reduce our ability to carry out even very simple cognitive tasks. Everyone should treat beliefs generated in these conditions with the deepest suspicion.

Second, even when mystical experience is not generated by the above kinds of conditions – and whether or not it simply comes unbidden or is invited by meditation, prayer, music, dance, chant, trance, or the like – there is no good reason to suppose that it is a reliable source of information that favours religious big pictures over other big pictures. Feelings of tranquillity, fear and compulsion, ecstasy and enthusiasm are not the sole preserve of the religious; naturalists also experience these feelings. Moreover, to the extent that we can give intelligible content to claims of being at one with nature, we can allow that even naturalists can have experiences of being at one with nature. Perhaps it would be odd for naturalists not to disavow belief with this content; but it is not at all odd for naturalists to allow that they are prone to 'sensings' that it is quite proper for them to reject as guides to belief.

Third, on the assumption that naturalists do have natural mystical experiences in which they have a sense of being at one with nature, there is a question about how these experiences should be explained. We all know that we are prone to a range of hard to interpret experiences: shivers down the spine, variations in mood and affect, feelings of being watched, intimations that we are looking at familiar things from completely new perspectives, and so forth. Sensations of being at one with nature are, at best, one more item to add to this list. Given that it is overwhelmingly plausible that, one day, everything on the initial list will be given a fully satisfactory unified explanation in terms of cognitive science and evolutionary theory – i.e., given that it is overwhelmingly plausible that we will have a fully satisfactory unified explanation of shivers down the spine, variations in mood and affect, feelings of being watched, intimations that we are looking at familiar things from completely new perspectives, and so forth, in terms of cognitive science and evolutionary theory – we have the best of reasons for thinking that we shall one day be able to account for sensing oneness with nature in terms of that unified explanation.

The upshot of our discussion is that there is nothing in religious experience that is better explained by non-naturalistic big pictures than by naturalistic big pictures. Even in the case of mystical experiences – after we have set aside the irrelevant, because merely hypothetical, case of salvific mystical experience – we see that naturalistic big pictures promise, and can be expected to deliver, fully unified accounts of hard-to-interpret experiences that non-naturalistic big pictures are unable to better, and that, in consequence, there is nothing in mystical experiences that is better explained by best non-naturalistic big pictures than by best naturalistic big pictures. As in the other cases that we have looked at thus far, best naturalistic big pictures are not explanatorily inferior to best religious big pictures.

14. Premise 2 (artifacts)

The term 'religious artifact' can be construed to include religious buildings, religious organisations, religious texts, and other 'constructed' religious objects. Religious artifacts that are of interest in the present discussion are those that have features that adherents of given religions claim are best explained by appeal to the exercise of non-natural causal power by non-natural causal agents.

The paradigmatic example – and the one upon which we shall focus – is provided by certain kinds of religious texts. In some cases, the mere *existence* of these texts is claimed to be best explained by appeal to the exercise of non-natural causal power by non-natural causal agents. In many other cases, the *content* of these texts is claimed to be best explained by appeal to the exercise of non-natural causal power by non-natural causal agents.

Many religions have sacred texts. We can do no more than give a very sketchy overview of a few cases.

The earliest religious texts that we have belong to ancient Egyptian religion: the *Pyramid Texts* (2400–2300 BCE), the *Coffin Texts* (2050–1800 BCE), the *Book of the Dead* (1700 BCE), etc.

In Hinduism, sacred texts divide into *Shruti* ('authorless' primary works) and *Smriti* (derivative secondary works). While some 'unorthodox' Hindu traditions did not recognise their authority, all of the 'orthodox' Hindu traditions recognised the four Vedas – *Rigveda, Samaveda, Yajurveda*, and *Atharvaveda* – as canonical principal texts. Each of the Vedas contains Samhitas (prayers, litanies, hymns, mantras, and benedictions), Brahmanas (records of myths and legends, explanations of rituals, and speculation about natural phenomena), Arankayas (philosophies of ritual sacrifice), and Upanishads (general philosophy). The earliest hymns in the *Rigveda* date to somewhere between 1500 BCE and 2000 BCE. The *Smriti* include the Vedānga (grammar, metre, phonetics, etymology, and astronomy), the Itihasa (the *Mahābhārata* and the *Rāmāyana*), the Purānas (myths, legends, and traditional lore), the Kāvya (poetical literature), the Bhasyas (reviews and commentaries), the Nibandhas (politics, medicine, ethics, culture, arts, and society), and other Tantras, Sutras, Shastras, Stotras, and so forth.

In Zoroastrianism, the primary texts are the *Avesta*, which date back to at least 1300 BCE. These texts include the liturgical Yasna and Visperad, the Vendidad (which lists manifestations of evil spirits and ways to confound them), the Siroza (invocation of the divinities that preside over the days of the month), the Yashts (hymns to various divinities), the Nyayeshes and Gahs (prayers for regular recitation), and the Afrinagans (blessings for special occasions).

In Confucianism, the primary texts are the Four Books (*Great Learning, Doctrine of the Mean, Analects,* and *Mencius*), the Five Classics (*Classic of Poetry, Book of Documents, Book of Rites, I Ching*, and *Spring and Autumn Annals*), the Thirteen Classics, and the Three Commentaries. The earliest parts of these texts – attributed to Confucius himself – probably date to somewhere around 600 BCE.

In Judaism, the primary sacred texts are the *Tanakh* and the *Talmud*. The *Tanakh* consists of the *Torah* (*Genesis, Exodus, Leviticus, Numbers,* and *Deuteronomy*), the *Nevi'im* (*Joshua, Judges, Samuel, Kings, Isaiah, Jeremiah, Ezekiel, Hosea, Joel, Amos, Obadiah, Jonah, Micah, Nahum, Habakkuk, Zephaniah, Haggai, Zechariah,* and *Malachi*), and the *Ketuvim* (*Psalms, Proverbs, Job, Song of Songs, Ruth, Lamentations, Ecclesiastes, Ester, Daniel, Ezra* and *Chronicles*). The *Torah* was most likely written down around 600 BCE, based on earlier oral and written sources; Jewish tradition maintains that the *Torah* was written by Moses.

In Buddhism, the *Tipitaka* ('Pali Canon') is universally taken to be a collection of sacred texts In Mahayana Buddhism – but not in Theravada Buddhism – the Mahayana Sutras are also taken to be sacred texts; and in Tibetan Buddhism the *Kangyur* and the *Tengyur* are also taken to be collections of sacred texts. The *Tipitaka*, which was composed from about 500 BCE, and written down during the first century BCE, divides into three parts: the Sutta Pitaka (the teachings of the Buddha), the Vinaya Pitaka (expected discipline for monks), and the Abhidharma Pitaka (special doctrines).

In Jainism, the primary texts are the *Agamas*: the twelve Angās, the six Chedasūtras, the four Mūlasūtras, the ten Prakīrnakasutras? and the two Cūlikasūtras. The Angās are the oldest and most central texts; they probably date to around 400 BCE. The oldest agama – one of the Angās – is the *Acharanga Sūtra*: it contains recommendations concerning self-restraint, abandonment of ego, overcoming adversity, perception of righteousness, detachment, destruction of karmas, service to elders, penance, austerity, and sexual reticence.

In Taoism, the principal primary texts are the *Tao Te Ching*, the *Zhuangzi*, and the *Daozong*; the first two of these texts date earlier than 300 BCE. The *Zhuangzi* consists of fables, anecdotes, parables, and allegories that valorise spontaneity of action – being one with the Dao – and freedom from merely human conventions, distinctions, and modes of thought.

In Christianity, the principal text is the Bible, which consists of the Old Testament and the New Testament. There is some variation across Christian sects in the exact contents of both volumes; however, the books of the New Testament are typically: the four gospels (*Mark, Matthew, Luke* and *John*), *Acts*, some Pauline letters, some other letters, and *Revelations*. The four gospels are narratives composed in the latter part of the first century CE; the earliest Christian documents date to as early as 50 CE. The development of the New Testament canon was a gradual process that reached its terminus at some point in the fourth century CE.

In Manichaeism, the principal text is the *Evangelion*. This gnostic gospel, written by Mani in around 200 CE, is one of seven original scriptures in Manichaeism. Only a small number of fragments of this work survive.

In Mandaeism, the principal text is the *Ginza Rba*, though there are many other Mandaen scriptures. It probably dates to around 200 CE, though some scholars place it earlier. The *Ginza Rba* is a compilation of liturgy, hymns, theological texts, didactic texts, and poetry. It consists of two parts – the *Right Ginza* and the *Left Ginza* – that are included in a single volume with each part upside down and back to front with respect to the other.

In Islam, the primary texts are the *Qu'ran* and the hadith. According to Islamic tradition, Muhammad received the *Qu'ran* from Gabriel between 609 CE and 632 CE; according to Islamic tradition, the *Qu'ran* is the most important miracle of Muhammad. The hadith – sayings attributed to Muhammad – differ among Sunnis, Shias, and Ibadis. According to the Sunni, there are six legitimate hadith, including the *Sahih al-Bukhari* and the *Sahih*

Muslim; according to the Shia, there are four entirely different legitimate hadith; and according to the Ibadi, the principal hadith is the *Tartib al-Musnad*.

In Shinto, the principal texts are *Kojiki, Rikkokushi, Fudoki, Jinnō Shōtōki,* and *Kujiki*. The earliest of these texts – *Kojiki* – dates to about 700 CE; it is an account of the origins of the four major Japanese islands, and the proper objects of veneration – Kami – including features of landscapes, forces of nature, ancestors of clans, great leaders, and the like.

In Sikhism, the principal texts are the *Guru Granth Sahib* and the *Dasam Granth*. The *Guru Granth Sahib* was compiled between the fifteenth century CE and the seventeenth century CE. It is regarded by Sikhs as a spiritual guide for all of humanity.

The texts that I have mentioned – and the many texts of religions that there is no space here to mention – have much in common. Often, they are literary exemplars; often, there are treated by some – but not all – adherents of given religions as accurate historical records.

Some arguments for the non-natural origins of one or another of these texts – to be found in many, but not all, of the religions mentioned – turn on the alleged literary merits of the texts. Given that most of these works are canonical literary works for adherents of the religions to which the works belong, any claim of absolute literary merit for any particular work is hopelessly controversial. Entirely unsurprisingly, there is no expert consensus about the comparative literary merits of the various works mentioned above.

Some arguments for the non-natural origins of one or another of these texts – again, found in many but not all of the religions mentioned above – turns on allegedly successful detailed predictions of future events in these texts. Given what is known about the historical redaction of most of these texts – and given the uncertainties involved in dating the initial composition and subsequent redaction of most of these texts – it is entirely unsurprising that there is no expert consensus on even one successful detailed prediction of a future event in any of the works mentioned above.

Perhaps the most common arguments for the non-natural origins of one or another of the texts – found in some, but not all, of the religions mentioned above – appeal to various types of confirmation of the material that is contained in those texts. Some point to the superiority of the distinctive moral and/or social teachings of given texts. Some point to advanced scientific knowledge that is contained in given texts. Some point to information that is contained in the texts that could not have been in the possession of those who compiled the texts. These arguments face various problems. There is, of course, no expert consensus about the superiority of the moral and/or social teachings of any one of the mentioned texts; there is no expert consensus that any advanced scientific knowledge is contained in any of the mentioned texts; and there is no expert consensus that there is any information contained in any of the mentioned texts that could not have been in the possession of those who compiled those texts. Given the many barriers to confident interpretation of these texts, the many uncertainties about their production and reproduction, and the depth of disagreement about moral and social matters, there is no prospect of expert consensus on the conclusions of any of these common arguments.

One final common class of arguments appeals to historical confirmation of the material that is contained in one or another of these texts. Given that we have historical confirmation for the natural events – i.e., events involving none but natural entities with none but natural causal powers – that are recorded in these texts, we have evidence for the reliability of those who compiled them; and so we have reason to take them at their word when they make claims about non-natural events, i.e., about events involving non-natural entities with non-natural causal powers. This type of argument faces at least two kinds of serious difficulties. First, the reliability of these authors concerning natural events is no more than the very weakest evidence of their reliability concerning non-natural events. Second, there is typically no evidence of the reliability of the authors concerning natural events. True enough, religious texts sometimes refer to genuine historical events involving genuine historical figures in genuine historical locations. But none of that comes close to establishing that the compilers of those texts are reliable recorders of natural events. What is missing from the historical record is independent confirmation of detailed description of any events in primary religious texts. Certainly, there is sometimes multiple detailed description of events in different texts within a given religion; but there is never good evidence that those reports really are independent, i.e., really are produced by figures working independently of one another.

The upshot of this discussion is that there is nothing in primary religious texts that creates an explanatory disadvantage for naturalistic big pictures. Obviously enough, every best big picture says that almost all primary religious texts are full of historical, moral, social, scientific, philosophical, and theological falsehoods. Every best big picture has to explain the existence and content of all of those primary religious texts. Naturalistic big pictures have a uniform story to tell about all primary religious texts. When we put this together with the previous observations about the lack of expert consensus on which are the best primary religious texts, we arrive at the conclusion that there is no reason to suppose that naturalistic big pictures are explanatorily inferior to other big pictures when it comes to the existence and content of primary religious texts. And from there, it is a very short step to the conclusion that best naturalistic big pictures score at least as well on explanatory breadth and depth in this area as best religious big pictures.

15. Premise 2 (communication)

Almost all religions involve alleged communication with, or by, non-natural agents. Almost all religions have specialists who are allegedly able to interpret *omens* set in the natural world by non-natural agents. Almost all religions have specialists who are allegedly able to *divine* future events with the aid of information that they elicit from, or that is disclosed to them, by non-natural agents. Almost all religions have *prayers* and *rituals* that are alleged to influence the course of future events via the intercession of non-natural agents. Almost all religions have specialists who are alleged to be in *direct or indirect communication* with non-natural agents. Here, I shall focus on divination, broadly understood.

There is an extraordinary range of human divinatory practices. I begin with a partial list of the various kinds of things that are taken to be suitable tools or materials for divinatory practices by some human populations: *animals*: ants, beetles, birds, crabs, dogs, fish, frogs, horses, rodents, roosters, snakes, spiders, wild hogs, and so on; *animals' behaviour*: flight, migration, noises (e.g., howling), production of tracks, and so forth; *animals' remains*: bladders, blood, entrails, excrement, livers, placentas, shoulder blades, urine, and the like; *atmospheric conditions*: clouds, lightning, thunder, wind, and so on; *celestial bodies*: comets, meteors, the moon, the planets, individual stars, stellar constellations, the sun, and so forth; *'elements'*: ashes (especially of incense or tree bark), burning coals, colours, dust, earth, fire, flames, ice, incense, minerals, molten metal, molten wax, oil, rainwater, smoke, soot, water, and the like; *environmental features*: lakes, lighting, mountains, oceans, rivers, rocks, seas, shadows, and so on; *foodstuffs*: barley cakes, cheese, chewing gum, eggs, flour, fortune cookies, gum wax, rice gruel, salt, wine, and so forth; *human appearance*: blemishes, bumps on skin, buttocks, eye colours, eyes, faces, fingernails, hair, hands, lines on foreheads, lips, moles, navels, palms, ridges on breastbones, shoulders, soles of feet, spots on skin, teeth, toenails, and the like; *human behaviour*: acting foolishly, becoming dizzy, blowing, boiling a donkey's head, burning straw with an iron, consulting computer oracles, convulsing, cracking a turtle's plastron via application of heat, crawling, doing double takes, feeling afraid, feeling itches, folding banknotes, folding paper, gazing (especially with reflective objects: crystal balls, mirrors, pools of water), glancing behind, hearing random shouts and cries in crowds at night, laughing, making second glances, moving fingers, nursing, performing (black) magic, playing four-handed chess, raving, sacrificing animals, sitting in a drawn circle, sleeping, speaking to the dead, summoning dead souls, swirling water in a cup, swirling wine in a brass bowl, walking, and so on; *human remains*: blood, bodily fluids, excrement, footprints, placenta, skulls, umbilical cords, urine, and so forth; *'linguistic' entities*: alphabets, books (e.g., the *Aeneid, Bible, I Ching, Iliad*, and *Odyssey*), dictionaries, films, guttural sounds, handwriting, initials, inscriptions, letters of the alphabet, overheard speech, poems, words, writing burnt into bark, and the like; *mathematical entities*: birthdates, fractals, lines, logarithms, numbers, and so on; *objects for casting*: bones, coins, copper bowls, cowrie shells, cylindrical tools, dice, divining rods, dominoes, electronic playlists, finger rings, gems, gongs, keys, Mah-jong tiles, Ogham letters, opele, pearls, pebbles, pendulums, rods, runes, shells, sticks, stones, weights, wheels, and so forth; *'occult' entities*: aerial visions, auras, demons, dragons, saints, spirits, and the like; *plants*: bamboo, barley, beans, fig leaves, figs (burnt), flowers, fruit, laurel wreaths (burnt), leaves, mistletoe, oaks, onion sprouts, palm nuts, rose petals, sage (burnt), wood, yews, and so on; *sharp objects*: arrows, axes, knives, needles, spindles, swords, and so forth; *sundry chance events*: accidental seeing, accidental hearing, ballots, divulged secrets, lots, meetings with strangers, things found on a road, wheel ruts, and the like; and *sundry objects*: altars, brushed cloth, candles, cups, fountains, hanging sieves, icons, idols, old shoes, Ouija boards, sacred relics, statues, and so forth.

This vast range of entities mostly fits into a relatively small number of very general categories: *chance artifacts* (i.e., artifacts that generate chance outcomes); *dangerous things; environmental things* (the heavens, the earth, and their constituents); *human things; linguistic and mathematical things; non-human living things* (animals and plants); and *sacred things*. (Perhaps we might further include the dangerous things under the chance artifacts, and group human things and non-human living things together as living things.) However, while it may seem that almost anything can be adapted to the purposes of divination, the practices of particular human communities are tied to a small number of specific instances that fall under our very general categories. Practitioners of divination inevitably claim a narrow range of expertise, sometimes – but not always – backed by historical tradition. While, in theory, proponents of divination could suppose that everything I have listed – and more besides – can be an appropriate focus for divinatory practice, it often turns out that proponents of particular divinatory practices are sceptical about the efficacy of some – perhaps even most – other divinatory practices. And, of course, where these divinatory practices are connected to religions, it is very often the case that adherents of a given religion condemn the divinatory practices of competing religions.

Given our previous discussion of miracles, scriptures, and mystical experience, it is clear what we should say about divination. At least in principle, naturalists have a comprehensive unified story to tell about all cases of divination – all cases of omens, all cases of prophecy, all cases of prayer, all cases of talking with or listening to non-natural agents, and the like. Every best big picture says that no more than a vanishingly small fraction of claims to successful divination are true. Best naturalistic big pictures say that no claims to successful divination are true. Competing best big pictures that claim that there is some successful divination have a very significant explanatory disadvantage compared to best naturalistic big pictures. Unless it can be shown – by methods to which all with relevant expertise agree – that a few claims to successful divination are in much better standing than all competing claims to successful divination, there is no reason for anyone to suppose that any competing best big pictures have greater explanatory breadth and depth than best naturalistic big pictures when it comes to the explanation of reports of successful divination.

16. Conclusions

In this chapter I have sketched a case for the claim that best big pictures are best naturalistic big pictures. That case relies on two claims. First, among best big pictures, naturalistic big pictures are minimal: they have fewer commitments than their competitors. Second, among best big pictures, naturalistic big pictures are maximal: with respect to breadth, depth, and adequacy of explanation, best naturalistic big pictures do at least as well as any other best big pictures. Given the further assumption – a third claim – that, if any best big pictures are minimal and maximal in the above senses, then those big pictures are the very best big pictures, it follows that best naturalistic big pictures are the very best big pictures. Hence, in particular, it follows that best naturalistic big pictures are better than best religious big pictures: naturalism defeats religion.

While the case for the first claim is relatively straightforward, the case for the second claim is clearly controversial. I considered a range of topics – 'general causal features', 'general design features', 'mental capacities and phenomena', 'reports of the naturalistically anomalous', 'religious experience', 'religiously significant artifacts', and 'religious communication' – for which I argued that naturalistic big pictures are maximal. However, there are plenty of questions. Have I covered all of the controversial cases? Have I given an adequate discussion of the controversial cases that I have considered? Am I right in thinking that evaluative and normative considerations are independent of causal considerations? And so on.

Moreover, there are questions about the third claim. Perhaps there are theoretical virtues that are not adequately accommodated in the approach I have adopted. Perhaps there is some completely different approach to the assessment of the comparative merits of big pictures that is required.

I do not claim that the case that I have set out is successful; I do not claim that anyone who fails to be persuaded by this case is irrational. What I have produced in this book – and, in particular, in this last chapter – is philosophy. It is a discussion of matters on which there is simply no expert consensus. So long as there are intelligent, sensitive, well-informed people who do not agree with what I've said, I have the best of reasons for supposing that the case that I've set out is not successful – even though it seems entirely compelling to me.

9 Conclusion

In this book, I have argued (a) that there is no such thing as naturalistic religion; (b) that it is not the case that science defeats naturalism; (c) that it is not the case that religion defeats naturalism; and (d) that it is not the case that science defeats religion. Moreover, while I have presented what seems to me to be a compelling case that naturalism defeats religion, I acknowledge that this case is not likely to persuade anyone (since it cannot persuade anyone who already accepts it, and is unlikely to persuade anyone who does not already accept it).

The arguments that I have presented depend upon substantive assumptions that I have made about the nature of naturalism, science, religion, and philosophy. The account that I have given for each of these things is controversial; in each case, it is a newcomer to the court of public opinion. So, apart from questions about what follows when these accounts are put together, there are also questions about the individual and collective adequacy of these accounts.

There are other controversial novelties in the views that I advance. I frame my account of naturalism in terms of causal powers. I defend the necessity of naturalism by appealing to controversial claims about modality and chance. I rely on an only partially articulated theory of big pictures, and some controversial views about theoretical virtues, in order to establish the framework within which the case for the superiority of naturalistic views is developed. And, no doubt, there are further controversial novelties in this work that have not yet registered with me. As with almost any work in philosophy, the views that are being developed are evolving together; there are bound to be ways in which they are susceptible to improvement.

While there are many who doubt that there can be anything of value in this book – including those on one side who think that philosophy of religion, if not philosophy more broadly, is a discredited waste of time, and those on the other side who think that naturalism is the worst of all possible big pictures and clearly the spawn of the devil – I hope that it has provided useful food for thought for some readers.

Bibliography

Abdul-Baha (2014) *Some Answered Questions* Haifa: Bahá'i World Centre
Addley, S. (2013) 'Atheist Sunday Assembly Branches Out in First Wave of Expansion' *The Guardian*, 14/09/13, https://www.theguardian.com/world/2013/sep/14/atheist-sunday-assembly-branches-out
Adherents.com (2017) 'Major Religions of the World Ranked by Number of Adherents' http://www.adherents.com/Religions_By_Adherents.html
Ano, G. and Vasconcelles, E. (2016) 'Religious Coping and Psychological Adjustment to Stress: A Meta-Analysis' *Journal of Clinical Psychology* 61: 461–480
Atran, S. (2002) *In Gods We Trust* Oxford: Oxford University Press
Atran, S. and Norenzayan, A. (2004) 'Religion's Evolutionary Landscape: Counterintuition, Commitment, Compassion, Communion' *Behavioural and Brain Sciences* 27: 713–770
Bahá'-ulláh (1990) *Gleanings from the Writings of Bahá'-ulláh*, edited by S. Effendi- Wilmette: Bahá'i Publishing Trust
Barbour, I. (1966) *Issues in Science and Religion* New York: Vantage
Barbour, I. (ed.) (1968) *Science and Religion: New Perspectives on the Dialogue* New York: Harper Row
Barrett, J. (2000) 'Exploring the Natural Foundations for Religion' *Trends in Cognitive Sciences* 4: 29–34
Barrett, J. (2004) *Why Would Anyone Believe in God?* Walnut Creek: AltaMira Press
Bashour, B. and Muller, J. (eds.) (2014) *Contemporary Philosophical Naturalism and its Implications* London: Routledge
Berezow, A. and Campbell, H. (2012) *Science Left Behind: Feel-Good Fallacies and the Rise of the Anti-Scientific Left* New York: Public Affairs
Bishop, J. (2007) *Believing by Faith: An Essay in the Epistemology and Ethics of Religious Belief* Oxford: Oxford University Press
Bishop, J. (2018) 'A "Naturalist" Christian Theism' in G. Oppy and N. Trakakis (eds.) *Inter-Christian Religious Dialogues* London: Routledge: 3–24
Black, A. (1989) *Man and Nature in the Philosophical Thought of Wang Fu-Chih* Seattle: University of Washington Press
Blasi, A. (1998) 'Definition of Religion' in W. Swatos (ed.) *Encyclopedia of Religion and Society* Walnut Creek: AltaMira Press: 129–133
Bloch, M. (1971) *Placing the Dead: Tombs, Ancestral Villages and Kinship Organisation in Madagascar* London: Seminar Press

Bodde, D. (1991) *Chinese Thought, Science and Society: The Intellectual and Social Background of Science and Technology in Pre-Modern China* Honolulu: University of Hawai'i Press
Bonevac, D. (2012) 'Two Theories of Analogical Predication' *Oxford Studies in Philosophy of Religion* 4: 20–42
Bonjour, L. (2010) 'Against Materialism' in R. Koons and G. Bealer (eds.) *The Waning of Materialism* Oxford: Oxford University Press: 3–23
Boyer, P. (1994) *The Naturalness of Religious Ideas* Berkeley: University of California Press
Brightman, E. (1940) *A Philosophy of Religion* New York: Prentice-Hall
Brooke, J. (1991) *Science and Religion: Some Historical Perspectives* Cambridge: Cambridge University Press
Chalmers, D. (1996) *The Conscious Mind* Oxford: Oxford University Press
Chalmers, D. (2010) 'The Singularity' *Journal of Consciousness Studies* 17: 7–65
Chambers, R. (1844) *The Vestiges of Creation* London: John Churchill
Comte, A. (1875–7) *System of Positive Polity or Treatise in Sociology, Instituting the Religion of Humanity*, four volumes, London: Longman, Green & Co
Craig, W. and Moreland, J. (2000a) *Naturalism: A Critical Analysis* London: Routledge
Craig, W. and Moreland, J. (2000b) 'Preface' in W. Craig and J. Moreland (eds.) *Naturalism: A Critical Analysis* London: Routledge: xi–xv
Crane, T. and Mellor, H. (1990) 'There is no Question of Physicalism' *Mind* 99: 185–206
Crosby, D. (2002) *A Religion of Nature* New York: State University of New York Press
Curlin, F. et al. (2005) 'Religious Characteristics of US Physicians: A National Survey' *Journal of General Internal Medicine* 20: 629–634
Dawes, G. (2011) 'In Defence of Naturalism' *International Journal for Philosophy of Religion* 70: 3–25
Dawes, G. (2016) *Galileo and the Conflict between Science and Religion* London: Routledge
Dawkins, R. (2006) *The God Delusion* London: Bantam
De Caro, M. and Macarthur, D. (2004a) *Naturalism in Question* Cambridge: Harvard University Press
De Caro, M. and Macarthur, D. (2004b) 'Introduction: The Nature of Naturalism' in M. De Caro and D. Macarthur (eds.) *Naturalism in Question* Cambridge: Harvard University Press: 1–17
De Caro, M. (2010) 'Varieties of Naturalism' in R. Koons and G. Bealer (eds.) *The Waning of Materialism* Oxford: Oxford University Press: 365–374
De Cruz, H. (2017) 'Religion and Science' *Stanford Encyclopedia of Philosophy* https://plato.stanford.edu/entries/religion-science/
De Cruz, H. and De Smedt, J. (2015) *A Natural History of Natural Theology: The Cognitive Science of Theology and Philosophy of Religion* Cambridge: MIT Press
Dembski, W. (2000) 'Naturalism and Design' in W. Craig and J. Moreland (eds.) *Naturalism: A Critical Analysis* London: Routledge:253–279
Dennett, D. (2006) *Breaking the Spell: Religion as a Natural Phenomenon* London: Allen Lane
Dennett, D. and Plantinga, A. (2011) *Science and Religion: Are they Compatible?* Oxford: Oxford University Press
Devitt, M. (1998) 'Naturalism and the A Priori' *Philosophical Studies* 92: 45–65
Draper, J. (1874) *History of the Conflict between Religion and Science* New York: Appleton

Draper, P. (2005) 'God, Science and Naturalism' in W. Wainwright (ed.) *The Oxford Handbook of Philosophy of Religion* Oxford: Oxford University Press

Durkheim, E. (1915) *The Elementary Forms of the Religious Life: A Study in Religious Sociology*, translated by J. Swain, London: Allen & Unwin

Ecklund, E. (2010) *Science vs. Religion: What Scientists Really Think* Oxford: Oxford University Press

Ecklund, E. and Scheitle, C. (2007) 'Religion and Academic Scientists: Distinctions, Disciplines, and Demographics' *Social Problems* 54: 289–307

Ecklund, E. *et al.* (2016) 'Religion among Scientists in International Context: A New Study of Scientists in Eight Regions' *Socius* 2: 1–9

Edis, T. (2007) *An Illusion of Harmony: Science and Religion in Islam* Amherst: Prometheus

Eliade, M. (1969) *The Quest: History and Meaning in Religion* London: University of Chicago Press

Evans-Pritchard, E. (1937) *Witchcraft, Oracles and Magic among the Azande* Oxford: Clarendon Press

Fara, P. (2009) *Science: A Four Thousand Year History* Oxford: Oxford University Press

Feldman, R. (2007) 'Reasonable Religious Disagreement' in L. Antony (ed.) *Philosophers without Gods: Meditations on Atheism and the Secular Life* Oxford: Oxford University Press: 194–214

Ferngren, G. (2002) *Science and Religion: A Historical Introduction* Baltimore: Johns Hopkins University Press

Feuerbach, L. (1841/1854) *The Essence of Christianity*, translated by M. Evans, London: John Chapman

Feyerabend, P. (1975) *Against Method* London: Verso

Fitzgerald, P. (1997) 'A Critique of "Religion" as a Cross-Cultural Category' *Method and Theory in the Study of Religion* 9: 91–110

Flanagan, O. (2006) 'Varieties of Naturalism' in P. Clayton and Z. Simpson (eds.) *Handbook of Religion and Science* Oxford: Oxford University Press

Frazer, J. (1890) *The Golden Bough: A Study in Comparative Religion* London: Macmillan & Co

Freddoso, A. (2016) *New English Translation of St. Thomas Aquinas's Summa Theologiae (Summa Theologica)* https://www3.nd.edu/~afreddos/summa-translation/TOC.htm

Freud, S. (1927/1928) *The Future of an Illusion*, translated by W. Robson-Scott, London: Hogarth Press

Gaukroger, S. (2006) *The Emergence of a Scientific Culture: Science and the Shaping of Modernity 1210–1685* Oxford: Oxford University Press

Geertz, C. (1971) 'Religion as a Cultural System' in M. Banton (ed.) *Anthropological Approaches to the Study of Religion* London: Tavistock: 1–46

Gillett, C. and Loewer, B. (2001) *Physicalism and its Discontents* New York: Cambridge University Press

Goetz, S. (2000) 'Naturalism and Libertarian Agency' in W. Craig and J. Moreland (eds.) *Naturalism: A Critical Analysis* London: Routledge: 156–186

Goodenough, K. (2000) *Sacred Depths of Nature* New York: Oxford University Press

Gould, S. (2002) *Rock of Ages: Science and Religion in the Fullness of Life* New York: Ballantine Books

Gross, N. and Simmons, S. (2009) 'The Religiosity of American College and University Professors' *Sociology of Religion* 70: 101–129

Guthrie, S. (1993) *Faces in the Clouds: A New Theory of Religion* New York: Oxford University Press

Hague, M. (2010) *The Promise of Religious Naturalism* New York: Rowman & Littlefield

Hall, D. (2010) 'Why don't we Practice what we Preach? A Meta-Analytic View of Religious Racism' *Personality and Social Psychology Review* 14: 126–139

Hampton, J. (1998) *The Authority of Reason* Cambridge: Cambridge University Press

Hansson, S. (2017) 'Science and Pseudoscience' *Stanford Encyclopedia of Philosophy* https://plato.stanford.edu/entries/pseudo-science/

Harris, S. (2004) *The End of Faith: Religion, Terror, and the Future of Reason* New York: W. W. Norton

Harrison, P. (2015a) 'That Religion has Typically Impeded the Progress of Science' in R. Numbers and K. Kampourakis (eds.) *Newton's Apple and Other Myths about Science* Cambridge: Harvard University Press: 195–201

Harrison, P. (2015b) *The Territories of Science and Religion* Chicago: University of Chicago Press

Hitchens, C. (2007) *God is not Great: How Religion Poisons Everything* New York: Twelve

Hocart, M. (1952) *The Life-Giving Myth and Other Essays*, edited by F. Somerset London: Methuen

Hooykaas, R. (1972) *Religion and the Rise of Modern Science* Edinburgh: Scottish Academic Press

Horgan, T. (2006) 'Materialism: Matters of Definition, Defence and Deconstruction' *Philosophical Studies* 131: 157–183

Hume, D. (1757/1956) *The Natural History of Religion* London: Adam & Charles Black

Irons, W. (1996) 'In Our Own Self-Image: The Evolution of Morality, Deception, and Religion' *Skeptic* 4: 50–61

Jackson, F. (1998) *From Metaphysics to Ethics: A Defence of Conceptual Analysis* Oxford: Oxford University Press

James, W. (1902/2012) *The Varieties of Religious Experience*, edited by M. Bradley Oxford: Oxford University Press

Jim, H. et al. (2015) 'Religion, Spirituality and Physical Health in Cancer Patients' *Cancer* 121: 3760–3768

Johnston, M. (2009) *Saving God: Religion After Idolatry* Princeton: Princeton University Press

Keil, G. (2008) 'Naturalism' in D. Moran (ed.) *Companion to Twentieth Century Philosophy* London: Routledge

Kenny, A. (1969) *The Five Ways: St. Thomas Aquinas' Proofs of God's Existence* London: Routledge.

Kenny, A. (2002) *Aquinas on Being* Oxford: Oxford University Press

Kettell, S. (2012) 'Has Political Science Ignored Religion?' *Political Science and Politics* 45: 93–100

Klass, M. (1995) *Ordered Universes: Approaches to the Anthropology of Religion* Boulder: Westview Press

Kitcher, P. (1992) 'The Naturalist Return' *Philosophical Review* 101: 53–114

Knowles, J. and Rydenfelt, H. (eds.) (2011) *Pragmatism, Science and Naturalism* Frankfurt: Peter Lang

Kohler, W. (1925) *The Mentality of Apes*, translated by E. Winter, London: Kegan Paul, Trench, Trubner and Co.

Kohut, A. et al. (2009) 'Public Praises Science; Scientists Fault Public, Media' *Pew Research Centre Report* http://www.people-press.org/2009/07/09/public-praises-scien ce-scientists-fault-public-media/

Koons, R. (2000) 'The Incompatibility of Naturalism and Scientific Realism' in W. Craig and J. Moreland (eds.) *Naturalism: A Critical Analysis* London: Routledge: 49–63

Koons, R. and Bealer, G. (eds.) (2010a) *The Waning of Materialism* Oxford: Oxford University Press

Koons, R. and Bealer, G. (2010b) 'Introduction' to R. Koons and G. Bealer *The Waning of Materialism* Oxford: Oxford University Press: ix–xxxi

Krauss, L. (2015) 'All Scientists should be Militant Atheists' *The New Yorker*, 08/09/15, http://www.newyorker.com/news/news-desk/all-scientists-should-be-militant-atheists

Kunin, S. (2003) *Religion: The Modern Theories* Edinburgh: University of Edinburgh Press

Laats, A. and Siegel, H. (2016) *Teaching Evolution in a Creation Nation* Chicago: University of Chicago Press

Larson, E. and Witham, L. (1997) 'Scientists are Still Keeping the Faith' *Nature* 386: 435–436

Larson, E. and Witham, L. (1998) 'Leading Scientists Still Reject God' *Nature* 394: 313

Lauden, L. (1983) 'The Demise of the Demarcation Problem' in R. Cohen and L. Lauden (eds.) *Physics, Philosophy and Psychoanalysis* Dordrecht: Reidel: 111–127

Lawson, E. and McCauley, R. (1990) *Rethinking Religion: Connecting Cognition and Culture* New York: Cambridge University Press

Leiter, B. (1998) 'Naturalism and Naturalised Jurisprudence' in B. Bix (ed.) *Analysing Law: New Essays in Legal Theory* Oxford: Clarendon: 79–104

Leuba, J. (1916) *The Belief in God and Immortality, a Psychological, Anthropological and Statistical Survey* Boston: Sherman, French

Lodi-Smith, J. and Roberts, B. (2007) 'Social Investment and Personality: A Meta-Analysis of the Relationship of Personality Traits to Investment in Work, Family, Religion, and Volunteerism' *Personality and Social Psychology Review* 11: 68–86

McCutcheon, R. (1999) *The Insider/Outsider Problem in the Study of Religion* London: Cassell

McInerny, R. (2014) 'Saint Thomas Aquinas' *Stanford Encyclopedia of Philosophy* https://plato.stanford.edu/entries/aquinas/

McIver, T. (1988) *Anti-Evolution: A Reader's Guide to Writings Before and After Darwin* Baltimore: Johns Hopkins University Press

McKinnon, A. (2002) 'Sociological Definitions, Language Games, and the "Essence" of Religion' *Method and Theory in the Study of Religion* 14: 61–83

Maddy, P. (2001) 'Naturalism: Friends and Foes' *Noûs* 35: 37–67

Maddy, P. (2011) 'Naturalism and Common Sense' *Analytic Philosophy* 52: 2–34

Malinowski, B. (1944) *A Scientific Theory of Culture, and Other Essays* Chapel Hill: University of North Carolina Press

Mander, W. (2016) 'Pantheism' *Stanford Encyclopedia of Philosophy* https://plato.sta nford.edu/entries/pantheism/

Manson, N. (ed.) (2003) *God and Design: The Teleological Argument and Modern Science* London: Routledge

Marx, K. (1844) 'A Contribution to the Critique of Hegel's Philosophy of Right' *Deutsch-Französische Jahrbücher*

Masci, D. and Smith, G. (2016) 'Is God Dead? No, but Belief has Declined Slightly' *Pew Research Centre Report* http://www.pewresearch.org/fact-tank/2016/04/07/is-god-dead-no-but-belief-has-declined-slightly/

Masters, K. and Spielmans, G. (2007) 'Prayer and Health: Review, Meta-Analysis and Research Agenda' *Journal of Behavioural Medicine* 30: 329–338
Mill, J. (1865/1993) *Auguste Comte and Positivism* Bristol: Thoemmes
Mirza, O. (2011) 'The Evolutionary Argument against Naturalism' *Philosophy Compass* 6: 78–89
Moran, D. (ed.) (2008) *Companion to Twentieth Century Philosophy* London: Routledge
Moreland, J. (2000) 'Naturalism and the Ontological Status of Properties' in W. Craig and J. Moreland (eds.) *Naturalism: A Critical Analysis* London: Routledge: 67–109
Moreland, J. (2003) 'The Argument from Consciousness' in P. Copan and P. Moser (eds.) *The Rationality of Theism* London: Routledge: 204–220
Moreland, J. (2007) 'The Argument from Consciousness' in C. Meister and P. Copan (eds.) *Companion to Philosophy of Religion* London: Routledge: 373–384
Moreland, J. (2009) 'The Argument from Consciousness' in W. Craig and J. Moreland (eds.) *Companion to Natural Theology* Oxford: Blackwell: 282–342
Moser, P. and Yandell, K. (2000) 'Farewell to Philosophical Naturalism' in W. Craig and J. Moreland (eds.) *Naturalism: A Critical Analysis* London: Routledge: 3–23
Nagel, T. (2012) *Mind and Cosmos* Oxford: Oxford University Press
Nielsen, K. (2001) *Naturalism and Religion* Amherst: Prometheus
Numbers, R. (ed.) (2009) *Galileo goes to Jail and Other Myths about Science and Religion* Cambridge: Harvard University Press
Oppy, G. (2013a) *The Best Argument Against God* New York: Palgrave Macmillan
Oppy, G. (2013b) 'Consciousness, Theism and Naturalism' in J. Moreland, C. Meister, and K. Sweis (eds.) *Debating Christian Theism* Oxford: Oxford University Press: 131–144
Oppy, G. (2014a) *Reinventing Philosophy of Religion: An Opinionated Introduction* Basingstoke: Palgrave Macmillan
Oppy, G. (2014b) 'Abstract Objects? Who Cares!' in P. Gould (ed.) *Beyond the Control of God: Six Views on the Problem of God and Abstract Objects* New York: Bloomsbury
Oppy, G. (forthcoming a) 'Against Idealism' in T. Goldschmidt and K. Pearce (eds.) *Idealism: New Essays in Metaphysics* Oxford: Oxford University Press
Oppy, G. (forthcoming b) 'Morality Does Not Depend on God' in S. Cowan (ed.) *Disputations: An Introduction to Philosophical Problems* New York: Bloomsbury
Otto, R. (1917/1923) *The Idea of the Holy* New York: Oxford University Press
Papineau, D. (1993) *Philosophical Naturalism* Oxford: Blackwell
Papineau, D. (2015) 'Naturalism' *Stanford Encyclopedia of Philosophy* https://plato.stanford.edu/entries/naturalism/
Paul, G. (2005) 'Cross-National Correlations of Quantifiable Societal Health with Popular Religiosity and Secularism in the Prosperous Democracies' *Journal of Religion and Society* 7: 1–17
Peacocke, A. (ed.) (1981) *The Sciences and Theology in the Twentieth Century* Notre Dame: Notre Dame University Press
Pettit, P. (1992) 'The Nature of Naturalism' *Proceedings of the Aristotelian Society, Supplementary Volume* 66: 245–266
Pew Research Centre (2012) *The Global Religious Landscape* http://www.pewforum.org/2012/12/18/global-religious-landscape-exec/
Pigliucci, M. and Boudry, M. (2013) *Philosophy of Pseudoscience: Reconsidering the Demarcation Problem* Chicago: University of Chicago Press
Plantinga, A. (1991) 'An Evolutionary Argument against Naturalism' *Logos* 12: 27–49

Plantinga, A. (1993) *Warrant and Proper Function* New York: Oxford University Press
Plantinga, A. (1994) 'Naturalism Defeated' http://www.calvin.edu/academic/philosophy/virtual_library/articles/plantinga_alvin/naturalism_defeated.pdf
Plantinga, A. (2002) 'Reply to Beilby's Cohorts' in J. Beilby (ed.) *Naturalism Defeated? Essays on Plantinga's Evolutionary Argument against Naturalism* Ithaca: Cornell University Press
Plantinga, A. (2007) 'Religion and Science' *Stanford Encyclopedia of Philosophy* http://plato.stanford.edu/entries/religion-science/
Plantinga, A. (2011) *Where the Conflict Really Lies: Science, Religion and Naturalism* Oxford: Oxford University Press
Popper, K. (1959) *The Logic of Scientific Discovery* New York: Routledge
Preston, J. and Epley, N. (2009) 'Science and God: An Automatic Opposition between Ultimate Explanations' *Journal of Experimental Social Psychology* 45: 238–241
Price, H. (2011) *Naturalism without Mirrors* Oxford: Oxford University Press
Quine, W. (1981) *Theories and Things* Cambridge: Harvard University Press
Radcliffe-Brown, A. (1952) *The Andaman Islanders* Cambridge: Cambridge University Press
Raphals, L. (2015) 'Science and Chinese Philosophy' *Stanford Encyclopedia of Philosophy* https://plato.stanford.edu/entries/chinese-phil-science/
Rea, M. (2000) 'Naturalism and Material Objects' in W. Craig and J. Moreland (eds.) *Naturalism: A Critical Analysis* London: Routledge: 110–132
Rea, M. (2002) *World without Design: The Ontological Consequences of Naturalism* Oxford: Oxford University Press
Reppert, V. (2009) 'The Argument from Reason' in W. Craig and J. Moreland (eds.) *Companion to Natural Theology* Malden: Blackwell: 344–390
Rios, K. *et al.* (2015) 'Negative Stereotypes Cause Christians to Underperform and Disidentify with Science' *Social Psychological and Personality Science* 6: 959–967
Robinson, A. (2007) *The Last Man Who Knew Everything* Harmondsworth: Penguin
Robinson, H. (ed.) (1993) *Objections to Physicalism* Oxford: Clarendon
Rosenberg, A. (1996) 'A Field Guide to Species of Naturalism' *British Journal for the Philosophy of Science* 47: 1–29
Rue, L. (2011) *Nature is Enough* New York: State University of New York Press
Sarot, M. (2011) 'The Cardinal Difficulty of Naturalism: C. S. Lewis' Argument Reconsidered in Light of Peter van Inwagen's Critique' *Journal of Inkling Studies* 1: 41–53
Schmitt, F. (1995) 'Naturalism' in J. Kim and E. Sosa (eds.) *Companion to Metaphysics* Oxford: Blackwell
Sjodin, U. (2002) 'The Swedes and the Paranormal' *Journal of Contemporary Religion* 17: 75–85
Spencer, N. (2014) *Atheists: The Origins of the Species* London: Bloomsbury
Spiro, M. (1971) 'Religion: Problems of Definition and Explanation' in M. Banton (ed.) *Anthropological Approaches to the Study of Religion* London: Tavistock: 85–126
Stace, W. (1952) *Time and Eternity* Princeton: Princeton University Press
Stark, R. and Bainbridge, W. (1987) *A Theory of Religion* New Brunswick: Rutgers University Press
Steadman, L. and Palmer, C. (2008) *The Supernatural and Natural Selection: The Evolution of Religion* Boulder: Paradigm Publishers
Steedly, M. (1993) *Hanging without a Rope: Narrative Experience in Colonial and Neocolonial Karoland* Princeton: Princeton University Press

Stenger, V. (2012) *God and the Folly of Faith: The Incompatibility of Science and Religion* Amherst: Prometheus

Stirrat, M. and Cornwell, E. (2013) 'Eminent Scientists Reject the Supernatural: A Survey of the Royal Society' *Evolution: Education and Outreach* 6 https://link.springer.com/content/pdf/10.1186%2F1936-6434-6-33.pdf

Stoljar, D. (2001) 'Physicalism' *Stanford Encyclopedia of Philosophy* http://plato.stanford.edu/entries/physicalism/

Stoller, P. and Olkes, C. (1989) *In Sorcery's Shadow* Chicago: University of Chicago Press

Stone, J. (2008) *Religious Naturalism Today: The Rebirth of a Forgotten Alternative* New York: SUNY Press

Stone, J. (2011) 'Is a "Christian Naturalism" Possible? Exploring the Boundaries of a Tradition' *American Journal of Theology and Philosophy* 32: 205–220

Stone, J. (2012) 'Spirituality for Naturalists' *Zygon* 47: 481–500

Strenski, I. (2015) *Understanding Theories of Religion: An Introduction* Oxford: Wiley-Blackwell

Stroud, B. (1996) 'The Charm of Naturalism' *Proceedings of the American Philosophical Association* 70: 43–55

Stump, E. (2003) *Aquinas* New York: Routledge

Talmont-Kaminski, K. (2013) *Religion as Magical Ideology: How the Supernatural Reflects Rationality* Durham: Acumen

Tillman, H. (1982) *Utilitarian Confucianism: Ch'en Liang's Challenge to Chu Hsi* Cambridge: Harvard University Press

Tremlin, T. (2006) *Minds and Gods: The Cognitive Foundations of Religion* Oxford: Oxford University Press

Turner, E. (1992) *Experiencing Ritual: A New Interpretation of Human Healing* Philadelphia: University of Pennsylvania Press

Tylor, E. (1871) *Primitive Culture: Researches into the Development of Mythology, Philosophy, Religion, Language, Art, and Custom, Volume 1* London: John Murray

Webb, M. (2011) 'Religious Experience' *Stanford Encyclopedia of Philosophy* https://plato.stanford.edu/entries/religious-experience/

White, A. (1896) *A History of the Warfare of Science with Theology in Christendom* New York: Appleton

Whitehorse, H. (2004) *Modes of Religiosity: A Cognitive Theory of Religious Transmission* Walnut Creek: AltaMira Press

Whitely, B. (2009) 'Religiosity and Attitudes towards Lesbians and Gay Men: A Meta-Analysis' *The International Journal for the Psychology of Religion* 19: 21–38

Whiten, A., et al. (1999) 'Cultures and Chimpanzees' *Nature* 399: 682–685

Wildman, W. (2014) 'Religious Naturalism: What It Can Be, and What It Need Not Be' *Philosophy, Theology, and the Sciences* 1: 36–58

Willard, D. (2000) 'Knowledge and Naturalism' in W. Craig and J. Moreland (eds.) *Naturalism: A Critical Analysis* London: Routledge:24–48

Williams, B. (2000) 'Philosophy as a Humanistic Discipline' *Philosophy* 75: 477–496

Wilson, D. (2002) *Darwin's Cathedral: Evolution, Religion and the Nature of Society* Chicago: University of Chicago Press

Wippel, J. (2002) 'The Five Ways' in B. Davies (ed.) *Thomas Aquinas: Contemporary Philosophical Perspectives* Oxford: Oxford University Press: 159–225

Worrall, J. (2004) 'Science Discredits Religion' in M. Peterson and R. VanArragon (eds.) *Contemporary Debates in Philosophy of Religion* Malden: Blackwell, 59–72

Wu, A. et al. (2015) 'Religion and Completed Suicide: A Meta-Analysis' *PLoS One* 10(6): e0131715
Yancey, G. (2012) 'Recalibrating Academic Bias' *Academic Questions* 25: 267–278
Ye, F. (2011) 'Naturalised Truth and Plantinga's Evolutionary Argument against Naturalism' *International Journal for Philosophy of Religion* 70: 27–46
Yinger, J. (1948) *Religion in the Struggle for Power* Durham: Duke University Press

Index

Actual Chance 19
Actual Naturalness 18, 19
alternative medicine 171
anaerobic marine bacterium 76, 79
anomalous beliefs 172
anomalous events and entities 169–73
anthropology of religion 147
applied sciences 127
Aquinas, Thomas 109, 113, 115, 116, 117, 121, 123–4
Aristotelian metaphysics 124
Aristotle 13, 113, 115, 123
Armstrong, D. 97
atheism 37
Atran, Scott 3, 31–2, 33, 41, 53
axioms: truth of 81–2

Bacon, Francis 128
Bacon, Roger 128
Bahá'í: and science 144
Bainbridge, W. 40
Barrett, J. 41
Behe, Michael 65–6, 67
beliefs: anomalous beliefs 172; sources of basic beliefs 91–3; truth of 80–2
big pictures: articulation 154; assessing comparative merits 24, 154; conflict between 93–4, 153; idealisation 153–4; internal review 154; method of assessment 154–5; in philosophy 106; propositions 153; theistic 93; theoretical virtues 154–5; as works in progress 21; and worldviews 20, 152 *see also* naturalistic big pictures
Bishop, J. 49–51
Boyer, P. 41
British philosophy of science 107–8
Buddhism: sacred texts 179; and science 143, 144

Caenorhabditis elegans 76–7, 78, 80
Catholic Church: and science 144–5
causal entities 12–14; natural causal entities 12, 14–17; non-natural causal entities 14–17, 46; spatiotemporal location 14
causal powers 12–13; natural causal powers 12, 14–17; non-natural causal powers 14–17, 46; types 12
causal reality 12; actual versus possible 17–19; final causes 50; first causes 13–14; infinite regress 159, 160; initial singularity 159–61; scientific method and 12, 16, 21, 25, 56, 156; as single, all-embracing spatio-temporal system 97 *see also* natural causal reality
Chalmers, D. 169
Chance Divergence 18, 19
Chinese religions: rejection of science 143
Christian fundamentalism: on history of natural reality 144; rejection of evolutionary science 143–4
Christianity: sacred texts 179
cognitive science of religion 148
Collins, Francis 138
Comte, Auguste 52
Confucianism 143, 178
Conservation of Naturalness 18, 19
conspiracy theories 171
Copernicus 145
Craig, W. 22, 24
cryptids 171
Cult of Reason 52
Cult of the Supreme Being 52

Damascene 113, 115
Daoism 143
Darwinian theory 104, 108, 143
Dawkins, R. 146, 147

De Cruz, H. 41, 136, 137
De Ente et Essentia (Aquinas) 116–17, 121–5
De Smedt, J. 41
defeater-defeaters 58
defeater-deflectors 58
deism 52
Dembski, W. 23
Descartes, R. 128
design discourse: and theism 65–7
Devitt, M. 99, 102
Dewey, J. 108, 109
divination 182–3
Draper, J. 145–6
dreams 174–5
Durkheim, E. 30, 31, 40

economics of religion 148
ecstatic mystical experiences 176
empiricism 105, 106
epistemological commitments of naturalism 99–102
evidence bases 57
evolutionary argument against naturalism *see* Plantinga's evolutionary argument against naturalism (EAAN)
evolutionary psychology: and theism 58–60
evolutionary theory: common ancestor for humans and chimpanzees 139–40, 143–4; rejection by fundamentalists 143–4; and theism 60–2

Feuerbach, L. 40
final causes 50
final physical theory 162, 164
first causes 13–14
formal sciences 127–8
Frazer, J. 40
freedom 13
French positivism 107, 108
Freud, S. 40
frogs 77, 78–9, 80

Galileo 128, 145
Geertz, C. 30, 31
German materialism 107, 108
God: as pure existence 124–5; uniqueness of 118–21
Goetz, S. 23
Gould, S. 141
Guthrie, S. 40

Hampton, J. 103
Harris, S. 146, 147
Hébert, Jacques 52
Herbert of Cherbury 52
Hinduism 178
Hitchens, C. 146, 147
human culture: naturalism and 4
humanism 13, 53–4
Hume, D. 40, 173

inquiry 86, 87, 89
intelligences 124
International Humanist and Ethical Union (IHEU) 54
intuitionistic research programs 106–7
Irons, W. 41
Islam: sacred texts 179–80
Islamic fundamentalism: and history of natural reality 144; rejection of evolutionary science 143–4

Jainism 179
James, W. 176
Johnston, M. 46–8
Judaism 178

Klass, M. 30, 31
Koons, R. 23
Krauss, L. 146, 147

Leiter, B. 103

McKinnon, A. 31
Malinowski, B. 40
Mandaeism 179
Mander, W. 44
Manichaeism 179
Marx, K. 40
material causal entities 13
material causal powers 13
materialism 105, 106
materialists 13
mental capacities and phenomena: in natural causal reality 158, 165–9
mental causal powers 12
metaphysical commitments of naturalism 94–7
metaphysical naturalism 45
Metaphysics (Aristotle) 13
methodological commitments of naturalism 102–3
methodological dispositions 86, 87, 89–91